A Devil on One Shoulder and an Angel on the Other

The Story of Shannon Hoon and Blind Melon

By Greg Prato

Printed and distributed by Lulu.com
Published by Greg Prato
Front and back cover, and dedication photos by Danny Clinch
[www.dannyclinch.com]
Book design and layout by Linda Krieg
Copyright © 2008, Greg Prato. All Rights Reserved.
First Edition, September 2008

ISBN: 978-0-615-25239-1

Contents

Introduction

It was a warm summer evening in 1993—July 9th in New Haven, Connecticut, to be exact. A few buddies and I had made the trek from Long Island, New York to catch a show by one of our favorite bands, Blind Melon, at a venue called Toad's Place. One small problem—it turns out that it's a 21+ entry, and another guy and I are the only members of our group who are old enough to get in. Standing outside of Toad's as show time grows near, it's looking pretty bleak—until we see a smallish, longhaired, hippie-looking figure walking down the street with a backpack on. "Hey guys," he says in a friendly voice—and compliments yours truly on wearing a Primus t-shirt. That was the beginning of my brief but memorable interaction with Shannon Hoon.

Never mind that his band was about to go on stage, he seemed more concerned with our dilemma after we told him about it. "Don't worry, this is what's going to happen," he said. "When we go on, someone inside is going to crack open the fire exit right there, then you guys gotta bum-rush the door." A few songs into the set, my friends and I are inside. Hoon announces from the stage that he's glad to see that the "young people" had made it in. After the show, we meet guitarist Rogers Stevens, a friendly guy, who like Hoon, likes to chat with fans. In addition to voicing his exuberance for the Butthole Surfers' CD, 'Independent Worm Saloon' (which he displays a copy of), the subject comes up of how Blind Melon appear on the verge of a breakthrough. "If we do become big, we won't change. Stick with us," he announces, before driving off in a van with his band mates. Stevens' words soon proved prophetic.

While that night's show would not be the best I'd seen from the band with Hoon (that would be a two-way tie between the first time I saw them, March 25, 1993 at the Wetlands in New York City, and the last, September 19, 1995 at the Tradewinds in New Jersey), the Toad's show is perhaps most memorable for me. Obviously, because of meeting two members of the band. But also, it showed that the band—and Hoon in particular—were really just like their fans, and honestly cared about them.

Ever since then, Blind Melon has been one of my favorite bands, and out of the 100+ shows I've seen over the years of other bands, there was nothing quite like a Blind Melon show—trust me. And while I've been lucky to see some of rock's best-ever frontmen live (Iggy, Ozzy, Alice, etc.), Shannon to this day remains one of the best frontmen I've ever seen, as his stage moves never appeared pre-planned—he simply moved and responded to where the music took him. He truly became one with the music when he performed. And of course, you've got to love a singer that stopped a show twice to stop crowd-surfing lunkheads from landing on fans crammed in the front row, before punching one of the goons in the face (yep, another show I attended).

And as far as Blind Melon's music, a word that I always felt described their music best was 'pure.' Out of all the rock bands of the era (and there were certainly quite a few great ones), Blind Melon was one of the purest-sounding rock bands out there—their albums sounded as if you were sitting right in the middle of their rehearsal space, listening to them let it rip. Take a look around at popular music nowadays—quite a few modern day rockers could learn a thing or two about real-sounding music from 'Blind Melon,' 'Soup,' and 'Nico.'

Although I didn't know Shannon personally, I can still recall the sadness, shock, and disappointment upon learning of his untimely death in October 1995. I was so positive that Melon were going to be one of those Stones/ Who/Zeppelin-type bands, that would make a career out of delivering one classic album after another. It's been nearly thirteen years since the release of the group's second album, 'Soup,' as I type this, and to this day, it's the rock album I return to the most, as it sounds as great today as it did back then. Whenever I'm asked what my favorite album of all time is, 'Soup' gets the nod time and time again.

If anyone's story deserves to be told, Shannon Hoon and Blind Melon certainly get my vote. Strap yourself in; it's going to be a wild ride!

Greg Prato (New York, April 2008)

p.s. Have questions or comments? Email me at gregprato@yahoo.com. Also, to see what I'm up to—and to view vintage Blind Melon pictures not included in this book—visit www.myspace.com/gregpratopage.

Cast Of Characters

[Note: Descriptions and titles reflect the time period this book takes place]

Tomas Antona [Alice Donut singer, toured w/ Blind Melon in '94]

Bill Armstrong [Friend of Blind Melon]

Nicholas Bechtel [Assistant to Blind Melon in '94]

Jerry Cantrell [Alice in Chains guitarist, toured w/ Blind Melon in '92]

Gilby Clarke [Guns N' Roses guitarist, toured w/ Blind Melon in '93]

Danny Clinch [Photographer]

Mike Clink [Guns N' Roses producer]

Colleen Combs [Axl Rose's personal assistant, friend and neighbor of Shannon Hoon in L.A.]

Paul Cummings [Blind Melon tour manager '92-'95]

Tim Devine [Capitol Records vice president of A&R]

Lyle Eaves [Blind Melon soundman '91-'95]

John Fagot [Capitol Records senior VP of promotion]

Brooks Byrd Graham [Wife of Glen Graham]

Glen Graham [Blind Melon drummer]

Jeremy Hammond [Capitol Records VP of marketing/product development]

Nel Hoon [Mother of Shannon Hoon]

Shannon Hoon [Original Blind Melon singer]

Mike Inez [Ozzy Osbourne and Alice in Chains bassist, toured w/ Blind Melon in '92]

Domenique Johansson [Capitol Records publicist, director of media]

Michael Kelsey [Styff Kytten guitarist - Shannon Hoon's pre-Blind Melon band]

Curt Kirkwood [Meat Puppets singer/guitarist, toured w/ Blind Melon in '94]

Jena Kraus [Friend of Blind Melon, sang on "Mouthful of Cavities" from 'Soup']

Duff McKagan [Guns N' Roses bassist, toured w/ Blind Melon in '93]

Hale Milgrim [Capitol Records president '89-'92, Capitol Records CEO '92-'93]

Stephen Moses [Alice Donut drummer, toured w/ Blind Melon in '94]

Mike Napolitano [Assistant engineer of 'Soup,' producer of 'Nico']

George Nunes [Capitol Records national sales department]

Owen Orzack [Soundman for Blind Melon from '93-'95]

Mike Osterfeld [Stage manager for Blind Melon from '93-'95]

Eva Pfaff [Capitol Records promotion rep]

Robert Plant [Led Zeppelin singer]

Jon Plum [Engineer of 'Blind Melon']

Marc Pollack [Friend of Blind Melon]

Barbara Prisament [Capitol Records label director]

Riki Rachtman [Owner of the Cathouse in Los Angeles, host of MTV's 'Headbanger's Ball']

Charles Raggio [Inclined manager/tour manager]

Craig Ross [Lenny Kravitz guitarist, toured w/ Blind Melon in '93]

Sissi Schulmeister [Alice Donut bassist, toured w/ Blind Melon in '94]

Shelley Shaw [Worked for Guns N' Roses and Blind Melon's booking agency, ICM]

Susan Silver [Soundgarden and Alice in Chains manager]

Lisa Sinha [Longtime girlfriend of Shannon Hoon, mother of Shannon's daughter, Nico Blue Hoon]

Denise Skinner [Capitol Records product manager]

Brad Smith [Blind Melon bassist]

Chris Smith [Brother of Brad Smith]

Kim Smith [Wife of Brad Smith]

Rogers Stevens [Blind Melon guitarist]

Marlon Stoltzman [Friend of Blind Melon]

Miles Tackett [Inclined guitarist/cellist - played cello on 'Soup,' played w/ Blind Melon at Woodstock '94 and MuchMusic: Intimate & Interactive]

Kim Thayil [Soundgarden guitarist, toured w/ Blind Melon in '91, '93, and '95]

Christopher Thorn [Blind Melon guitarist]

Heather Thorn [Wife of Christopher Thorn]

Travis Warren [Current Blind Melon singer]

Brian Whitus [Friend of Shannon Hoon from Indiana, husband of Melissa Whitus]

Melissa Whitus [Friend of Shannon Hoon from Indiana, wife of Brian Whitus]

Buz Zoller [Flowerhead guitarist, toured w/ Blind Melon in '92 and '93]

Dedicated to the memory and music of Richard Shannon Hoon
September 26, 1967—October 21, 1995

MuchMusic Audience Member: If you were given a chance to write an autobiography, what would you begin your first paragraph with?

Shannon Hoon: "Why?"

Shannon's Upbringing

Richard Shannon Hoon is born on September 26, 1967, in Lafayette, Indiana.

Nel Hoon: A lot of the magazines or papers made it out that Shannon had a terrible childhood. Well you know what? Shannon was spoiled rotten from day one. He was born out of love and no one that I know ever disliked Shannon…except maybe the police [laughs]. But he was totally spoiled rotten. So if I ever did anything wrong, or if his dad ever did anything wrong, we did spoil him so much. My daughter Anna [Shannon's older sister] always said, "Shannon was the 'chosen one'—he was the one that got the loads of love and affection." And she always said that he was special—more so than her or Tim [Shannon's older brother]. Nobody ever talks much about my Tim, but he's a great guy. My only two grandsons are in the military right now. My one grandson has been in Iraq twice already, and I think he's getting ready to go back a third time. [Anna] also said that maybe God knew that Shannon wasn't going to be here as long as everybody else. So maybe that's why he was so special.

Shannon Hoon: I'm from Lafayette, an hour outside Indianapolis. We have nothing but cornfields. The kids in my area tassel corn. Tasseling corn is like when you pull out that little tassel at the top of the corn stalk. I don't know why you pull it out.

Nel Hoon: We lived out in the country all the years that Shannon was growing up [in Dayton, Indiana]. It's six miles from Lafayette, but we lived even further than that—we lived on gravel roads. He ran around using a stick for a gun—climbing trees and all that. We drove him 15 miles to school. He was a good student—he was rowdy but kept his grades up enough so he could stay in sports, because he loved sports. The worst punishment he could have was if he got a bad grade and couldn't wrestle or play football.

Shannon Hoon: I was such a jock. I couldn't enjoy a game of pinball without wanting to beat my opponent.

Nel Hoon: The way he got into karate was when he was really young, he was hyperactive. He couldn't even walk though a room—he was always running. He was such an ornery little kid that really, I didn't even visit my family much because it was like, "Oh no—Nel and Dick [Shannon's father] are coming to visit, and they're going to bring Shannon!" It was one of those things—they loved him, but he was a holy terror. So I took him to the doctor. At the time, they were giving Ritalin—I didn't want him taking some sort of drug, so I thought, "O.K., we've got to do something, because he's just way out of control." He was very small—there were three karate schools at the time, and there was only one that would take his age. He was very successful—by the time he was nine, he had got first-degree black belt. He was an amazing, energetic, little competitor at that age. We traveled with him though—his dad and I took him to seven different states, and he never didn't come home with a trophy. Ever. He grew up being competitive.

Shannon Hoon: I have a relationship with my mother, which is the best. I was groomed to be an athlete like my father.

Nel Hoon: I can't remember when I didn't know [Dick Hoon], actually. Shannon was a lot like his dad—in many ways. He did drink a lot—but he was a wonderful dad, he really was. A lot of people got the idea that he wasn't, but Shannon was his life. Dick was a bricklayer and I was a manager of a bar in Dayton.

Michael Kelsey: Seventh grade. I always noticed his energy. The kind of energy that makes you laugh even when nothing funny is said. Giddy—the kind of personality you gravitate towards.

Brian Whitus: How I met him was wrestling practice in junior high. What I thought of him was just a little, wiry, mean kid [laughs]. That's how we got to know each other—through the sport thing. There on out, we got in trouble. I recall a wrestling match—we were a couple of weight classes apart—we were in high school at this point. Shannon was beating this guy pretty good, and I remember Shannon picked him up, turned and looked at our wrestling group, and gave us all a big wink, before he slammed him down on the ground. He was pretty much the life of the party. Most definitely kept you in stitches—as far as the laughter is concerned. Shannon walked in a party; everybody stopped and noticed him. He was a good-looking guy in high school—short hair and whatnot.

Lisa Sinha: We went to high school together—McCutcheon High School—that's how I met him. It would have been '84. We met through sports. He was very popular—everybody liked him. He was a hardcore wrestler, I was a gymnast, so we had practice near to each other. We were all kinda flirty [laughs]. And we ran track, so everybody's together—all grades. He was a pole-vaulter, and I was a high jumper, so we were right next to each other—we'd all hang out. He was also a football player.

Nel Hoon: If Shannon didn't want to do something, Shannon did not do it. I think the newspapers said that he did [sports] for his mom and dad. Well, of course we wanted him to—it was the thing to do to keep kids out of drugs. Shannon especially, needed to be busy. He was great at any sport he ever did. It was easy for Shannon to stay in sports, because he actually loved it.

Shannon Hoon: I was raised in an environment where if you were far left in any manner, you were pretty much condemned. You know, I go back home now and look at pictures, and I'm this sharp-dressed, shorthaired jock. I can see the denial in my eyes in those pictures, man. I will never forget all the time I lost trying to get along with people who really, deep down inside, weren't important to me.

Brian Whitus: Most of what we did either had to do with fighting or girls. I remember one Halloween party, we got in a big old ruckus—a four on four fight. This guy had Shannon on the ground—I took the guy off Shannon. Shannon was a black belt in karate, and I remember holding the guy down. Shannon came up—it was like slow motion—and kicked the guy in the back of the head. I was just like, *"Nooo!"* Needless to say, that guy threw me off like a sack of potatoes, and pushed Shannon off back in the crowd. At that point, someone pulled a knife out and stabbed Shannon in the back—gave him 17 stitches. The funny thing is, the guy that Shannon had kicked grabbed a hold of Shannon, and said, "You need to go to the hospital!"

Lisa Sinha: He was a fighter—but his dad was a fighter.

Nel Hoon: If there was trouble somewhere in town, you could bet Shannon was involved. It may be helping a friend. If there was a fight in a bar and Shannon was there, he always got involved. He would choose the underdog and help him out, because Shannon was very tough. One of his cousins had gotten into a fight, and he wasn't big enough to defend himself, so Shannon took on the fight. Nine out of ten times, Shannon would be the one that would go to jail. It was mostly just being rowdy and opened his mouth when he should have kept it closed so many times. If Shannon was on the scene, the police were going to take Shannon to jail. It was pretty painful for me, because I didn't think it was always Shannon's fault. I think a lot of the times he was picked on by the Lafayette police. Any time you create a name for yourself in that respect, if you're there, you're the one that's going to jail.

Shannon Hoon: Nothing major. Just fighting or maybe hanging out with kids who had burglarized a place and not telling on my friends. But in a small town, they'll [get] you five or six times for fighting, and next thing you know, you're up for a habitual-criminal charge.

Lisa Sinha: I started dating him the end of my junior year. I was 17, I think he was 18. It would have been '86. I'd heard stories about him, so I was a little worried [laughs]. Not worried, but a little cautious. I had class with this girl, and she's like, "I know somebody that wants to go out with you—Shannon." I'm like, *"Oh my gosh."* He was wild and liked to have fun. What did I hear about him? Just that he got in trouble. At the time, I was pretty tame compared to that. Stories that they'd go out and run from the cops, get in fights. I hadn't really dated that many people before him. So, I feel he corrupted me [laughs].

Melissa Whitus: I was the 'tag along girl,' meaning I was with Brian. I worked at Dog n' Suds—a local hotdog stand. They always came in there. Lisa will tell you that too, she'd say, "Why do we always go to Dog n' Suds on Friday nights?" And then Lisa started putting two and two together, she's like, "Wait, I think you like that little girl that works there." I was younger than all of them. Shannon got kicked off the lot plenty of times—for skateboarding. My boss would go out and [say], "Get the hell off my lot," 'cause he thought they were a bunch of juvenile delinquents. *They kind of were.*

Brian Whitus: I recall us getting drunk a few times and me being jealous of him flirting with my girlfriend.

Melissa Whitus: I wasn't very adventurous, but we had a park here in town. He convinced me one night…we were supposed to meet [Brian] at a party, and he fibbed and said that Brian was at his apartment. He in fact wasn't, and Shannon was trying to, well, it was kind of a 'guy competition thing.' He thought he could woo me, but it didn't work. The one thing that he convinced me to do—sneak in a park and go down the slide. That was like the worst thing we ever did. Then we snuck into Ross-Ade Stadium, which is Purdue's football field, and we ran around the football field in the middle of the night.

Brian Whitus: [Shannon and Brian] pulled over to the side of the road and got into it—just us two—got back in the vehicle and drove on.

Shannon Hoon: My family was broken up when I was like 16 years old, and at that age it seemed really hard on me. I'd been accustomed to holidays spent together as a family, and all of a sudden it wasn't there anymore. I found it really hard for me to deal with and understand. I was also torn between two parents, being put in the position of having to choose which one I wanted to live with and, in turn, risking losing the other one's love.

Brian Whitus: Close to his mom. I would call it dysfunctional—nothing was ever good enough in his parents' eyes. One night, we came to his dad's house—his dad was drunk. He opened the door and literally laid Shannon out right in front of me. But that being said, they would do anything for him, too. I remember Dick bought him that Trans Am. He pulled up with that Trans Am in the McCutcheon High School parking lot. Shannon at that time, we were in track—he was a pole-vaulter. Drove up with that car for him, and had a pole vault pole tied to the side of the passenger door. [Shannon] had several cars—he had a gold El Camino, some silver little car. But I would say he probably drove that his junior year. I think he wrecked that, and then took over his dad's El Camino. He probably wrecked that one, too.

Lisa Sinha: As far as Nel went, very lenient, as far as never wanting to tell him "No." And I know how that is—you don't want to tell your kids "No." But she really needed to. She loved her son dearly. She would have killed somebody to protect him. I think she was a little too lenient. As a teenager, he could get away with murder. His mom would always bail him out. The consequences were never too harsh. At one point, we looked at the stack of papers and were like, "This could be bad if you get one more." He never did jail time, but I'm shocked.

Shannon Hoon: I was a prick 'til I was 17. Where I come from…I love it, but you were subliminally scarred being raised in that type of community. I was raised almost to be a little shaky about people who came from a different walk of life than I did. I don't think I was prejudiced, but I could have become that way. I suddenly realized I'd spent 17 years not getting on with anyone at all. Your parents didn't even have anything to do with it. It was just the air about the place.

Brian Whitus: He didn't really do the drug thing, other than occasional pot smoking. At one point, I remember he and my brother got put in jail—this didn't have anything to do with fighting, this had to do with vandalism over at one of the apartment complexes. They took some stuff out of there—him and a couple of other guys—and they got thrown in jail for that. Neither one of them got a record for it or anything like that. Another time, it was fighting—him and my brother were running through Purdue campus, being chased by cops. They both got caught, got thrown in jail.

Lisa Sinha: They used to drink in high school pretty heavy. Maybe a little marijuana, some acid. He was dabbling—it was just recreational.

Melissa Whitus: One time they beat the shit out of a bunch of guys at a party, brought the keg back to my mother's house, and my mom was totally fine with that. My house was 'the party house.' But I never did it—I was always 'the mother.' I always took care of everybody.

Brian Whitus: Our athletic director was kind of a dickhead. So Shannon and I were drinking one night, and we decided…this is really mean. We built a seven foot cross—[the athletic director] is not black or anything like that, no prejudice—buried it in his front yard, doused it with gasoline, brought it clear out to the court, and caught it on fire. [The athletic director] found out about it and confronted us in school about it. At that point, I think Shannon was driving a Trans Am. Left the building, pulled the Trans Am up on the sidewalk, and peeled out on the sidewalk. He used to have a key to a fitness center downtown. We used to take girls from school, sneak in there at midnight/1:00 in the morning, do our thing. I remember when he graduated high school, he was shaking the principal's hand, and Shannon had Vaseline all over his hand!

Shannon Hoon: I didn't realize until I was eighteen years old that I was living my life for my parents. That's when I started dabbling with LSD. I was more into tripping than smoking pot. I like hallucinogens. I would listen to Pink Floyd for hours. It helped me get a fix on what was really important to me.

Nel Hoon: I had always heard Shannon sing. He could sing *anything*—rap, country. One time, he hurt himself in football, and we were going to a hospital in Indianapolis. I said, "You can have the radio as we're going down and I'll get it as we're going back." At the time, I was listening to country music. I had the country station on [and] Shannon could sing right along. I remember him singing along with Hank Williams Jr.—I had no idea he knew that music. After he got out of sports is when he got into music. And I mean *seriously.* At that time, his dad and I had divorced, and I lived in an apartment in town. He came to visit one day, and said, "Mom, this friend of mine that I went to high school with wants me to sing in his band. What do you think of that?" I said, "I think it's great." He said, "I've wrote a song. I'm going to sing it, and you tell me what you think." He sang this song—I wish I could remember which song it was, because I've never been able to remember which song he sang for me that day—with no guitar, because he didn't even know how to play guitar at that time. But he sang this song, and I thought, "Oh my God, he has a beautiful voice."

Brian Whitus: I remember a couple of concerts we went to were Judas Priest… it seemed like no matter what concert we went to, somehow, he always got backstage passes. I couldn't even tell you how, but he always did. I remember him being in the video of one of Mötley Crüe's—he was in the audience. They took the camera through the audience, and there Shannon was. I know he listened to Bon Jovi—when he first started singing, in Mike Kelsey's mom's garage, he sang "Wanted Dead or Alive." That was the first time anybody ever heard him sing.

Shannon Hoon: Singing made me feel good. And finally I was around people who thought it was alright to sing.

Michael Kelsey: After high school he hung out a lot around my house. I was always recording and playing. After a few times he mentioned that he wrote some songs and sang. He had said that before, but I didn't take it too seriously. Then one night he started singing a song that he wrote about Lisa. I put some chords to it and we played around with it for a little. I was impressed because I thought he was just a big talker, but the singing and lyrics came from a real place. He always joked about us starting a band. After that night I was pretty caught up on the idea of having a frontman like Shannon. We got a mutual friend of ours to play bass, Brian Bundy, and we spent a while looking for a drummer. Eventually, someone told us about Barry Koch—he fit in perfectly. We spent all of our time practicing in Nel's basement. Barry had the name Styff Kytten from some earlier band name brainstorm sessions years before. As soon as he said it, we knew that was the name.

Nel Hoon: After I realized that he was going to sing, I called a friend of mine, Larry Gould—he taught guitar. So I bought Shannon a guitar and sent him over to Larry.

Brian Whitus: In Mike Kelsey's garage, I was in awe. And it was just playing around. Then he went back another day sober, and I was just shocked. He'd never done anything like that before. The song "Change," he strummed that on the guitar for years down the basement on Central Street. They played a lot down the basement on Central Street.

Nel Hoon: That was when we lived at Central. I knew he was writing a song, and I think he didn't want me to hear it until he had it completed. I was in the living room and he was sitting on the front porch—the windows were up. I could hear him very clearly singing "Change," and I thought, "Oh my God, that's the most beautiful song I've ever heard." And truly, it ended up being just that. So pretty soon, he got with the band, and the band set up in the basement. They put up walls so the whole neighborhood couldn't hear them practice. But inside the house, it was terrible—no matter where you were. I would be sitting on a chair and watch my candelabras bouncing up and down on the dresser—that's how noisy it was. But Shannon only got better and more serious about his music.

Lisa Sinha: That was a wild time—the Styff Kytten days. Slightly heavy metal era, with big hair, tight pants. They played all over the place—all the local bars. There was one place; I think their first show ever, called the Good

Time Bar. And fights would take place there, or girls that would like Shannon would spill drinks in my face [laughs]. Styff Kytten had a huge following—they could pack Nick's, which was someplace that Blind Melon played at one point. I remember they did some really huge outdoor parties [and] a lot of the bars around town—even in Purdue they played, they had people that followed them up to Monticello. That's when the trouble began as far as his 'partying ways.'

Michael Kelsey: I was always entertained observing Shannon's way. I would see Shannon do things that would piss people off one night and then those same people would be buying him drinks the next. I was always amazed. One night he lost his voice and we had to try to pull the gig off without him. Towards the end of the night after he had drank quite a bit, he got on stage—some impromptu 'whisper jam.' Most of it was incoherent except for the part about jumping off the stage onto the big birthday cake on the front row table. I was able to give a quick five-second "Move!" warning before Shannon became airborne and landed butt-first on top of the cake. There was a lot of anger that night from the first three rows, the bar owner, and staff. A few days later…everyone loves Shannon even more.

Lisa Sinha: The wild crowd that he started hanging out with—they were friends with Axl [Rose, Guns N' Roses singer—originally from Lafayette, Indiana]. I didn't really hang out with that crowd—they didn't like me [laughs]. They all hated me; in fact, they threatened to beat me up [laughs]. So they hooked him up with Axl. Shannon was the type of person—he would just approach people. He was not scared at all to approach *anybody*. He would not have been scared to approach the President of the United States. So he was like, "Hey, we're from the same town. When I come to L.A.…." And Axl liked him—he was younger than him. They became friends.

Brian Whitus: We were at a party somewhere in the middle of town, and I remember Shannon and Axl Rose walking down the road from the party, just talking. At that point, Axl already had made it.

Shannon Hoon: I remember we were in a bar called Magoo's in Lafayette back when I used to really drink a lot, and I was trying to sing some Bad Company songs that I kept forgetting the words to. Axl, who was in town for awhile, was there trying to sing it with me but I kept screwing it up. Fortunately though, Axl's a pretty forgiving guy.

Lisa Sinha: Shannon and I were kind of broken up, and he was dating this other girl. He was starting to dabble in cocaine and harder acid. He hooked up with this crowd that was doing that. He got screwed up, and he and I weren't getting along. It's a small town. One night he called and we were talking. I could tell that he'd been drinking or something. We're on the telephone, and he says, "I'm going to kill myself." I freaked out, and this is after a period of time of he and I fighting—you know how teenagers fight. So I drove there—my poor parents, they were like, "Oh my gosh, what's next?" When I get there, I don't even know what he had ingested. But I know he had taken all the pills in the house, drank cough medicine, drank beer, booze—who knows. It was really scary and horrible. He was wild and crazy. It was some of the 'Guns N' Roses/Axl Rose friends' that were over there. People kept dropping by and phone calls were being made to come over and help control him. Because he told me, "If you call 911, *I'll kill you*" [laughs]. I was scared of him at one point—I didn't know what to do.

As it progressed over a period of a couple of hours of fighting—one guy came over and tried to get him to go to the hospital, this was the 'Axl Rose friend,' I mean, falling down in the bathtub—you just can't even imagine some of the stuff I witnessed. Fighting, fighting, and then finally, a group decision to call 911, and we did finally—because he was on fire. I feel like I'm painting this picture of a madman, but he had moments like that. He was calm, cool, funny, happy—but in the matter of a second, if something triggered him, *he'd go off*. And there was no controlling him—*at all*. The ambulance came and took him away—he was in pretty bad shape. I think he spent a couple of days in the hospital. He had to get his stomach pumped. It was this triangle of things he was unhappy with—he and I weren't getting along, he was kind of dating somebody else, they were doing drugs. I don't know, he was just that kind of guy that was dramatic in a lot of ways. Never quite satisfied.

Shannon Hoon: I'd basically backed myself into such a corner at home that I wasn't going to lose anything by leaving.

Nel Hoon: He got so serious, [and] told everybody, "I'm going to L.A." He really gave everybody in Styff Kytten a chance to come with him if they wanted to. Some of them might not show up for practice, and Shannon would get furious with that. At the time I knew this friend—a D.J. at Indiana University. He went to see him and said, "Shannon can make it—he has a great voice." [Shannon] was doing a cover of "Born to be Wild," and he said, "That was the best version that I've ever heard." It wasn't long after that that he and I went out to this hotel where I was working. It was about 3:00 in the morning and he was getting his music ready—to make a [demo]. I think it had four songs on it and there was a picture of Shannon. We made a whole bunch of tapes so he could pass out. And I remember on it, it said, "I'm from the Midwest—I'm a singer looking for a band."

Lisa Sinha: When I got out of high school, I moved to Chicago to go to a school for fashion. At that time, he would come up to Chicago or I would come home every weekend. So that's really the story about our relationship— we dated off and on. I went to college at Purdue—I transferred—he hung around Lafayette for a period of time when I was in college. He ended up moving to L.A. I think a lot of that triggered, "O.K., I'm acting crazy, I'm hanging around with these people that are doing drugs." It made him say, "I'm going to go to L.A." The funny thing is the first time he ever went to L.A.—the first time he ever flew—I was a freshman in college, and we went to my aunt's house in L.A. Then the next time he came out to L.A., I went to L.A. on spring break—he came out, loved it, went back, prepared to go to L.A., and then moved to L.A. after that.

Nel Hoon: When he told me he was going to California and was going to get signed to a major label, that didn't surprise me really. Before he left for California, I said, "Honey, when are you coming back?" He said, "When I'm signed to a major label."

Shannon Hoon: Well, people in Indiana like to get drunk and fight, and now that's very disturbing to me. When I lived there, yeah, we'd get drunk, and if you couldn't find someone to fight, you'd fight your friends. Pretty pathetic. And going back, I saw that time had stood still. And it's still standing still. But at least I understand it now.

Lisa Sinha: I remember him telling me—this is when we were young—that he would die by the time he was 30. I remember being furious with him—I couldn't believe he would say such a thing.

Glen, Brad, Christopher, and Rogers' Upbringing

Glen Graham is born on December 5, 1967 in Columbus, Mississippi, Brad Smith on September 29, 1968 in West Point, Mississippi, Christopher Thorn on December 16, 1968 in Dover, Pennsylvania, and ... Rogers Stevens on October 31, 1970 in West Point, Mississippi.

Rogers Stevens: I lived [in West Point] the first 18 years of my life, as well as Brad and Glen. When I first started playing guitar, I was into heavy metal bands, like AC/DC and Mötley Crüe. But that was some kind of repressed sexual thing rather than the music [laughs]. My mother forced me to take piano lessons when I was a kid—I did end up learning a lot from that, despite my efforts to get out of it. And down where we came from, there's not a lot of outlet for this stuff. There's a lot of church music and country music, but there was nothing as far as a rock scene or any other people doing what we were trying to do.

When Brad and I were doing high school bands...we had known each other since we were much younger—I mean, we were in Cub Scouts together. The age of six/seven/eight years old. He got a guitar first, and I would go over his house because I was friends with his younger brother. So he was playing guitar, and I ended up really wanting one. I got him to show me stuff—we were playing all this awful heavy metal music. It wasn't that it got a bad response or people threw tomatoes at us—it got *no* response. Other than, "Well, we'll just let them do their thing, and they'll grow out of it." My hair looked like a pineapple and I was wearing tight pants—they thought that we lost or minds.

Glen Graham: I'm from Columbus, Mississippi—about 15 minutes from West Point. When I was in fourth grade, I saw Kiss on television, and that did it for me. My aunt had given me all the Beatles records through 'Rubber Soul' when I was about ten, and she later initiated me into the later Beatles and the Rolling Stones. I started playing in bands when I was fourteen years old. I did rockabilly stuff, and a bunch of cover bands—everything from '80s heavy metal to things like Hüsker Dü, the Replacements, and Soul Asylum.

I was in tenth grade—it was October of '82. I started falling out of the group of people I'd been hanging out with for a long time. I was heavily into rock music and I was playing in a band of older guys. Over a period of a year or so—leading up to the fall of '82—I started becoming withdrawn. I told my parents, "There's something wrong with me." They took me to a psychiatrist, and the psychiatrist said, "This kid is screwed up and exhausted—let's keep him for a week." So they did. At the end of that week, I was discharged from the hospital. About two weeks later, there was this trip to Washington D.C.—this school trip had been scheduled months in advance. I didn't feel up to going but since it was already planned, I went anyway. The guy who was chaperoning the trip was also our swim coach and history teacher at the high school—I'd been on the swim team since I was five. When I got on the bus, immediately, I knew something was wrong with me. I felt very odd, didn't seem to recognize anybody.

By the time we got to Chattanooga, Tennessee—and this is leaving from Columbus, Mississippi—six hours down the road, *I was tripping my ass off.* Had no experience with drugs of any kind—never had anything to drink, never smoked a cigarette, and at that point didn't know acid existed, much less what its effects were. Apparently, I flipped out in ways that no one has ever told me—I'm sure it was not pretty and probably very frightening for most of the people on the trip. Namely, whoever gave me the acid. I found out a few years ago that it was a *massive* dose. I have almost no memory of that trip—I blacked out. I remember waking up in the hospital a month later, and didn't get out of the hospital until the middle of January. It was unpleasant to say the least. I came back to school, and everybody who was on that trip thought I was a narc. Crazy high school logic—"Oh, dosed kid goes to mental hospital … must be a narc." It kind of focused me on music. I started playing with these guys from Starkville, Mississippi, and played with them through 1990—right up to the time I joined Blind Melon, really.

Rogers Stevens: Glen was in another band called Café Des Moines, that were actually really cool. They were more into that whole southern/alternative scene that was happening—R.E.M., Guadalcanal Diary. When I was fourteen and in all my heavy metal glory, Glen and them were playing Cream songs and doing cooler stuff—writing their own songs.

Glen Graham: Jim Mathus—the Squirrel Nut Zippers guy—was in [Café Des Moines]. He left, and then we started a band called Birdy. Pat Sansone—who just started playing with Wilco—was in that band.

Christopher Thorn: I was born in Pennsylvania, a little place.

Heather Thorn: We're both from Pennsylvania—we both met in the third grade and started dating when we were seniors in high school. We couldn't wait to get away from the town to be honest. We grew up in a town called Dover—outside of York, Pennsylvania. It's a really close-minded kind of little city. There's a lot of Pennsylvanian Dutch there, and it's where the Amish community is in that area. Christopher and I were in high school, he was playing guitar, and our goal was to basically get out of there as soon as possible. [Chris' high school band, Rot] played around the tri-state area all the time. It was a total speed metal band—a group of really good guys. Christopher loved doing the music and he loved the guys, but that wasn't really his true calling, as far as music goes—he grew up listening to Zeppelin and the Grateful Dead. Even though they were successful for that area, he knew that wasn't where he was going to end up. Live [the band] is from York, but we didn't go to the same high school. We didn't get to know them until we left York, really.

Glen Graham: [Rogers and I] were on the swim team together. In the late '80s, Brad and Rogers had a band. They were called Concrete Jungle. It was like a Guns N' Roses cover band, basically, and Brad sang. I remember seeing them one time in a field behind a club, out in the prairie—between Starkville and Columbus. They were on a flatbed trailer, and there were 15 people there—their girlfriends, the two other bands in a six mile radius, and the club owner. These guys were nuts. Where we grew up—when we grew up there—there was no radio to speak of. The FM radio was strictly top-40. There was nothing but AM and soul stations. These guys didn't hear any of the cool, old rock stuff until much later than most people do. None of us had older brothers who were into this stuff or anything. We all came to it late.

Brad Smith: We felt that Mississippi wasn't for us. I don't know if it was subconscious or what, but I never saw my future in Mississippi. When you get obsessed with music and songwriting, you're totally withdrawn, you're basically a loner in a way. And Mississippi didn't have a lot to offer in terms of supporting that obsession or art form. We always got magazines like Metal Hammer, Hit Parader, and Circus, and you're like, "Fuck it, it's all happening in L.A."

Rogers Stevens: It dawned on us when I was a junior in high school. Brad and I had this diabolical plan to [move to Los Angeles] together. He went off to college, and I still had two years of high school left—we were playing together the whole time. So he went to Mississippi State, which is in the next town over. We sprung it on my family towards the end of my high school days.

Glen Graham: As far as musical influences, by the time I got into college, I was listening to all the '60s bands—everything from the Grateful Dead to Led Zeppelin. I got really immersed in all that stuff—Cream, Buffalo Springfield. And the band I was playing in at the time, we were really trying to do improvisational stuff—kind of like Cream. Blues-based improv. We did poorly, but it was really fun. It was good training for this Blind Melon thing.

Heather Thorn: [Heather and Christopher] went to college for a couple of years—he was doing communications and I was doing whatever. One day, we were like, "Do you want to move to L.A.?" "O.K." It was back in '88 I think that we moved out here.

Christopher Thorn: I moved to Los Angeles I think when I was nineteen. For all the same sorta cliché reasons—to become a rock star. In Pennsylvania, we didn't exactly have a music scene. I figured if I was going to give it a shot, I should move to a place that the business actually was.

Brad Smith: We had big balls and little brains, and moved to Los Angeles to take our chance. We didn't know it was a chance at the time, but looking back on it, it was insane. We just followed our dreams. We had really good support from our families. They thought it was going to be a flash, and we'd be back in six months. But we stuck it out. That was in 1989.

Axl and Shannon

Shannon arrives in L.A. (via bus) in 1990, and an old friend lends a hand—Axl Rose. In the midst of G n' R's sessions for 'Use Your Illusion,' Axl invites Shannon to sing on the soon-to-be G n' R classic, "Don't Cry," and to appear in its bombastic video.

Shannon Hoon: We've been friends for five or six years. He used to live in Indiana.

Colleen Combs: I met Axl when I still lived in Sacramento—I was in high school. We used to go to Los Angeles to see shows, and I worked for Tower Records in Sacramento. Axl worked at Tower Video on Sunset at that time—we're talking '85, somewhere in there. When I was in grade school and junior high school, coincidentally, my local neighborhood garage band was the band that turned into Tesla. That's Tom Zutaut, who was later involved in Guns N' Roses. The original singer of that band moved to Los Angeles and as Tesla became Tesla, they got a new singer. I ran into him on the Strip, and he worked at Tower Video with Axl—he introduced him to me. This was before Guns N' Roses existed. Axl and I sort of became pen pals—we used to write to each other. When I moved to L.A. in the summer of '85, I ran into him again, and became friends that way.

Shelley Shaw: I got a job working for the head of worldwide music at I.C.M. [International Creative Management]. I knew a lot of acts; I'd traveled, and got to meet the managers. I'd been to L.A. a lot and I had a core of friends there—somehow I met Guns N' Roses. I went to see them at the Roxy, and went over to Geffen—I knew John Kalodner. He gave me 'Live Like A Suicide' [G n' R's 1986 E.P.]. I was like, "This isn't really what I saw at the Roxy last night, but O.K." Anytime I got $200 in my pocket, I bought a ticket to L.A., went out, and saw people. So we ended up signing them—I'd bring back things for my boss and he'd listen to them. It was amazing to me that nobody had Guns N' Roses yet.

Over the years—from '87 to '91—Axl and I became really good friends. It's really hectic for people to go through that kind of growth through the public eye and be famous…and be 25. Axl had a 'seen it all/done it all' reputation—but on a lot of levels, he was really naïve. So there was a lot to go through—I was the same way, so we got along really good. We were really close. I remember he said a friend of his in high school had rung him up-her little brother was going to L.A. to try and make it in music, and would he keep an eye out. That was Anna, Shannon's sister. So he said, "Yeah—give him my numbers." I think he got there sometime in 1990. I think it was Axl that had a picture of him on the fridge, that was clipped out of the Lafayette paper. It was Shannon deserted at the Lafayette bus station—sitting there for two or three days. There was a bus strike.

Shannon Hoon: We're both from the same town; he went to high school with my sister. We ran around with the same crowd, but I never really hung out with him in Indiana because I'm a few years younger. Out in L.A., there's a handful of people who are from our community. I'd sometimes run into friends who were from Lafayette and it was such a breath of fresh air. It felt like you were going home without going back home.

Colleen Combs: Axl told me Shannon was coming to L.A., and asked me to help him settle in. I remember Shannon already having been at parties via Axl. Shannon came by my place—Axl told him he was going to Vegas to marry Erin [Everly]. But I wasn't talking to Axl very much at that period, and Shannon was going out with him a lot. A month after that, Axl was calling me again. I ended up being a personal assistant to him. [Shannon] really had this idea of me that I was this Rolodex of Los Angeles, because of all the nightclub work I did—I knew a lot of people casually and the city pretty well.

Riki Rachtman: Axl at that time was always great about helping his friends out. Obviously, Axl was a very influential part in Shannon's success. And Shannon would do anything for him—just like Axl would do anything for his friends. If you were at the Cathouse, and somebody said something bad about Axl, Shannon would just hit the guy in the face.

Bill Armstrong: I was playing in bands—we were all musicians in town, everybody trying to get a band together. Axl was a big fan of Shannon's. He really loved the way Shannon sung, and felt like, "Here's a guy from my hometown, and I'm going to do anything to help this guy out."

Shelley Shaw: In 1990, it was the holidays—I think that's when [Axl] had been through a really quick divorce with Erin. He was sad and living at the studio—he was in a really bad way. I remember Shannon looked after him and stayed there with him. But he was like, "I've got to go home to Indiana to see my family on Christmas Eve." Somehow, he got a hold of me—I still hadn't talked to [Shannon]—"I've got to go, and I heard you might come in. This is what's going on."

I kind of took over, and then when I left, he came back. We were like 'ships in the night'—it was really weird. When I got there, [Axl] was sleeping a lot and going out to eat—there was no recording going on. He was just living there and he had a lot to say. It was more like Axl always needed somebody—he loved to sit and friggin' filibuster. They were doing the sessions for 'Use Your Illusion,' and I remember Axl was like, "My voice just isn't there for these high bits—I've got to get somebody in there to help." So he brought in Shannon to see if he could do some things. I still hadn't met him. It was like this myth—this little 'charge' that had been sent from the cornfields to have Axl look after.

Shannon Hoon: I still think of Axl as a friend, but we don't sit around talking about the music business or publicity stunts, because that kind of talk doesn't matter much to either of us. We always seem to find much more interesting things to talk about.

Mike Clink: Shannon was great. He was this shy little kid, that used to sit in the back of the room. And he would come night after night after night—sit there and listen. He was a sponge taking it all in. At that time, Blind Melon didn't exist—he was just doing demos every once in a while at home, and he would come in and play them for me. Trying to get my reaction on them. But he was still searching for his sound.

I think we had decided to get a whole bunch of people—with a bunch of different textures. We had some girls coming in singing—just a ton of people. When he did the vocals, he had a really great, smooth, pretty voice. It added a nice little texture to the songs. My first impression was of him being this shy little kid from Indiana, who was a friend of Axl's. He was very respectful of everybody's space—he never got belligerent. He was there to take it in and experience the events.

Duff McKagan: He was a good guy. He was a friend of Axl's, so he was hanging out quite a bit in the early days of Guns N' Roses. A fucking hell of a singer. He sang on "Don't Cry"—he was around a lot, before that even.

Shannon Hoon: I got to know the rest of the band through him, and that day I just happened to be in the studio and they asked me if I wanted to sing on that one track.

Nel Hoon: He was very excited. The fact that he was on the "Don't Cry" video and the song—I have to give Axl credit, that he did help. I know that now Axl's not the most popular guy—I still think he helped Shannon out.

Michael Kelsey: Before Shannon met Axl, he had gotten a hold of G n R's demo from mutual Axl friends. He was bent on [Styff Kytten] doing a tune on the tape that hadn't been released. So we were doing a version of "Don't Cry" years before he ever recorded the actual studio version with Axl.

Shannon Hoon: It was just a couple of friends getting together to sing a song. As far as the big deal that was made out of it, that was your fault, not mine.

Bill Armstrong: I remember going out with Shannon and Axl, when Shannon was singing on the 'Use Your Illusion' records. One night, we were standing on Sunset Boulevard, and this car pulls up out of nowhere, and it's Axl. He goes, *"Hey you fuckers—jump in the car!"* We all get in, we got driving around town listening to rough mixes in the car, and went to a couple of parties together. It was just surreal. And then Axl drops me off at my house! Shannon used to live maybe a block and a half away from me, so we'd see each other all the time.

Riki Rachtman: The way I knew about Shannon was pretty much from Axl. I had an office in Hollywood that handled all my clubs, my apparel company, and a lot of my appearances through MTV and radio. So Axl said, "Look, there's a friend of mine that is coming into town and he needs a job." If there was somebody from the old days, he always helped a lot of his friends—where he had either an old friend write a video or get a job in the band. He'd always done a lot of help for me, so whatever he wanted; I was like, "Yeah, no problem."

Shannon Hoon: If I had to deal with half the stuff that [Axl] has to deal with, then I'd be mad! I think everyone would!

Colleen Combs: [Shannon was] completely jazzed. That was one of those things where…that world is so huge. There's such a difference between having to play covers back in your hometown, moving to a place like L.A., where you can play all original stuff, and get shows. It's a bit strange when some of your friends have already made it, because you can *see it*—it seems so real, it's not like winning the lottery any longer. It seems like a really accessible thing. And really, at that time, it was an accessible thing—a lot of people were being signed.

Axl was living pretty large, so anyone coming in at that point didn't see Guns N' Roses when they were struggling and living in their practice space. By that time, he had his condo up on Sunset, I think, and money to buy other property. Everything was huge—he had that custom convertible BMW. I'm guessing what it would look like to Shannon, but Shannon was enthusiastic about almost everything. When I say he was sweet and nice—a lot of things really made him excited. And all of Los Angeles to him was huge, exciting, and completely open to him—he was always meeting people, getting invited places, and going places.

Brian Whitus: I recall when they did that video on the roof. Shannon wore that outfit—the blazer shirt and jeans. Axl went and changed his clothes to kind of simulate Shannon. Shannon laughed about it—"*That guy took my idea!*"

Shannon Hoon: They had one hell of a catering situation at that thing.

Bill Armstrong: I think Axl saw a little bit of himself in Shannon. Shannon definitely had some 'Axl-like qualities.' Not as far as being a dictator or any of that kind of stuff—more along the lines of living life by the seat of his pants.

Shannon Hoon: I don't really want to talk about that any more. It seems like such a long time ago to me now, but that's all everyone seems to think about. It's not something I feel is relevant to what I'm doing now.

L.A./Blind Melon Forms

Hoon, Smith, Stevens, and Thorn arrive in Los Angeles at various points between 1988-1990, and all four small-town boys eventually cross paths to form Blind Melon. Graham is the last piece to the puzzle. Thanks to Hoon's association with G n' R, the group creates a buzz amongst record labels—without even having played a proper gig yet.

Shannon Hoon: I moved out there [to Los Angeles] and was attacked by all these different sides of life that are out here, and I learned to deal with a lot of things. Where I come from, a lot of people can't deal with people who are gay, and when you're brought up around a society that doesn't accept people for what they are, regardless of whether they're gay or black or whatever...if you're brought up in a society like that, it's hard to not become that way. When I moved out here, I was so happy that I could be friends with people who are gay, I could push all the stereotypical ideas that I was subjected to growing up aside. The only people that can't deal with it are small-minded people who are really unhappy with themselves, and they take it out on other people who are happy about the way they are.

Colleen Combs: People have an impression that big cities are unfriendly, and I have an opposite opinion of cities. If you know someone new is coming, you try to set them up with all your friends. Just like if you meet someone who you know is brand new and kind of green, you push them in the right direction— "Don't go east of this block, don't look for work there it'll it never happen, this place is a scam." The first time I remember being with Shannon, I had a motorcycle—I'm quite small, I had a little Honda—and Shannon wanted to drive around to construction sites. That seemed like the oddest thing to me—I didn't know anyone who did something like construction. I mean, Shannon was a pretty healthy, normal guy—he wasn't like 'heroin chic.' So I thought he was a bit out of his head—that he could just go to random sites and that they would hire him on a construction crew. But that's what he wanted to do, so that's what we spent the day doing.

He ended up moving into an apartment right in front of mine—an old, sort of Hollywood neighborhood. There was a house in front, a guesthouse in the middle of that, and then a guesthouse behind that—he lived in the front house. Our block was a really popular block. The rest of the guys that lived there were all improv actors—they were part of the Groundlings. So we had a very non-rock environment. They thought we were interesting and we thought they were interesting. I think of things when I think of him like… lizards get trapped in your apartment a lot—they run in under the door. Lizards for some reason freak me out, and Shannon would always come over, help collect them, and put them in a fishbowl. We would get on my motorcycle and go to Wattles Park and let them go, and talk about how if we had a lonely lizard, maybe that lizard would go find another lizard and they'd be happy together. We'd be like, "Stay out of Hollywood, what are you doing? Stay in the park—the park's nice!" There's people that you can call at 2:00 in the morning, and you know that even though you're disturbing them, they'd always come help you. Shannon was one of those guys for me.

Rogers Stevens: We got there and we were just blown away. We thought we were going to meet up and get into cool bands, but we were really fresh off the farm. We didn't have any fucking idea what was going on. We got there and thought, "We'll just go see where all this music is coming from." We went and saw what was happening on the Sunset Strip and all those bars, and it was completely ridiculous. We were pretty discouraged—we didn't know where to go look for any other types of scenes. We were trying to survive. But we knew other things were going on, it was just a matter of time until we met other people.

Brad Smith: It was the remnants of the metal scene, which was ultra sad. We got here, and that was part of the allure when you're reading magazines in Mississippi, is that out here, it's O.K. to be a freak. But the saving grace of the

L.A. scene at that point was Jane's Addiction. It tore my fucking head off and changed my life—Perry [Farrell] made me feel like it was O.K. to be different and write your own songs from the heart, even if they don't sound all nice and shiny. If you have the fire to deliver it, that's all that matters. So Jane's Addiction was one those saving graces when I moved to L.A., because I was depressed from the music scene. It was just horrible.

Shannon Hoon: It's hard to find people who like the same music that you do, especially in a place like L.A., where we got together. There are so many different types of music in the city—glam, metal, you name it. It's a lot like a broken mirror—bits of music everywhere, like pieces of shattered glass—but no one, single, solid chunk. It was a challenge just to find each other, but then again, maybe it was meant to happen.

Rogers Stevens: I was in a band, and then I got Brad in the band, I think it was called the Glass Grenades. But these things would last two weeks, because you would see an ad with someone looking for one member, not two members. And we were a pair. So we were testing the waters, doing other things, and meeting other people. That's how Brad met Christopher.

Brad Smith: It was tough for the first couple of years, and then I found Christopher through the Music Connection. I was actually going to play bass in his band, and then once Rogers and I got a foothold and found a drummer, I called Christopher, and said, "Come play in our band."

Christopher Thorn: I went on a bunch of auditions. I was in this sorta folk rock band, and that's how I met Brad. The project I was working on at the time didn't work out, but Brad and I stayed tight. Then he called me—he and Rogers had met Shannon.

Brad Smith: We tried out a bunch of singers, and we found Shannon through a mutual friend—he came in, sat down with an acoustic guitar, and played "Change" as his audition. We were like, "O.K., this is it, this is so right." And he had the same kind of background that we did—moving from a small town.

We kinda wore that on our sleeves. At the time, right before Nirvana and Pearl Jam dropped, it was unique for a band to have that stance. When Shannon came in, all those songs that I had started on, he took them to full realization. Easily. It was a struggle for me—I can write songs, but I don't think I was as prolific as Shannon. I definitely don't have the voice he had—he had an amazing voice. He came in and he made it easier for everybody. He just seemed like a bro from Mississippi. I swear to God, it was like, "Let's smoke some weed and go out to the train trestle!"

He was completely unpretentious, unaffected by L.A. thus far, and he felt like one of us immediately. We were very congenial people—we felt that way about a lot of people initially, until they played guitar, and we're like, "Oh, I don't know if this is going to work." But Shannon, from the first three or four notes, you're like, "Jesus Christ—*this is great.*" It wasn't really a hard decision to make, it was almost immediate. Rogers I think had the first meeting with Shannon, called me up, and said, "Brad, you gotta go down, right now, to the rehearsal space and meet this guy Shannon. I'm telling you, he's the guy—he's amazing." It was the first guy that I ever heard Rogers get pumped up over. There was never a moment in the Blind Melon career where I felt like I had 'made it.' I think the closest I ever came to feeling like I made it was when Shannon walked in the room and played "Change," I felt like I made it in a weird way. I knew it was so good, undeniable, and unstoppable. It was like the missing piece of the puzzle on how to become a great band.

Christopher Thorn: Brad called and said, "We found this singer and he's really great. Come over, we're looking for a guitar player." I went over, and they had set up a little practice space at the home of the original drummer. I walked in and they were working on a song that kinda sucked, to tell you the truth! It never made it to anything more than a four-track demo—I think it was called "Rebirth." It was really cheesy—it was a lot more metal-y, in a *bad* way. But when I heard his voice, I thought, "Holy shit"—he totally blew me away. He might have played me "Change" that night too, on the acoustic. I was totally into it—we started practicing in the back house of the original drummer's parent's house in Westwood. And that's how the band started.

Immediately, I thought he was it. You know when somebody has whatever that is that you want for a lead singer? I'll never forget going home to my girlfriend, and going, "Oh my God, this guy's the shit!" And people wonder about Shannon—did he get that way because he became famous or was he always like that? Shannon was a rock star even if he was going to work on a construction site. Yeah, the fact that he was in a band, that worked out really well for him. If he was at the 7-11, you'd walk in and think, "This guy is a rock star." He just had that incredible energy—talked non-stop, was hilarious, slightly demented, and had that incredible energy.

Rogers Stevens: He would *not* shut up. I remember that first night that we decided we were going to be in a band, we'd gotten really drunk. We were crashing out at the living room of my apartment, and he tried to pick a fight with me! He got mad because I was laughing at him—he had said something really stupid. That was the thing about Shannon, he'd say everything that came into his mind. A lot of the times it would like, "Why did you say that?" He was on the phone, trying to get a cab to drive him back to Indiana, and I'm laughing even more. Miraculously, he didn't throw a punch. It could've ended right there.

Shannon Hoon: L.A.—after being out there for a while, I found myself surrounded by a lot of people, and the only thing they really had was who they knew. All they could talk about was who they knew, how they knew them, what parties they'd been to, and what rock stars and movie stars they hung out with. It was all part of the big city attitude, and I was subjected to a lot of people like that. Meeting up with Brad and Rogers was real refreshing.

Lisa Sinha: Shannon liked those guys from the get-go. They truly became friends, not like, "We're gonna play together and be a band." They wrote all their songs, but they were all buddies and had girlfriends. They truly had a relationship.

Nel Hoon: When I went out to visit him, he took me to the Cathouse. The line was around the block. He said, "Come on mom, we're going up front." He knew the people at the door, and they let us go walking right in. He was really proud—he introduced me to so many people that night. I just thought, "O.K.—he's going to make it in this town." That was only about a few months after he left, because I couldn't stand him being so far away and I couldn't see him. So I went out there. I wanted to see his surroundings—where he lived, who were his friends, and meet the people he knew. Shannon seemed totally fine—I saw no signs of him doing any drugs whatsoever. I didn't even see any signs of him smoking pot. And that was my first introduction to the restaurant, Johnny Rockets—I loved that restaurant, so we went there almost every day. My next visit out, I took my daughter Anna and her daughter, Grace. L.A. was great.

Marc Pollack: Guns N' Roses played the Pantages Theater, and I remember we all went there with Shannon. We were sitting in our seats, and from the stage, Axl Rose requested Shannon's appearance on stage. Shannon had to go running through the audience to get up on stage to sing "Don't Cry." When Guns N' Roses played the L.A. Forum, Shannon played the first night, and then was asked *not* to play the next couple of nights [laughs].

Nel Hoon: I have a great picture of Shannon and Donald Trump. A big 8x10—Shannon sent it home to me. I'm sure he thought I would be impressed. There were a lot of celebrities that had heard Shannon sing. I remember I was visiting Shannon in L.A. and Guns N' Roses [performed] at the Great Western Forum, and Shannon introduced me to Johnny Depp. I was just so starstruck that I was meeting 'Edward Scissorhands.' He knew everybody.

Riki Rachtman: We met Shannon, and I hired him in my office to answer phones at first. He was just this normal kid—really funny. Nothing that you would think with the Blind Melon stuff. I mean, Blind Melon was kind of 'happy flower hippie stuff'—he wasn't like that. He was just this cool kid—he used to hang out at all the clubs. He would come into our office and tell us stories like, "Check it out, I met these two girls this night, I was doing one…"—he would tell us all these crazy sex stories about all the girls he was hanging out with. He was really loving being part of the 'L.A. scene' at the time. It seemed like he was kind of naïve. I remember I took him to Vegas—he'd never been to Vegas, he was just blown away. He had a very good relationship with his mother—his mother was awesome. We would talk to her all the time. [Shannon] didn't work at the Cathouse—I had a company called 'Rachtman Entertainment,' and he worked at Rachtman Entertainment. When we did the Cathouse in Arizona, we had like a hundred or so people from Hollywood come down, and because he worked for me, I said, "Here Shannon, you drive everybody from the hotel to the club." Which was the stupidest idea in the world, because he was just *smashed out of his brain*, driving people. But that was Shannon.

Gilby Clarke: That's what I remember Shannon from—the Cathouse days. He was just a kid that hung around—it was kind of a small circle, the 'Cathouse gang.' Some of us went every week—it was just our kind of bar that we went to, hung out, and got in trouble with. He looked like everybody else. With Blind Melon, it was more of the 'hippie vibe.' Then, it was more of the 'metal vibe.'

Colleen Combs: We hung out a lot, and it tended to be after I was done working or after he had come home. So really, what we would do is talk about his night, and what was going on. And that's where I think I get that strong impression of him looking at Los Angeles like it was this huge wonderland, and sort of open to him. Whereas some people get to Los Angeles and it's intimidating, cold, or scary—too freaky for them—Shannon thought that everything was interesting. A lot of times, he would turn around and try to turn it into songwriting—different, weird people he saw. He knew Drew Barrymore from somewhere—they may have met at a party. I remember passing Drew on Sunset Boulevard and her yelling out the window to Shannon.

Marc Pollack: My roommate was Bill Armstrong. Rogers used to work with Bill at a rock memorabilia store on Melrose—I met Rogers through him, Shannon through Rogers, and then the rest of the band. In my little apartment there on Sunset, the band would practice acoustically. I remember I'd get up early and go to work—leave for the day and come home at 6/7:00. I'd walk in, and in my living room, they're sitting around on the couch and on the table in a semi-circle, jamming. Playing tunes from the first record.

Christopher Thorn: We had gone on a few meetings with this original drummer, and we realized he was just not happening. We were all from small towns, we didn't have this sorta 'L.A. attitude,' and he really thought that he knew better than us. And he wasn't that good—that's the truth.

Glen Graham: I got a call from Rogers out of the blue. He said, "We've got a band and we need a new drummer. Will you come out and do this?" And I took that to mean, "You've got the job, come on out and be in the band." Little did I know, I was *auditioning*. Rogers sent me a tape. I was living in a house with a bunch of people—this is Chapel Hill, North Carolina. This is as far from L.A./late '80s music as you can possibly get. I put this thing in the cassette player in the kitchen. And I just thought immediately, "O.K., I see what they mean—this will work. People will like this." It was not something that I was necessarily into at the time, but I knew the way that I played drums, if they would let me play the way I wanted to play, I would be able to slightly steer it away from the metal thing. They were a *heavy metal band*, and had "Change" and "No Rain." The rest of the stuff was totally different. I had no money or anything at the time—I was driving around in a Ford Escort. I had my little four-piece kit, my chopping block, knives, and my jam box. I moved out there just spur of the moment, and ended up sleeping on the floor of an old band friend from Mississippi for about a month. And oddly enough, living directly across the street from Christopher and Heather. It was like a block off Hollywood Boulevard. I was doing phone surveys—where you annoy people endlessly about things that don't matter. Trying to keep them on the phone for five bucks an hour.

Christopher Thorn: The band never really found its sound until Glen joined the band. Glen was such a big part of that sound, because nobody plays drums like Glen. And Glen turned us on to so many older records that we didn't even know about. Glen's one of those guys who listens to everything—he was really great at 'the history of rock.' He could tell you musicians, song titles. Any great record, he knew about.

Glen Graham: I met Shannon hours after I got there. Rogers was working at the Rock Store, on Melrose. I remember going there, and then very shortly after that, going to Shannon's apartment, where Shannon was eating Chinese food. I remember him putting fourteen packets of soy sauce on his lo mein, which was already the saltiest thing on the planet. He was newly into Chinese food. *"This stuff is great man, you've got to try it!"* But my impression of him was, "This guy is perfect" [laughs]. He's nuts, he's loud—if two of you were in the room, he would still be on 'ten' the whole time. Just one of those guys that's meant to front a band. The first time we played together was maybe two days later. It was like, "Wow, cool—this guy can do all those heavy metal vocal stylings, but he doesn't sound like a heavy metal singer." I'd never played in a band with a guy that could do the David Lee Roth super-squeaky thing. It was just amazing to me. Not that he used it, but he could do that stuff. I was blown away, but at the same time, I was sort of afraid—to be perfectly honest. Because you could see that this is your future Jim Morrison—over-the-top guy, running on fumes, with no ability to put on the brakes.

Lyle Eaves: Back in Starkville, Mississippi, there's a small music scene. I was a sound engineer there, and I worked with Brad, Rogers, and Glen. When they all took off and went to L.A., I stayed in touch with them and kept saying, "When you guys get ready to go out on the road, I want the job." I was the very first person hired—before they'd even recorded an album. I lived with Shannon and Rogers when I moved out there. It was pretty much [a] non-stop party—a lot of fun. We'd go out, and the goal was to get [Shannon] home in one piece every night. We went out seven nights a week when we were in L.A. The Cathouse a lot, and a club called Peanuts.

Bill Armstrong: Shannon—just like all of us at the time—would drink a lot. We would all go out and get wasted. But he was also a black belt in karate. So Shannon drunk plus black belt in karate always led for adventures [laughs].

Lyle Eaves: At his drunkest—he would decide to pull that out. And it usually ended up with him busting his own ass—trying to karate kick somebody.

Riki Rachtman: Shannon was a bit of a scrapper. Shannon was always getting in fistfights—*always*. He would get drunk and was a little troublemaker—but he was a blast to hang out with. One time, I think it was right before I was going to go to New York for MTV, I used to have…it wasn't a gang, it was just a group of guys that were called 'the Alumni.' There were like ten of us. One night, I didn't go out with them—Shannon went out with them. Shannon ended up getting into a fistfight with the guys in the band Vio-Lence, which was a San Francisco metal band. He was a guy that whenever trouble started, he had your back.

Lyle Eaves: He definitely was Dr. Jekyll and Mr. Hyde. Within two or three days of me moving to L.A., we went out one night. We were living in a little guest house out back, and there was one driveway going to the back of the house, [which] everybody parked their cars in. So, if you needed out, you had to get people out of the front house [to] move cars. We came in, Shannon's trashed, [and] Rogers wants to go see this girl. We go up to tell this guy in the front house—it's like 2:00 in the morning—"You need to move your car so we can get out." He comes out, sits in the car, and Rogers is in there running his mouth, drinking more. Forgets about it, and the guy is getting pissed sitting out in the driveway. So he comes in and starts raising hell—trying to start a fight. He got dragged out of bed. So Rogers is outside arguing with the guy and I'm trying to get the guy away. I finally talked the guy into getting in his car. When I turned around, Shannon comes running out of the house with a steak knife! Bear in mind—I've been there like three days, just met this guy. I tackled him with a *steak knife*, and he starts trying to stab me with it! I had to wrestle him down and get the knife away from him. I mean, I'm not a huge guy, but I was bigger than Shannon. It ended up the guy finally moved his car and Rogers' drunk ass gets in his car—backs right into the large house, and backs all the way down the side of it, and leaves. The next morning, Rogers pulls up, and I said, "How's your car look?" He was like, "What do you mean?" I said, "Go look at the passenger side of it." The whole side of it just had this huge yellow crease from the brick on the front house all the way down it. It was something like that non-stop with Shannon.

Riki Rachtman: He was in our office one time, and he comes in with this cute little dog [named Wooh]. He went into the pet store, grabbed a dog, and ran!

Colleen Combs: You know how he got his pug? That's Shannon. Y'know, "Look at the puppy I got—I liberated him." I rarely remember Shannon ever saying something was difficult or bad. When he had the pug was the same time he had a girlfriend for quite a while—and they had kind of a messy break-up. And even that, he'd sort of laugh about everything—really easygoing and happy, all the time I ever had any experiences with him.

Heather Thorn: Right in the beginning of the band, he kicked in our door in L.A. One night he got really drunk, came home to Rogers, Rogers couldn't deal with him being so wasted, so Rogers took [Shannon's] dog. Brought him over to our house, and then Shannon came beating on the door in the middle of the night. Finally, the cops showed up and had to haul him away. In the process, he would knock on the door, "Just give me my dog, just give me my dog!" We'd be like, "Shannon, just go home—*you'll sleep it off.*" Then he'd go, "O.K. guys, I'm really sorry." And then we'd say, "O.K., then just go home." And then he'd flip out. We lived in a courtyard apartment, so eventually the cops came and took him home.

It was like that literally from the day I met Shannon. He was always that guy—he was a big sweetheart, but he was also a mess. Especially when he drank—he was really violent when he drank. It was like, "God, can't you just smoke pot?" [laughs] His heart was always in the right place. Like when I was saying Shannon ended up kicking down the door, his way of apologizing for that, my birthday was the following week. He showed up at my birthday and he'd written a song, framed it, and sang it to me. It's great, it's about he would 'leave farts that wouldn't stink if I'd forgive him' [laughs]. He was so great at apologizing. He hated when he fucked up, and he was a really good guy underneath it all. He would fuck up so bad, but he would turn around, and he's so sweet that you can't not love him.

Rogers Stevens: At the beginning, there was kind of bouncing around, until we got this house that [Shannon] and I lived in. Which there's pictures of that house—of us sitting on the front porch with flannel shirts on. I was there for less than a year with Shannon. It was just a little bungalow backhouse in Hollywood. Shannon was a complete neat freak. So living with him, you never knew what hour of the day he was going to be scrubbing under the toilet with a toothbrush or something. It was one of those character traits that threw me about him—how clean he was. He was obsessed with it. He would cook things like Chef Boyardee raviolis. Almost domesticated, in a way. He liked to keep his home area like 'the home'—[he'd] go out and be a jackass somewhere else. We never had parties there.

Kim Smith: I met Shannon first—in April of 1991. We had a party at our house—I had already fallen asleep. When I woke up the next morning, he was already a legend in our house. I lived with four girls, and all I heard was "Shannon Hoon, Shannon Hoon, Shannon Hoon!" I was like, "Who was he?" You have to remember, we were 22 at the time, so all these girls in my house were 'claiming' him as their boyfriend. That next day, I went to the grocery store with my friend Mia, who lived with me. And Shannon happened to be there with Rogers. He acted like I knew him forever—like he'd met me the night before or something. He just had that huge personality, and instantly, we were all friends. He started hanging out at our house, we started going out to different clubs. One night, we were all meeting up at Riki Rachtman's Cathouse, and he brought along Brad. Shannon called the next day after, he's like, "Hey—*my bass player thinks you're cute.*" I'm like, "Ugh, the last thing I want to do is date a musician." Because all my friends were into musicians. But Brad was the nicest guy—he wasn't your typical 'musician' in that way. Shannon was, though [laughs]. So Brad and I started dating in May of '91. Honestly, even before Blind Melon was big, *everyone* knew of Shannon Hoon. He was just out and about. And the party did not start until Shannon was there. Very friendly to everybody—he was such a good guy. It was pretty apparent from the very beginning of meeting Shannon that he did everything in excess. He wasn't 'the moderate drinker' or 'the moderate drug taker.'

Marc Pollack: I was dating this girl, and she was living with her boyfriend at the time. She wanted to move out of her apartment on him, and we were up pretty late the night before the move was going to happen. Shannon made a decision that he didn't think that it would be good for me to help this girl move, because if the boyfriend was there, it would get ugly. He and another friend of ours got up earlier than me the next morning, got in the moving truck, and moved the girl for me. Without me even asking. It's just a nice gesture—he was looking out for his buddy. That characterizes the kind of guy he was a little bit.

Glen Graham: That was Rogers' selling point—"Shannon's friends with Axl, and we're going to try and be managed by the same management company that does Guns N' Roses. And if we do that, we'll be touring with them." This is total bullshit, total speculation on his part. To my astonishment, both of those things happened. So that was just good luck. Plus, Shannon was the kind of guy that would go to a record company, and say, "I want to speak to whoever…Ahmet Ertegun," and get up there. Actually be able to sit there and make the people listen to him play acoustic guitar and sing. I don't remember exactly who he did that with, but he did that more than once. How the hell do you do that? Shannon was good at first impressions.

Rogers Stevens: I never went down to the ['Use Your Illusion'] sessions, but we did stuff with Axl here and there—outside of the studio. I'm not sure what point in the process they were. I went over to his apartment a few times—he was living off Sunset in some condo. Just temporarily. Went to the movies— of all things—with Shannon and Axl. That was really when [Guns N' Roses] were at their peak. People were freaking out that he was there—they couldn't believe it. We went to the Mann's Chinese Theater right there on Hollywood Boulevard. It was 'Mortal Thoughts' starring Demi Moore and Bruce Wil- lis. By the time I was getting to know [Axl], he took off on that big tour. My impressions of him was he seemed like a 'for real' guy. I got on well with him. It's difficult to imagine what they went through—it was just so out of control, their level of fame.

Lyle Eaves: I was really impressed with the band the first time I heard them play—they were better than I was expecting. I knew there was a lot of hype around the band, because of Shannon's connection to Guns N' Roses. I really hadn't heard any of the music—other than a couple of demos—until I went out there. They had a rehearsal, I sat and watched them, and I was pretty blown away.

Colleen Combs: The demo was made, and they didn't have to do the circuit like people did. Some people come to Los Angeles to start bands, and they're playing shows over and over again, hoping that A&R people will notice them that way. And it seems like Blind Melon had gone in the other direction— they had a demo tape, and *then* they had interest.

Glen Graham: When I got in the band, it changed. I brought them back to, "Let's listen to some Traffic, let's listen to some Allman Brothers." Christopher was a huge Led Zeppelin fan, and that really hadn't entered into the thing yet—it was still Guns N' Roses/Jane's Addiction. It took a while to get things smooth, musically. But it was fun and really not that hard. We were practicing an hour a day—we were living all over Los Angeles, and we practiced downtown, an hour away. So every day we would pile into someone's car, drive to the practice room totally burned out from our day jobs, run the set, work on a couple of tunes, and that was it. So my initial impression of the band was, "This is certainly not what I would have chosen if I was putting a band together myself. But it's perfect for me, because I think I can bring something to it that would fuck it up in a good way" [laughs].

Rogers Stevens: We never did any shows until Glen was in the band. We didn't have a name, or we hadn't really decided on a name.

Glen Graham: I remember the first show was Tranca's, and it was a little place in Malibu. It was painted aqua on the inside. We had this group of people that followed us around. When I say 'group,' I mean ten people. I remember it being very, very shaky. We just hadn't done anything. I mean, we'd all played in bands, but these guys had not played in a band for so long…the difference between the practice room and playing in a club with nobody there was really kind of shocking. I was a little freaked out about that. And then we did some weird things, like back rooms of clubs in Hollywood. I don't remember much about them, except that they were put together by our lawyer at the time, who was trying to get us signed.

Shannon Hoon: Back then we were just waiting for the right time. We didn't like all the politics that were involved with the clubs. People just needed a little less attitude. That whole heavy metal attitude scene was going on at that time and we didn't fit into it.

Riki Rachtman: Shannon used to come into our office every Monday or Tuesday, and he'd go, "Hey, I got the idea for the name of our band—*Brown Cow.*" And we'd all laugh, "That's the stupidest name I've ever heard!" Then he came in one day, "I've got a better name for our band—*Blind Melon.*" I go, "That's a stupider name than Brown Cow!"

Brad Smith: My dad used to yell [the phrase 'Blind Melon'] to friends that lived next door to us. They were all very into the '70s groovy thing. Blind Melon is indirectly from a Cheech and Chong comedy record. Cheech says "What's happening, blind melon?" in a Mex-American way. That's how they referred to each other for a while. It's one of the colorful random things I remember from my childhood. I guess it made an impression, because they would literally yell it back and forth across the street.

Riki Rachtman: We did either a New Year's show or my birthday party—I can't remember which one. We used to have tons of bands play, and I let Shannon's band play. Doors opened at 8:00, they went on at like, ten to 8:00. But people were starting to notice.

Lyle Eaves: My first week out there, they played the Cathouse. We opened for a band that was supposed to be up and coming, that didn't really go any-where—Liquid Jesus. They were friends with them. It was really good—I wish there was a tape of it. I still have my setlist, that Shannon wrote. Gene Simmons was standing beside me and David Briggs was there—I was this kid from Mississippi, completely freaked out about the whole thing. But it was a good show. Seeing Shannon in all of his glory for the first time made an impression. I thought, "These guys really are the real deal. This is going to work." There were a ton of industry people there, because [of] the hype and the buzz about the band. I remember Christina Applegate being there. There was a lot of celebrities to see them the first time.

Christopher Thorn: It happened fast for us, as far as getting things up and running—we had an attorney. We weren't really prepared, we had a few songs, and this attorney shopped them. And before I knew it—I was only in the band a few months—we were having lunch and dinners with record companies.

Kim Smith: They had a few of songs—"Soul One," "Mother," and "No Rain." They had taped them on a four-track or something.

Chris Smith: Brad used to send me demos from California—that's all I listened to. Me and all my buddies in Mississippi, we were already all over it.

Michael Kelsey: I always got an occasional phone call with the latest updates. When the Blind Melon thing started coming together he was low-key about it. So I assumed it was nothing special and that he would have some different news on the next call. Every phone call had some good news about their journey and he always said it in that same humble way.

Colleen Combs: There was something about Shannon to me…comparatively, if I think about Eddie Vedder and Axl—who I've both worked with—he was always honest about it. I don't remember it ever becoming something he had to do or that he really even had any alternative agenda to get to somewhere with it. It was just really who he honestly was. There's something about a singer's personality—you tend to meet them, they look you right in the eye, you feel like you're engaged with them. Shannon had that same quality, but you didn't feel like he was doing it because he knew you were a reporter doing your job with him. It was something he would have done if he met you randomly, on the street somewhere.

Riki Rachtman: He would get drunk—he would have fun like everybody else.

But the drugs were just not good for Shannon—there are no two ways about it.

Shelley Shaw: It was the end of September 1991, and Shannon and I were talking on the phone a great deal—it was before we met in person but we had already signed them as a client. I was flying into L.A. to meet them for the first time, and when I got to L.A., I checked my home machine and there was a long message from Shannon saying that he really needed to talk. He had been at a party all night and a kid had overdosed and died at the party. Apparently, the kid was lying on the floor maybe in the kitchen of this house where the party was, and there was activity around getting help in another room. Shannon said that he sat on the floor with the body of this stranger and just watched his face, looked long and hard into his eyes, and stayed there like that for a long time. And that he was contemplating his own behaviors and mental processes around wanting to get high. Went home, stayed up all night, and had gone through the Yellow Pages marking psychiatrists' phone numbers to try and call later in the day to go and get help, and never end up like that dead party guest. He did not follow through.

Capitol Records/Chris Jones/'Sippin' Time Sessions'

Blind Melon inks a deal with Capitol Records, Chris Jones signs on as their manager, and the group promptly records—and shelves—an E.P., 'Sippin' Time Sessions.'

Rogers Stevens: We did it in a really stupid way. Because labels jumped all over us because of Shannon's connection with Guns N' Roses, we were doing things like renting out rehearsal halls, and playing there with these people sitting there watching us. Showcases for just the heads of the labels. We did those kinda shows for like ten labels. And it was really weird—it was a different time in the industry. I'm not sure that would happen now.

Glen Graham: We did a lot of showcases. Our lawyer at that time wanted to also manage us, which was a conflict of interest—that's how we managed to move him out of the picture as soon as we got signed. He lined up all these labels—just about every label you could think of. We'd have dinner with them and then do a showcase with them. And you'd go to like, 'Joe's Garage,' Frank Zappa's place in the Valley, set up in a room that's got the padded cell set from the "Metal Health" video from Quiet Riot lining the back wall. I remember doing the showcases—there you are, in a theater with two rows of seats, which were folding chairs. And literally, suits walk in, and do the little 'Phil Hartman nod.' Then you walk over there, they say some bullshit to you, and that's that. This went on for a few months, and then one day we got a call. Every week, another offer would come through, and then people would retract the offers.

Gene Simmons wanted to manage us, too. The thing that people don't know about Gene is that he is the guy who supposedly resurrected Liza Minnelli's career. I remember David [Rudick, Blind Melon's subsequent lawyer] sitting us down very carefully, and saying in no uncertain terms, "[Gene] wants to start a management company. He understands the tides are turning. The shape of the hard rock scene is moving from L.A./glam to a Nirvana thing. He understands that you guys are 'next up,' so he wants to get in on this." We went to his house thinking bats, fire breathing dragons, and Vincent Price as the butler, but at this time he lived in a rather modest 80's contemporary home. Nothing like the 'Family Jewels' house. I think he lived next door to Kenny G. He explained that he owned fairly modest homes all over the world and that we should spread out our wealth rather than concentrating large sums in single properties or ventures. So far this has not been a problem.

We're sitting up in the second story of his guest house, which is like a Kiss shrine and over the fireplace is a circle of 22 overlapping platinum Kiss albums framed in this gigantic 5 1/2' by 5' shadowbox frame. And you realize "Wow, Goddamn...Kiss really sold a lot of records! I hadn't listened to these guys since I was a kid, but man, they did not stop." And then Paul Stanley came in, and that was weird. I think he had been egged on by Gene—"You've got to come see these guys." And Paul sat there with his little white Espadrilles on, legs crossed, jangling his gigantic ring of keys. Basically looking off into space, while Gene told us about the topsy-turvy world of heavy rock. "It's just a business." He's showing us all this *stuff*—his trophies. It's like being in some sort of seminar for insurance or something. It was nice—I did my little Gene Simmons impersonation for him in the driveway. "You guys need to put the make-up back on and get back together." He looked at me like, "Yeah, *like we haven't thought of that.*" But that was a personal thrill for me, because I mean, Kiss, when I was in grammar school, they were the shit.

Tim Devine: I was headed to see a girl named Elaine Summers at a club called Molly Malone's—on Fairfax Boulevard in L.A. As often happens, the set time got pushed back an hour. I was hanging out at the club with nothing to do, when her attorney grabbed me and said, "Why don't we go out to the car and I'll play you some of the other bands I'm working on?" So we went and we drove around for a while—listened to a few things—including a tape of a band called Head Train [one of Blind Melon's early names]. I thought it sounded very interesting, very unusual. It was this kind of jam-y, swirling demo, and the lead singer had a very unusual voice. Now, I didn't think the songs were all together, but I thought they had at least one of the elements that someone like me is looking for in a band—their own unique, distinctive sound.

From there, we went back in and saw the other act—not sure if she ever got signed or not—but I stayed in touch with their attorney, followed up, waited to hear more material and developed a genuine interest in what this Head Train band was up to. You hear thousands of tapes in the course of doing an A&R job and it's still truly rare—the ones that jump out at you and say, "Here's somebody who has been able to put together a sound, a vibe, or an attitude that you haven't yet heard before. And have it work." So naturally, I wanted to follow up.

I think from there we set up a showcase so I could see the band in a rehearsal setting. Which I did, and the same thing struck me—the same quality that seemed to show the seeds of something magical in the demo tape were even more apparent in the rehearsal setting. We booked them into a room at a place called Leeds Rehearsal Studios, out in North Hollywood. I went down and watched them play for probably about a half hour. The thing I remember distinctly about it was that they did four or five songs and that was it. I liked what I saw, so I asked if they could do a couple more songs—which is something that I rarely do, quite frankly. And they said, "No." "What do you mean, 'No'?" "That's all we have." So this was a band that had not been together that long, and it was very unusual for me to even consider a signing insofar as I don't think I ever signed a rock band that had not already been out gigging.

Glen Graham: All we were interested in was getting signed. When you're going through it, it feels agonizing. The amount of money they were talking about were big amounts to any kid working minimum wage. But you don't really understand what that translates to as far as starting your career. When we finally got the O.K. from Capitol, it was just like, "O.K., great." I think they got a bidding war started—I can't remember between who. It was just typical L.A. bullshit. "Oh, I hear these guys are doing something. They have Axl Rose [behind them]. I've got to check that out!" It snowballs, and then, "I've got to have them! No, *I've* got to have them!" So we got a really good deal at the time, for a band that had five songs. But showcasing was weird. Somebody from the Turtles came down to one showcase and I remember after we played—and the guy had no idea who played what in our band—the guy turns in our general direction and blurts out, "Yeah, well you guys are great, but I don't like the way the drummer and bass player play together." We're looking back at him like, "Yeah, well we'll get right on that. Next..."

Tim Devine: I had decided after several rehearsals that it was time to try to make a deal. At that point, we had all been listening to these demos in the office and were excited about what we heard. It was then that I decided to bring Hale Milgrim down to rehearsals. Hale was an old friend of mine. We had worked together in the '80s at Warner Bros. Records. Hale was head of merchandising at the time, and made all the cool buttons, posters, and campaigns for retail, and I was a product manager, which is basically an in-house manager or marketing guy. I was handling acts like U2, Prince, Devo, Bob Marley, Black Sabbath, Thin Lizzy, Tom Verlaine, and a bunch of others. We had a great relationship, and I brought him to a rehearsal room in downtown L.A. that was a very tiny room—perhaps less then ten feet square. It was tight and cramped but this was a room that the band was using on a monthly basis. I think we might have even been paying for it. It was very loud—as you can imagine in this tiny rehearsal cage. This was in a building—I believe it was the Downtown Rehearsals—which is a big warehouse complex housing probably 300 bands at any given time. It's about a six-story building with endless hallways of rehearsal rooms. Again, you could easily see the raw talent that was on display that day.

Hale Milgrim: As it turned out, Shannon was sick at that rehearsal. And it *still* sounded fucking great—like there was a charisma. Shannon, and the rest of the band, there was such a positive energy towards what they were doing. It seemed like they'd been doing this for a long time—which was strange, because they hadn't. It was just clicking—the band seemed like they had much more history than I would normally think at that stage of the game. Subsequently, we met and talked, and I totally got what they were trying to do. Or at least it seemed to me it wasn't anything strange—but it was absolutely different for that time period. It was more like something I would have heard out of the Grateful Dead—years earlier. And being a longtime Deadhead, for me, there was a special little magic that they had—with their own spin to it—that made it very interesting. Right after I saw them that night, I knew I wanted to sign them. It wasn't like I had to go see them three more times, or I had to see them in front of people—I knew they were special.

Tim Devine: As he and I sat in that room we knew we were on to something special. So we got into a negotiation with the band—there were several other labels starting to be in pursuit at this point as well. We moved in and I had had a pretty good relationship with their lawyer—the guy who turned me onto the tape back at the club in Fairfax months before—and we had them over to meet the people at the company. We ended up signing them in an outdoor signing ceremony on the roof of the famed Capitol Tower in Hollywood. It was a rainy day. We opened a big bottle of champagne and they stared out over the L.A. landscape, and I think realized this was the beginning of the possibility of their dream coming true. It was their first major connection with the so-called 'Hollywood star-making machinery.'

Rogers Stevens: They paid us more money—that's pretty much it. And there were a couple of people at the label that we really got on well with—Tim Devine and Simon Potts were really good to us. And the president of the label, Hale Milgrim, that guy was a real gem in the music business. You just don't run across people like him any more—they're rare. He was really committed to us, and allowed us to take our time, make our own record.

Shannon Hoon: We knew we wanted to have a hand in everything concerning the band because we knew that this was our future. We maintain 100 percent creative control over everything we do, be it our CD packaging, the artwork, whatever. A lot of people go to independent labels so they can do that, because most of the majors don't want to turn over that control to the talent. But we established those terms well in advance, long before we ever had signed our contract.

Nel Hoon: He was very happy. Just the fact that they had signed a record deal, I think he felt like he had achieved everything that he had ever wanted to achieve in his life.

Hale Milgrim: I always thought that this was going to be one of those two or two and a half year projects, that would slowly gain momentum, and that we would hopefully sell a couple of hundred thousand copies. That would be a great start, and then they'd do the second record and then we do half a million, the third record, blah blah blah. Keep on building it with a stronger foundation each time, with a bigger tour set up, and more and more of a fan-base.

Shelley Shaw: They had a gig at the Cathouse. I remember Axl's assistant, Colleen, worked the coat check or the ticket thing. So I rang her up from home, I go, "Put the phone on the counter and let me hear the show!" It was so ridiculous when you think of today and computers. It's like 4:00 in the morning here. It wasn't what I expected at all—it's very fusion-y. It was really different. It was still the heyday of 'butt rock.' I liked the major chords—there was something that was really appealing to my ear. I tried to get a hold of Joey [Blind Melon's then-manager] the following week—I think that show was a Tuesday. But he went away. I guess I got Shannon's number from Axl—I called him directly. I was like, "That was great, I'm Shelley Shaw." And he goes, "Oh my God, Shelley Shaw!" Because y'know, we had heard each other's names for two years or whatever. He goes, "God, I'm glad you called, because all these agents out here are going crazy—they were at the show." And I go, "Joey's out of town?" You know how it is—people make dumb decisions because they're not 'pro' yet. By the time Joey got back, it was in the bag.

Bill Elson, my boss, was going to L.A. I was like, "You've got to go see these guys, *at their house*, and meet them." So he went, spent the afternoon with them, called me, and goes, "I don't know how you do it, but you always find these magical creatures on God's great earth. These guys are *so special.*" He didn't see them play or anything—just as people. They were remarkably different than the rest of our roster, who was Dokken, Metallica, and these kinds of things. They were raised well, most of them had good educations, they were nice guys. It was right at 'the shift.' Shannon and I guess the whole band decided that Bill was the most professional guy that they had met. They were like, "Anybody who wants to manage us has to speak to Bill Elson at I.C.M." Every manager in the business was flooding Bill with calls. He comes into my office and says, "What have you got me into?" It was really hard for him, because he was the number one agent at the time and it was a big deal. Remember those crazy bidding wars people used to have? He kind of was enjoying it—it wasn't anything new to him in one way, but in the other way, he wasn't used to being that close to the talent that early.

I remember they were like, "Well, we like Chris Jones at Big F.D.," I don't know if it was called that at the time. Guns N' Roses' manager was Alan Niven, and Doug Goldstein was their tour manager. As things go, they stressed each other out—I think it was mostly Axl and Alan not getting along toward the end, or just getting really weary of each other. And then they sort of let Alan know that they didn't want to stay with him, and Doug took over. It was a pretty organic process. And then Doug set up his own management firm, and brought…Chris Jones was a manager, but Chris Jones was an assistant at I.C.M. in New York, just like me. So he and I had desks—we had a wall partition between us. He was lovely. He was smart, raised well, we were both really straight people—didn't really drink, no drugs ever, went to college. We both had similar 'centers' and we got along really good. I can't remember why he moved to L.A., but he ended up in L.A. somehow. And then he needed a gig—maybe we put him there, maybe we got him together with Doug.

Glen Graham: It was like, "O.K., cool. You're like…*a manager.*" [Chris Jones] was young. We always thought he was a lot older than he was, but he was close to our age—he was just much more mature than we were. Here he was married—he already had a kid.

Hale Milgrim: Chris, to me, was absolutely critical in helping us work with the band and the company to set up the programs. He was phenomenal. I can't tell you how great he was to work with. It's all about timing and putting together the team, and it's about the set-up. The set-up that we did—

and [Chris] was involved—I'm so impressed with him. The band absolutely responded when we asked management to do something. They bent over backwards for everything that I ever asked for.

Rogers Stevens: We decided we were going to make an E.P. ['Sippin' Time Sessions']—it didn't go very well. We weren't ready to record the songs, we needed to play more live. At the time, we were immature, and I remember blaming [the E.P.'s producer, David Briggs]. In hindsight, that's not the case—it was more our fault than anybody. God rest his soul, he passed away a few years ago. He was really fun too—always had tons of great stories about the legends that he worked with. We had some crazy times with him. We went up to this place called Indigo Ranch, which was John Barrymore's ranch, in Malibu, which was gorgeous. There's a studio in there now, and that's where we made it. We did it partially at Sound Studio and then we mixed there. That was really fun—I remember that was the first time I ever smoked pot, and they have these two-track masters of 'Dark Side of the Moon' there just sitting in the vault. So I took it out and put it on—this was out in the woods. I was scared shitless.

Glen Graham: We requested David Briggs and got him. He turned to me and said, "O.K., what do you want?" I was like, "Well, I want you do what you used to do. The reason why you're sitting in this room is because we like the stuff you did with Neil Young." It would be like somebody to say to me, "Hey, we want to hire you to be our drummer—we want you to play exactly the way you played in Blind Melon!" He didn't go for it and wasn't going to have anything to do with it. None of us knew enough to speak up. He would stand in the studio in the dark and do his 'David Briggs dance.' He would conduct in the air—not look at us, and just make all these gyrations. See, I'm a night person, and the other guys in the band really are not. To this day, I get up at 3:00 in the afternoon, and I go to bed around 7:00. I've done this since about probably I was 19 or 20 years old. So on this mixing thing with David Briggs, he was 'Mr. Coke'—I wasn't a coke person—I'd sit there stoned out of my gourd. Sit there at the table, and he would tell me all of these stories. All these things that went in one ear and out the other, and then I read the

Neil Young thing, 'Mansion on the Hill,' and all of those stories were in there [laughs]. He was a really sweet guy, who we made a terrible record with.

Heather Thorn: Me, Christopher, and Shannon got up at the break of dawn, and had gotten our friend's dog. A massive white dog. We had this idea that we were going to do a shoot for [the cover of the E.P.]. We got the dog all muddy and tried to make it look like he was digging in trash. So we were trying to get this dog to look in this garbage can. The only way to do it was to get a hot dog—Shannon was hiding back there with a hot dog, to make the dog's nose stick in.

Glen Graham: I was totally against it coming out. There's footage of us on ['Letters from a Porcupine'], sitting in London Bridge at the control room, pretending that we're a band, doing interviews. And just before that, we had a huge argument about the 'Sippin' Time Sessions,' and how I thought it'll be disastrous if it comes out, because this is 'last decade's kind of stuff.' It has a couple of songs on it that ended up on the first record, but it sounds too heavy metal. It's produced in a real shrill sort of way. I think everybody was glad [it was never released]. Of course it will come out at some point, I'm sure [laughs].

Tim Devine: "Dear Ol' Dad," "Soul One," "Tones of Home," "Seed to a Tree," and "Mother." The most incredible songs from the E.P. were the two that didn't make the album—"Soul One" and "Mother."

Brad Smith: The way Blind Melon operated, it was a very democratic process—majority process. Sometimes, the best stuff never happened, because there was a bunch of stupid people in the band all at the same time [laughs]. People become more stupid on certain topics than others—we're all pretty much boneheads.

Tim Devine: It's sad, because ["Mother"] is perhaps one of the most powerful songs they've ever written. It is a potent, tour-de-force of a song. It's too bad that it never saw the light of day.

Rogers Stevens: That song, I heard it recently—I hadn't heard it since we did it back then, and then I completely forgot about it. I thought it was O.K. It seemed to be an environmentalist's song, and I didn't know if we were such a 'message band,' y'know? It sounded odd to me in the context of the other songs and what the other songs were about. All of a sudden, there's this political message in the middle of the record with all these personal songs. Maybe I was wrong, but it seemed like maybe we needed to go and do more of that if we were going to do that. I think it requires a lot of energy to back up a song like that. To put something out like that, you really should live by it, I suppose.

Tim Devine: We decided to use the E.P. as an 'internal teaser' to the various people that worked at the label, as well as starting to spread it around a bit with tastemakers, agents, writers, etc.

Durham/Sleepyhouse/Soundgarden Tour

Realizing that L.A. is not for them (and not exactly beneficial to Shannon's health), the group relocates to a house in Durham, North Carolina, dubbed 'The Sleepyhouse,' to rehearse/write for their full-length debut. Blind Melon also open a series of shows for Soundgarden around this time.

Glen Graham: There was some confusion after we got signed as to what we were going to do. We decided to convince the label to give us money to live for a year, so we could actually write an album—because we didn't have any material. At that time, we were going to stay in L.A. Well; I *did not* want to stay in L.A. Over a period of about a month, I tried to convince everybody that we should go somewhere else. "Let's go to a college town. Let's go to Chapel Hill, North Carolina. Let's go to Athens, Georgia. Let's go to Austin. Let's go to *anywhere*." They looked at me like, "You've got to be kidding." Because we had girlfriends in tow, who were not interested in being away from L.A. They were having a ball.

Chris Smith: I was living in Mississippi, and they were coming from California, going to North Carolina, to write songs for their album. They were going to stop in Mississippi for a couple of days and recharge their batteries. Brad, Christopher, and Shannon ended up living with us at my parents' house—three of us in the guesthouse and one inside with my parents. The guesthouse had pinball and bumper pool—a lot of money traded hands over that bumper pool table. Shannon and I hit it off because we were similar—we were both pretty wild. They were rehearsing for some shows they were going to do, and that night we were driving home on these gravel roads from where they were rehearsing back to the house. We had all been partying a little bit. Shannon started agitating me on purpose, one thing led to another, and told whoever was driving to pull the car over. We got out of the car—on a gravel road, in the middle of the night, in Mississippi—and just went at it. For no reason other than we were both a little drunk and wanted to be crazy. That kind of sealed our friendship, because we got up the next morning—I was on my way to the big house to tell Shannon, "I'm sorry," and to see if he was O.K. And he was actually on his way out at the same time to tell me the same thing. One of us was holding our neck, and the other was holding our back. From then on, it was a lot of good times with that guy.

Christopher Thorn: So we moved to North Carolina, which was the best thing for us. We lived in a house together on Trinity Street in Durham.

Kim Smith: The best memory of that is the very first night I got to the Sleepyhouse. Shannon had his room all decked out—he had tin-foiled all the windows, so it could be totally black. We were watching 'The Shining.' He had been smoking a bunch of pot, and he had himself *so freaked out*. At that point, it was just me, Brad, and Shannon—I don't think the others were there yet, they were driving from Mississippi. That was our first night in that house. He didn't want us to leave and go upstairs. He was like, "Man, I'm kind of freaked out after watching that!"

Shannon Hoon: We established a lot of unity in the band, which obviously made our music more real, and from what I can see, 'real' is very in now. Besides being able to concentrate full time on music, if any problems arose while we were under the same roof, we were able to resolve them immediately. And we had to, because if we didn't, it was like five minutes later we'd be running into each other in the kitchen.

Brad Smith: [Rogers] didn't take off his pajamas for a week!

Rogers Stevens: That's where we wrote most of the first record—it kinda gelled. And we were going out every week and playing gigs at this place called the Brewery.

Kim Smith: We went to those shows and they were fun. I mean, they didn't draw big crowds—it was the local people that knew Blind Melon was in town. They were just getting their shit together at that point.

Christopher Thorn: My memories of that time are great, but they're also a little hazy—we were smoking a lot of pot. I remember waking up in the afternoon, smoking pot, and jamming all night long. More than anything, we bonded as 'brothers.' In L.A., we were all living in separate places. It was actually a good rehearsal for having to spend a long period of time in a van together. So we wrote songs in the Sleepyhouse—we became much better musicians there. We'd work on songs during the week, and every Thursday, we'd go [to the Brewery] and test out the songs. We were also packing up and going to anything that was within three or four hours of Durham. We'd put a couch in the back of a U-Haul, put the gear in, and all ride in the U-Haul.

Brad Smith: We had all our gear in the living room. We would work when we wanted to, or when we all happened to be in the same room. We never had a designated time—it was so casual. We had no structure whatsoever—it's amazing that we got anything done. Those were crazy times—I lived in L.A. for four years, and then found myself in Durham. I didn't know anybody— it was really weird. We smoked so much weed—I don't even know where it came from. I think Shannon always facilitated 'the buy' from whoever the powers that be. I was doing a lot of painting, growing weed and reading books on how to grow weed. And I had my vinyl album collection—I didn't have a CD player back then, just vinyl.

Lyle Eaves: [Brad] had a closet lined with tin foil and grow lights—the whole nine yards.

Shannon Hoon: My lungs are still recuperating. We were in a part of the country where there's a lot of dirtweed, so it took a lot of smoking to enhance my mood. The better the brand, the less damage to your lungs, because you don't have to smoke so much. Lately, I've been smoking the better brands.

Lyle Eaves: The house was an old boarding house—there were enough rooms for band members. I remember them drawing straws to get the rooms, and of course, the master bedroom Shannon ended up with. Even though he was drawing straws, that's just how his luck went. He always got the best of everything. The instruments were set up in the little living room, where I was sleeping. I still smoked cigarettes at the time—I set the sofa bed on fire one night, after an all-night partying session. Shannon woke me up with the couch on fire and me in the middle of it. We had to drag that thing out on the front porch and hose it down. He was pretty upset about that. It was kind of a hippie section of town—a lot of college students—so I don't think anybody really paid any attention to us. Shannon was real obsessive compulsive. The house had roaches. My memory of him in that house—other than them jamming all the time—was he was obsessed about the roaches. He was always buying roach poison and spray. He even ended up getting a 'roach necklace' tattoo, because of that whole experience.

Glen Graham: We didn't leave the house—we were such heavy potheads. Brad's growing dope in his room, Shannon's got foil on his windows, and we were all sleeping very, very late. You'd get up, eat something, smoke dope, and then walk into the front room—we had our little set up in there to play. We were there I don't know how many months. Maybe three or four. But I think we wrote "Deserted" and "Time." The saying goes, "They holed up in this house in North Carolina, did a bunch of [songwriting]." No. We smoked a bunch of dope and wrote two songs. But it was very good, because we played every day. We played a lot.

Shannon Hoon: Everybody slept all day long, then we'd get up and play from about three to six in the morning. We barely left the house. And when we did go out to visit our families for Christmas, we looked pathetic—just pale and white with dark circles under our eyes. I kept wondering what our relatives must've been thinking.

Lyle Eaves: Brad's wife, Kim, was around some, Heather was there. I know Glen met Brooks while we were there, and they started dating.

Brooks Byrd Graham: I'm from Alabama. We met at a wedding—my best friend from childhood and his best friend from childhood went to college together at the University of Mississippi. They met there, got married, and had us in their wedding. That was in January of '92.

Glen Graham: My memories of playing come later—they don't really start until the Soundgarden tour, which was when we were living in North Carolina. That was great.

Lyle Eaves: Chris wanted them to get out, do some live shows, and get a little bit of road experience—to hone their songs in front of an audience. Of course, nobody had any damn idea who they were. I think it was just me and the band—there may have been one guitar tech with us. We were in a van—a lot of really cold weather. They got a good reception [in] a lot of the places. But we were inexperienced at touring—real unorganized, not knowing what we were doing. And just broke—making a hundred bucks a show, there wasn't a lot of room for amenities at that point.

Susan Silver: The management company that managed Guns N' Roses was overseeing them. So we were friendly with them, and I think the guys had met at the Concrete Convention—Soundgarden played and Temple of the Dog played a couple of songs, and Blind Melon played on that one. They were just all so incredibly likeable. It was so refreshing—to hear acoustic [music] and have that little bit of southern rock in there. And the eerie thing was that Shannon bore at least an energetic resemblance to Andy [Wood, late singer of Mother Love Bone]. And a little bit physically—in that cherubic, wide eyed, lovin' life kind of way that Andy had. Shannon had a similarity to him— the long wavy hair and open heart. So there was a healing in that—Shannon could come into our lives after we'd lost Andy. A great storyteller and such a great energy to be around.

Kim Thayil: Shannon was a great guy. He was definitely full of life. He reminded me of Andy Wood. The day we met—I think we were in Colorado—he did some kind of back flip over this crowd railing by the stage. They were getting ready to do their soundcheck—it wasn't the show. We were sitting out in the theater, checking out their soundcheck. I remember how animated he was—he had this charismatic flamboyance that was cartoon-like. This weird, rock hyperbole that Andy certainly had. He was very much like him in his demeanor.

Shelley Shaw: Those are the real first set of dates that we booked for them. I went out on two dates—Columbus and maybe another city—and their van broke down. They went to rent [another vehicle], and they all came back really sheepish. They go, "Shelley, none of us are 25 or over, and we're not allowed to rent a car. Can you rent it for us?"

Christopher Thorn: For starters, I'm a huge fan, so for me, I felt totally privileged to be on that tour. That was one of the first tours we were on, that we actually played every night. I remember learning a lot. One of my first memories of that tour was in St. Louis. When you play local clubs, you can kinda go on whenever you want. They might say your set time is 9:30, but whatever, if you go on at 9:40, it's not the end of the world. For us, I remember a big lesson was we were opening up for Soundgarden, and we went on fifteen minutes late. We only had a half hour set, so 10:00 rolls around, and they pull us offstage! And we're like, "We only played a few songs, what's going on?" And it was like, hey—*this is the real world*. You can go on whenever you want, but you're going to end at 10:00. We learned a lot from watching a band that was at that next level.

Glen Graham: The first show was at Mississippi Nights in St. Louis. Matt Cameron had this drum riser, and Mississippi Nights is like a big barn, with a high stage. His drum riser was four-and-a-half feet tall—his drums were situated so that they hung out over the edge of it. He was very close to the ceiling. We just felt, "What is this?" You couldn't hear—it was deafeningly loud. The next show was at a theater, then they had the whole production—the eight-foot drum riser, the '70s walls of Marshalls. They might have even had stairs like Kiss had. It was hysterical. Once you saw the whole thing, you're like, "These guys are funny—they're great." And nobody, I mean *nobody* in their fanbase—except maybe the people in Seattle—got it. These guys are the Beastie Boys' first record. [The audience] took it at face value. "*These guys are* *a bad ass metal band.*" Yes, well, they're kind of making fun of you. They were great—they were nice. I think that might have been their first pretty big tour. And of course, they got extremely huge.

Rogers Stevens: I had a real epiphany seeing them live. I was such a metalhead when I was a kid, then totally got out of it. To see a really good heavy band that was really modern—it moved me.

Shannon Hoon: It was long enough for me to realize that Soundgarden is as awesome as I always thought they were.

Lisa Sinha: That he was *really* psyched about. That was one of the tours that he was so proud to be on. He really liked Chris Cornell and all those guys. It was a real band to him—he loved their music and loved hanging out with those guys.

Lyle Eaves: Shannon and Chris hit it off really well. They hung out a lot—so did the crews. Chris would eat with the band and hang out. In Atlanta, Shannon made a fork necklace for Chris, which I helped him make on the sidewalk outside of I think the Roxy. There was a guy who lived where we lived in L.A., and this guy had this necklace—a fork that all the tongs were turned out. It was professionally done and perfect looking. Shannon liked the necklace, and he wanted me to help him make one—he was going to give it to Chris Cornell. We got a propane torch and a regular fork—it was kind of gnarly looking, the thing we came up with. But Shannon liked it and gave it to him. Chris has worn it—I've seen him on TV with it on. On that tour, Shannon gave me his wallet to keep—that was when he really started his whole stagediving thing. And the wallet got lost. It had Chris Cornell's phone number in it—that's the reason he was pissed. And it had a couple of Valium in it too, I think.

Kim Smith: They were going to be playing the Limelight in New York in December [1991]. So I flew from L.A. That was one of the biggest shows that I had seen them play that year. People were going crazy and Shannon was a maniac—just all over the place.

Shelley Shaw: I remember they played the Limelight. Slash was in town and got up on the stage, and took over the show. It was a nightmare—the band was really pissed off in the dressing room. Shannon was sitting with me and my boss, with his head in his hands. And then he jumped up, started bouncing off the walls, kind of disappeared, and left the whole band in there yelling at each other. And yelling at Chris Jones, like, "What the fuck?! This guy just ruined our show!" I remember [Slash] got up there and he was doodling on the guitar. He was really drunk and I think fell off the stage. Oh my God, it was such a nightmare.

G n' R played the Garden that same week. Shannon and I went to the show together...actually, the whole band went. I was like, "You fucking hypocrites, what are you doing here?" Shannon I think got up on stage and did a song or two. I remember the band was really looking around impressed and awe-struck—they were being treated really well. They were just amazed by the people backstage. They *tortured* [Shannon] about this, and then it really pissed me off to see them basking in it. I was really annoyed. But then I was really glad, because if you flip it over, they were supporting him. So maybe that made it a little easier.

Jena Kraus: When I was young, I won a model search contest with the Ford Modeling Agency, and that got me to New York. I was still a teenager. I was a singer—I didn't want to model, I didn't stay with that. I was living in Manhattan, looking for a band, and networking. I went out one night, and a friend of mine was having a record release party at the Limelight. I think it was December 9, 1991. This guy introduced me to Shannon. We shook hands and walked away. I'm walking around and I'm feeling all alone—I look over and there's one other person who's standing alone in the room, and it was Shannon. We smiled at each other, and then I walked away. I went to another room, and the same thing happened, and then it happened again—but I still didn't talk to him. I walked down these steps that were next to the stage, and I see that there's a band that's about to go on, and it's the dudes I was introduced to. Nobody had heard of Blind Melon at the time. I look over, roll my eyes, and said to myself, "*This band is going to suck.*" Not because of the way they looked, just because I was jaded with everything.

So I started to walk away, they started to play, and I totally stopped dead in my tracks. I'm like, "Wait a minute—this doesn't sound like all the other bands I hear. *This is really good.*" It was really real—before he even started to sing, I could feel this music. And then he started singing—I just got this smile on my face. I was blown away. And Shannon's melodies sounded very familiar to me—so I connected with this music in such a deep way. It felt like home. And his voice—I love singers, but the way I felt his voice is different than anything I've ever experienced, before or after. Afterwards, I feel like I couldn't even talk to them—which is so unlike my character. I felt like they weren't even going to understand what I had just experienced. Earlier in the night, my friend Danielle had been talking to Rogers for a good couple of hours. After the show, she said, "They invited us to go out to eat with them afterwards." And at that same time, another friend of mine was like, "I'm going to this bar, the producer Nile Rodgers might come—you might be able to sing for him." I was always trying to get people to listen to me sing, so I could try and get discovered. At that one point, I had to make a decision—do I go hang out with this amazing band that just blew me away, or do I go try to sing for a producer? I chose to try to sing for the producer, even though my heart didn't want to do that. I never did get to sing for that producer.

Shelley Shaw: I remember in December '91—it was right before they were going to go [and work on the record]. Shannon was at my apartment in New York, and his mom had a lot of stress. She was trying to make ends meet, and as I remember, she was working at some kind of book-keeping job for a small business. And she lost her job. He was just so despondent beyond all words. He was like, "I think I have to walk away from all this and go home and take care of my mother. I can't let her live like this." I mean, he was *wrecked*. It was amazing—I'd never seen him this low. I said to him, "You can give so much more to her if you just give it a little time. One day at a time, patch together whatever you've got to do to help her out there, but stick to this thing. Give this thing that you have on the books for 1992 a chance. You can make such a better life for her after." And he was so angry. He was like, "None of that matters! What matters is that she's O.K. What you're talking about doesn't make any sense to me—that's fantasy, that's fairy tales, that's ten years down the road. I've got to go home and help." But he didn't do it—he didn't go.

Seattle/120 Minutes Tour/'Blind Melon'

Leaving Durham, Blind Melon set up shop in the then-leading rock music hotspot, Seattle, Washington, to record their self-titled debut with Rick Parashar, at London Bridge Studios. But in the middle of the sessions, the group accepts an invite to tour alongside Live, Big Audio Dynamite, and Public Image Limited, as part of MTV's 120 Minutes Tour.

Lisa Sinha: [Lisa and Shannon] were always talking on the phone—we never really ever lost contact. We still cared a lot about each other. I knew I had to finish college, and then if things were meant to be, then things would be. Once they got signed, they went up to Seattle—because that was when grunge and all that was starting. That's when I finished college, and moved to Seattle on April Fool's Day. I'll never forget, I was like, "Is this a bad sign?" But it wasn't—it was all good.

Kim Smith: We shared an apartment with Heather and Christopher, up on Capitol Hill. And Shannon and his girlfriend Lisa lived there also, at the time. We were all living at Seattle.

Shannon Hoon: We weren't in any hurry to make our album. We didn't want to put something out that didn't represent the band well.

Tim Devine: Rick Parashar was just coming off the success of the Pearl Jam record ['Ten']—he was sort of *the* Seattle-based rock producer of the day. I arranged for him to come to a rehearsal. Next thing we know, we were booking time and heading off to Seattle to record the album. The studio was a big cavernous room, but not a slick kind of studio that you would find in L.A. or New York. It was in a warehouse district, yet it had a similar vibe to their music—a little rag-tag, definitely imperfect. It was the place and the time and the environment that made sense for the recording of this record. They weren't about to become a slick, glossy, mass-produced kind of rock act. We had an organic, rootsy, disheveled, and very earthy approach to this record. It couldn't have gone any other way.

Rogers Stevens: That was really fun—definitely one of the high points of our band life. None of the bad stuff had really happened and it was a very optimistic time. Working with Rick Parashar—him and his brother, Raj, were so connected. This whole really fun nightlife scene. So we experienced a fun, decadent time. We were around each other all the time and really got to know each other—over that and North Carolina. And Rick had a really good rapport with the band, he was able to coax the record along to get where it was, without getting too heavy handed about it. Because I can only imagine what it must have been like for him—it was obvious that there were a lot of things we were pretty naïve about. And it was also obvious that there was a lot of volatility amongst the people in the group. But we got it done. It sounded like the way we wanted it to be. I remember at the time Brad being really unhappy with it. But looking back on it, I'm sure he'd feel otherwise.

Brad Smith: I remember it being really easy. You look back on those times, and you're like, "Aside from all our dope smoking and disagreements we may or may not have had, we had our shit together musically." We would play two or three takes of a song, and that was it. That was the song. There was no chopping on the tape machine—the only thing that maybe got overdubbed were some guitar solos and the lead vocals. And that's that—that was the record. I look back on those times and I'm like, "There's a real sense of musical purity and performance to those records." I think that's what's missing from today's records—that purity in terms of performance. Is that really what the band sounds like if you go and see them live? Blind Melon really captured that, as did a lot of bands during that exact period—post-hair metal, but pre-rap rock. There was a certain amount of realness to those performances that people captured on tape. And that's kind of gone—I think the allure has been replaced by other things like accuracy and stereo wideness. There's certain things that are great about today's recordings, but y'know what? Nobody performs like those bands back then.

Shannon Hoon: Anyone can go into a studio and make a slick, high-produced album, but that's something we didn't want to do. It sounds good to have those human touches on a recording, like when one plays acoustically and you hear the guitar being hit by the pick. That kind of stuff delivers a real raw and natural sound.

Lyle Eaves: I know they had a lot of contention with the producer, Rick, who's a great guy, but he wasn't around as much as he should have been during the recording sessions. He left Jon [Plum, the engineer] there by himself most of the time, and the band was pretty upset about that—they thought that he should have been producing more of it.

Jon Plum: They were into smoking pot, and Rick's atmosphere when he's running a session—it's very professional. He wants everything set up just right and he'll go until 8:00 at night, and then it's done. He encouraged the band not to smoke pot during the day when they were tracking. Just to focus and work hard. Every night this would happen—Rick would leave, they would all smoke pot, and I would stay engineering, so I could keep the session running. And then they'd go out and play the song again that they'd been working on that day—completely stoned. Nine times out of ten, that was the 'magical take.' That was the joke of the session—the end of the night, everyone knew that was going to happen.

Rogers Stevens: It was Seattle, and we were all partaking in 'Seattle's finest.'

Jon Plum: London Bridge at the time owned a house about a mile away that they lived in. They spent a lot of time decorating and making it their home. I remember they decorated the studio—they put up tapestries and had candles. Shannon would drip wax everywhere. We'd have all these music stands, and he'd sit and make little wax art projects.

Glen Graham: The general rule for me was 'stay as far away as possible from Shannon when he was recording.' We recorded and then he came in afterwards. Basically, for both the albums, when he came in to do his vocals, he was coming off of a six-week to two-month full-on, throw down party. And having all of a sudden to calm down. Which is difficult to do, after you've been smoking, drinking, and doing whatever else you're doing all day and all night for a long time. I avoided him [laughs]. He could be very volatile. He wasn't a self-conscious person in general, but he was very self-conscious about doing his vocals. And I'm very direct. The less said the better. It was more blatant on the second record—he was covering up a lot of it on the first record.

Christopher Thorn: I think we all felt a part of the writing process, because so much of it was morphed and jammed out. The first record was like, "Oh, I have a little riff here. Will that riff work with your riff?"

Rogers Stevens: Christopher and I really started gelling. I'd only been playing guitar for four or five years when we did that first record. I really learned how to play with these guys. My style came from trying to fit in around Christopher a lot. I got so deep into that thing with two guitars—the way Christopher played and anticipating what he was going to do—not really talking about it, just doing it. I've always loved two guitar bands—the Stones, the Beatles, or even Guns N' Roses. I feel like you really need that to make harmony, which is what I like. If you look at Derek and the Dominoes, with Duane [Allman] and [Eric] Clapton, I like what happens when guitars are slightly out of tune with each other. They do this thing that makes it sound a lot fatter, when things are out of tune.

Brad Smith: A lot of the lyrics on that first record intertwined, because there wasn't any hesitation in changing the lyric if it was better. If someone wanted to change one of my lyrics, it wasn't a fight; it was very open and easy. It always became better when someone made a change.

Rogers Stevens: We did that video ['Dear Ol' Dad'] for nothing. We did that in Seattle when we were recording the record. We had already tracked that song, and we needed to get something before we went on the MTV tour, so they could play it on '120 Minutes.' This guy came with Super 8 cameras, shot that video in a day or two, and put it together. It's very cheaply done, but it's cool because it's got that sort of 'we did this ourselves' feel. All the performance stuff was shot in the main tracking room at London Bridge Studios. Did some really cheap lighting effects, and our instruments were already there, so we just did it like that—in a few hours. Then just roamed around Seattle. I remember driving to some ski slopes an hour outside the city. People do nonsensical bullshit in videos I suppose—didn't really have to have a reason for anything. We found ourselves trying to do stunt photography—flying down the mountain. People smacking their heads and getting concussions.

Glen Graham: The '120 Minutes Tour'—which was in the middle of recording the first album—was an absolute disaster.

Christopher Thorn: That was also a really good thing for the band, because we had the pre-tour recordings, and went out and toured for six weeks.

Tim Devine: MTV does not package their tours lightly, and for a band with an unreleased record to be out on a MTV-sponsored tour was quite a feat. A group of us from the label had been traveling—both to the South by Southwest convention in Austin, TX and the N.A.R.M. convention in New Orleans. I had some of the label executives carry on from the two conferences, and we flew into Miami to see the start of the 120 Minutes Tour. Showtime was supposed to be 7:00, we decided to all meet in our hotel lobby to grab a drink at about 6:00. We walked across to the venue and got there at 7:00. We saw the band backstage by their truck. They were all excited to see us and wanted to know what we thought of the show. We thought they were joking, but it turned out we missed them! I remember Christopher saying to me, "We just played—the promoter moved the show up." So because of a curfew in Miami, at the last minute the promoter bumped the show up an hour. Nobody told us and probably half the people that planned to come see them that night ended up missing their performance.

Glen Graham: I remember riding around in a damn RV, with ten people in it, getting the odd Motel 6 room to take a shower in. That was the 'super, super budget tour.' It was like, "We have to do this tour, why not?" I remember Live—we thought those guys…there's absolutely no way in the world that those guys are going to amount to anything. It's not possible. They're doing something that was just completely…*U2 exists*. And the world surely does not need a 'youthful U2.' Of course, we were very wrong. Very nice people, but we were shocked. And it was just the weirdest thing in the world—it was Big Audio Dynamite, which was cool to meet Mick Jones, but it was [adopts British accent] "Mick Jones traveling circus, with this rave party with Mick Jones." Every night they had some [party], which was basically like an 'x fest.' At the time, we were just pot smokers—this was kind of like, "What? You're going into the basement of a bank, taking ecstasy and dancing for nine hours? O.K., *we're sleeping in a Winnebago*. I don't think we can work that in!" And then Public Image Limited—there's Johnny Rotten. As far as I remember, exactly the same on and off stage. That's who he is. And I remember that was the tour where we realized we were going to have to get earplugs, because it's impossible to play in these gigantic places. We were playing in like airport hangers—terrible venues. Big metal buildings. The sound is coming off the back wall. We went on first, and there was nobody in there, so it's like you're playing in a warehouse. It was impossible to hear.

Rogers Stevens: [John Lydon] would always call us "stinky hippies." I know he and Shannon had conversations. I had a favorable impression of him.

Owen Orzack: They were the opening band on the 120 Minutes Tour, and I was the monitor engineer for the tour. Had never heard of them, knew nothing about them before the record came out. That was my introduction to them. Normally, if you end up mixing monitors for [an opening band], they're supposed to pay you. Well, I remember after a few shows, I was wondering, "Hmmm, I haven't gotten money from anybody—maybe I go should follow up on this." They were in a motor home—they weren't even in a bus or a van. I remember sticking my head in, and I just went, "Eh…don't worry, we'll catch up on the *next* tour." I ended up staying in touch with everybody—especially Lyle. Lyle mixed the sound that the audience heard, and I mixed the sound that the musicians heard. Lyle would record all the shows off the board—some of those board tapes were released as b-sides. Shannon was a total stickler for recordings. He wanted every show recorded, but he had to control the recording—Lyle didn't keep anything, he gave it to Shannon or management. Shannon was always afraid about bootlegs. He was the worst bootlegger going, I mean, he had that video camera all the time—he bootlegged everything. But God forbid if he saw a video camera in the audience—he would freak out.

Paul Cummings: I was the merchandise guy—I was on the 120 Minutes tour. I worked for Brockum—they were a merchandise company. I was doing Live and Blind Melon. That's the first time I met them. I ended up driving the motor home most of the time. They were pretty green. They seemed happy to just be out there playing. It was kind of surprising that a band without a record was on that tour. Kind of an odd package—it did O.K. business. Originally, I got a hotel room because I worked for a different company and they paid for my hotel. [The band] got one room to split between them. So whoever wanted to crash on the floor or in the extra bed was fine.

Lyle Eaves: A good example of Shannon if you told him not to do something he'd do it—on that 120 Tour in Chicago at the Aragon Ballroom, we did two nights. For some reason, they had chairs on the floor one night, and one night they didn't. They told the bands not to encourage the mosh pit, because they were trying to keep the kids in the seats in the rows. We were the first band on, and Shannon comes out and says, "What the fuck are you guys doing in these chairs? Feel free to stand up and throw those things to the back of the room." So 3,500 kids stand up, take these chairs, and start chucking them to the back of the room. Piled them up. And Shannon ended up paying for like 300-400 chairs that night. Because he had to buy them, he ended up keeping one—for the rest of the tour, rode around with it in the bottom of the R.V.

Lisa Sinha: I went to the Chicago show. For me, it was the first time ever seeing him on a big stage, so it was really huge for me. I know he was really excited, because it was really their first tour.

Jena Kraus: I was always asking people, "Have you ever heard of Blind Melon?" And nobody had. It was in late March or early April, I went out this one night to the Trocadero in Philly. I was underage and I had really horrible fake I.D.—I didn't like being told no, so I'm arguing with the bouncer over my I.D. I look down, I see this newspaper and this ad that says 'Blind Melon'—they were playing on the 120 Minutes Tour at that point. I just couldn't believe I'd found them again, because they hadn't even done the first record yet. I didn't get tickets for the show—I figured I could get them when I went there, which was pretty dumb. I went to the show and got there late. I can't get in, I'm standing in the rain, and I can hear them playing. I'm standing by this back door, and then Mick Jones walks by me and says, "Hey, do you need tickets to the show?" He brought me in, introduced me to his band, and told me which way to go to where the audience was. As I was walking, I see this paper sign that says 'Blind Melon' with an arrow. I followed the sign and ran right into Rogers. I reminded him, "You met my friend Danielle in New York." He was like, "I'm headed to the R.V., I have a tape of the show—do you want to hear it?" I went to the R.V. with him, listened to one or two songs, and then everybody got on the R.V., and they were like, "We're leaving." And Rogers was like, "Do you want to come with us?" I did, and that's how I met them.

The first thing that happened that night—I had never smoked pot before. So I'm sitting there on the R.V., and they're like, "Jena, you smoke pot?" "No, never smoked pot before." "*You've never smoked pot before?*" They said it like they knew something I didn't—I guess something in my personality, I seemed like a hippie stoner. I remember Shannon being like, "Well, you're in luck—we've happened to travel to every state, we've tested all the pot there is to test, and tonight, we happen to have the best pot...from Seattle, Washington!" He pulled out this huge bag of pot and I smoked for the first time. They got me stoned, and Rogers was very technical in explaining how to use a bong. He's like, "This is the carburetor..." So we're sitting at a table—Shannon's sitting in front of me, Rogers is next to me, and Glen is next to Shannon. They're passing the bong around and they forgot that I had never smoked pot—they were caught up getting stoned and laughing. I just kept on smoking and I didn't realize what was going on either. And then all of a sudden, I was *really* stoned. I had fun for about five minutes, and then I got so paranoid and freaked out. When I was sitting on the R.V., I'm the only girl with all these guys, and [Shannon] is like, "Y'know Jena, we're not a 'groupie band'." Maybe some people would be insulted, but the way people were treating me because I was so young and a girl trying to get in a band, when he said that, those guys just seemed so much different than any others that I had met. They accepted me for who I was and weren't making any judgments—they weren't assuming anything. They were down to earth and real. I feel like I'd met a lot of people that weren't respecting me as woman—they were assuming that I was a girl hanging out with guys, so I must be a groupie. So he said that, and right then and there, I felt like these were such good people.

Chris Smith: There was nothing like seeing them live. I'd been hearing the songs all along, so I was used to hearing them come out of the stereo. To see them live was something completely different. Probably my favorite performance—that is actually on video—was the song "Time" when they played at the Ritz in New York City, [on] the MTV tour. It was the last night of that tour, and "Time" live was the most amazing thing ever. They did this thing in the middle where they broke the song down, and went into this instrumental jam. It lasted ten minutes—just amazing. Shannon jumping in the crowd—you could tell he was so into it. The next night, they played at the Limelight—it was just Blind Melon. After the show, Shannon gave me some really strong acid. We hung out for a few minutes, and I said, "If I take this, you're not going to leave me, are you?" And he's like, "*No, no, no.*" So I took it, we were hanging out and partying, and the next thing I know, Shannon is gone. I'm straight out of Mississippi in New York, and here I am on acid and left all alone.

Danny Clinch: I was on an assignment for the band Live—on the 120 Minutes Tour. I was waiting for Live to do their set and setting up to take a picture of them backstage. I saw the Blind Melon guys kicking around, and I started talking to a couple of the guys—asked them to stand in for some Polaroids. We just kind of hit it off. At that point in my career, I was really trying to let people know what I was doing, and I carried a portfolio around all the time of some of my photographs. I busted it out and showed it to them, and they were digging the pictures. I think Domenique [Johansson, Blind Melon's publicist] had something to do with reconnecting us, and getting me in there to shoot them for publicity in New York. I shot them in New York City shortly after that—they were all hung over, because they had played some big gig the night before. [Shannon] came down, and something wasn't right with this guy, I'm like, "What is up with this guy?" And he's like, "I shaved my eyebrows off!" I have these really funny pictures of him—simple close-ups of him looking into the camera. You're looking at him, and you're like, "Something's not right." I was like, "I love this band—I'm going to try and photograph [them] whenever I can."

Christopher Thorn: We came back in and did the second half of the record. We were really firing on all pistons at that point.

Jon Plum: I've seen it every single time—when a band goes on the road, they come back so much better. I remember seeing them a couple of times—they played at RKCNDY I think—and thinking Shannon had a cool voice, but had a hard time singing in key. And then later on, after getting some serious touring under his belt, his pitch was much better. Eddie [Vedder] was the same way—Eddie had a pretty hard time in the studio when I worked with him. Singing in pitch. Layne [Staley] was the same way.

Shannon Hoon: I get asked a lot what each song is about, but even my idea of the songs changes from time to time and place to place. We're playing these songs every night, and a lot of them start to take on new meanings that don't even match up with the original lyrics sometimes. I think that's the way it should be. I don't like to explain what my songs are about, because I like to have my version and let the listener have his or her version. That keeps it from getting monotonous for all of us.

Brad Smith: I wrote ["Soak the Sin"] about tripping in the desert. The whole band went out to the desert, and we saw Liquid Jesus play—it was out near Joshua Tree. I think it was some kind of homegrown festival. It was maybe

3-500 people out there. I was driving back out into the desert after coming to Los Angeles. So the song was a little about just driving in the desert and realizing how far you've come in your musical journey. And how good it feels to go back home and get re-grounded. Because we were out in the desert trip-ping, taking acid, and drinking—it was just insane. It was really kind of a warped reality out there. They had these fires next to these cliffs—all the rocks were 'breathing'—and Liquid Jesus was playing. The chorus is "I'm going to tell my momma, I love her so, and thank you for giving me these bones of gold"—it's a homage to your mother, home, where you come from, and your roots. At the time, those types of sentiments when you're that age have such a huge impact on you. They still do the rest of your life, actually.

Rogers Stevens: I remember that one being written in Mississippi, when we went down on our way from L.A to North Carolina. We stopped off at my hometown, and set up. "Soak the Sin" was done there, and a few others. It was just about our time together and the beginning of this thing.

Christopher Thorn: That riff came out of a jam we did at Sound City that I just started playing, and somehow morphed into part of "Soak the Sin."

Rogers Stevens: ["Tones of Home"] was written right as we met [Shannon]. I remember that Brad wrote the first verse, I wrote the second verse—the lyr-ics—and Shannon finished it off. But it was really about how we got out there and we were completely disillusioned—that L.A. wasn't what we thought it was.

Shannon Hoon: The song was about leaving home and adapting. It's the kind of stuff we all have to deal with. When we came to L.A., for example, it was very much like a carnival atmosphere. Then when we went to Durham, it was basically just a college town mentality. And now when we're back in Indiana, I have to readjust to the attitudes and lifestyles there.

Brad Smith: We all took hands in writing that song—I think I wrote the cho-rus. That song was 90% done before Shannon became part of the band. He just walked in and laid down that third verse like no problem. There were a lot of 'works in progress' going on.

Glen Graham: To me, that's one of the worst performances on record—bar none. I remember we did 40 takes of the thing, and it was a nightmare to do. I've listened to it since—recently, actually—and I don't really hear the crappiness anymore. But for a long time I thought, "*This is a disaster.*"

Christopher Thorn: I remember parts of that were 'jammed out,' so to speak.

Rogers Stevens: ["I Wonder"] I had the main riff to. I brought that riff in, and we built the song off that. It's one of those escape-ism type vibes to me, that Shannon wrote the words about. But I remember that riff, because I had that opening big rock riff for a while. Before the band was even formed, I was playing it in my bedroom in Los Angeles.

Brad Smith: I think Shannon wrote the lyrics, maybe I wrote the chorus.

Rogers Stevens: Christopher had the riff at the beginning of ["Paper Scratcher"] and had that chorus-y, sing-song-y thing. We just put the song together around that. It was about this guy that we used to see all the time—he was a homeless guy, that was right around where Shannon and I lived. He would have these magazines or catalogs—ripping pages out of—scratching stuff off of, like the private parts of the people. Really odd. He was obviously mentally ill. So that song is about that guy. We would give him money all the time and talk to him—some days he would be totally sane, and other days, he'd be just gone.

Brad Smith: Shannon came up with some really clever lyrics about that guy. A few years later, there was a "Change" [single] cover, and he took a picture of him—he's on the cover.

Shannon Hoon: I'm not about to sing something that one of us hasn't experienced.

Rogers Stevens: "Dear Ol' Dad" was written about [Shannon's] girlfriend. We had that piece of music—it was built around Brad's bass, and then we put the chorus in. It was written about…he had a girlfriend that was living out there at the time—a bit of a wildcard. There was some stuff that she revealed to him about her father, and he wrote the song about it.

Brad Smith: That was my attempt at playing something that was slightly Chili Peppers-ish, as a bass player. I had this groove thing worked up with Glen— that's where the song started. That was one of the first super-collaborative Blind Melon things. We recorded all that music without lyrics, and Shannon had a four-track recorder at his house. I think "Dear Ol' Dad" sat around for a couple of months, before the vocals even got on it. Shannon waited on inspiration, and wrote that song I think about his girlfriend at the time, Heather, who became a Born Again Christian. Her dad was always sending her money, and she was blowing it in irresponsible ways.

Rogers Stevens: ["Change"] blew us away right off the bat. It has those bigger than life lyrics. Part of it was almost like a Hallmark card. Just the lyric, "Life is hard, you have to change," I mean seriously, you could see that on a Hallmark card! In a way, kind of corny, but in a way, profound. He had that ability to say really simple things, that everybody could relate to, and that was one of those songs. It was just instantly perfect.

Brad Smith: I wrote ["No Rain"]—I played it on Venice Beach for quarters for maybe a year before Blind Melon was even together. I used to play in a band called the Guppies—it was me and my girlfriend at the time. This seriously hippy dippy scene. We were going to be like Fleetwood Mac or something—or so I was told by the other girl in the band. It was a husband and wife, and me and my girlfriend. We did this Mamas and the Papas harmonies type thing. It was super gay, but fun. At the time, I thought I was writing it about my ex-girlfriend, and the truth was, I was writing it about myself. You get so overwhelmed by Los Angeles or any big city when you come from someplace like West Point, Mississippi. The song is about depression, and finding excuses not to be happy, or finding excuses to be a loner, because it feels good to be unhappy. You get to the point where you're struggling so much; you couldn't imagine it being any other way. Every other type of mood that you may have seems foreign. Like, you'd rather be sullen instead of happy in some ways. So "No Rain" was about that, and it was about latching onto someone that you could have a connection with, and that's all you really needed to be happy. As unhealthy as it may or may not be—if you could just be with this one person, and have that as home base as your familiar face in this world; that is all it takes for you to be happy. Which isn't necessarily healthy, but that's just the way it was for me.

Christopher Thorn: I remember when Brad played me that song on his four-track. The part that now Rogers plays—the guitar part—Brad actually whistled it. I remember driving to Vegas for either Brad's 21st birthday or his girlfriend's birthday, and he played the song on the way up. This is before the band—we were just friends. I remember thinking, "That's a really good song," and just how funny the whistling part was.

Glen Graham: I don't have a lot of memories of the actual recording, except "No Rain," I do remember this. Those guys recorded it, and I said, "Look, just record it and I'll overdub the drums." I'm glad I did that, because it did work out well—not that overdubbing the drums had anything to do with the success of the song [laughs]. That took me about six minutes, and…wow [laughs]! They played it, I played shaker. I went back and did two takes—we took the first half of the first one, and the second half of the second one. That's where all the income was generated. For me, it took seven minutes to basically not have to work for fifteen years. It's the weirdest seven minutes of my life.

Brad Smith: ["Deserted"] is about coming back from the desert. We were tripping on acid, and I was still tripping when I got home the next morning, at 10:00. The song is like, "Man, I've got to get sober—I'm tired of tripping my balls off. I'm completely exhausted, dehydrated, hungry. I just wanted to be in my bed and 'unstoned.' I walked in the door, grabbed my guitar, and wrote that first verse—just *done*. It came so fast, it was ridiculous. The next day, I played it for everybody. Usually for me, the best songs that I write are like that—you feel like someone gave them to you, and you actually owe somebody else for the song that you produced.

Rogers Stevens: That song we wrote in North Carolina. That was one of the ones that came out of us setting up in a room and playing all night. It was written mostly about this party that we went to in the desert in California one time, where we all took acid, drove out to the desert, and there was this huge crazy party. Just random, out in the desert—thousands of people. Sort of what Coachella is now—except it was completely non-professional and done without any sort of money or anybody making money.

Glen Graham: That was an unbelievably bizarre evening. LSD and scorpions. I don't know where we were—east of L.A. somewhere. Low, pointy mountains—we were in this canyon-y area. It was very dark when we got there, and Liquid Jesus had brought this generator and a truck. They had plywood set up on the sand. The wind was blowing like crazy, so sand is blowing everywhere. Everybody is on acid. That was my first experience with scorpions. You're sitting around and tripping, sitting on a rock or something. You've got the moonlight, and you see these things—"God, that looks like a scorpion. Is it a scorpion?" That was in the early days of Brad and Rogers taking LSD—I think Christopher, Shannon, and I were introduced to it a lot earlier.

Shannon Hoon: Songwriting has become a therapeutic artery for me. Music is like this invisible person that's always around for a good discussion. My songs are always about some real emotion I'm feeling, so they become kind of a mental journal and a mental journey. It's been a great feeling to therapeutically bleed myself with music. But I have to be careful. If you force too much into the music, you give yourself a hernia. Songwriting is the way I reflect, but it's also like a great tasting candy—you have to be careful not to eat yourself sick with it.

Rogers Stevens: "Sleepyhouse" was a song that I wrote the music for, brought it into the group—had it sort of arranged and done. We put it together in the house in Durham. It's about our experiences there, after leaving L.A.—going there to work and getting away from the hectic stuff. We ended up in a cool musical environment. Some of the guys who ended up being in the Squirrel Nut Zippers, just a bunch of other local musicians—that's what the references to 'the yellow house' is. It's a house we ended up going to—in Chapel Hill—where a bunch of those people lived. A flophouse. We ended up playing with people who were playing horns, accordions, and all kinds of weird things. I think the rest of it is about that house, which is in Durham—right off the campus at Duke University.

There was a cool thing that happened regarding that song—when we were in Seattle, we were working with Rick Parashar. He's Indian, and he took us to I think the University of Washington—there was an event where Usted Sabbi Kahn played the sarangi. We went and watched him play—it was amazing. He must have been at least 80 years old—he was renowned in India as a master of that instrument. I think 'Usted' means master. Rick knew him, and asked him to come to the studio. That's how we got him to be on that recording. I remember Christopher and I had a couple of really big guitar amps that we put in rooms off to the side, and he sat in the main room. He rolled out a carpet and he chewed on these spices that they chew on when they go into this trance-like thing when they're playing. He had this yellow foam coming out of his mouth. We must have played for half an hour straight—Christopher, I, and him—and we were getting all this weird feedback and turning the amps up loud. There's recordings of it somewhere and it's kind of cool. We ended up using a segment of what he did, but he played for an hour—it was amazing.

Brad Smith: I think I wrote a verse of that—I think Shannon wrote the first verse. We finished that in the Sleepyhouse. It was another piece of music we had recorded to cassette that sat around for months and months. When we got to North Carolina, we had an eight-track by then—we re-recorded that music, and Shannon buckled down one night and started finishing the lyrics. And I had some stuff that was laying around on a piece of paper. He cranked out that chorus—I remember when he came up with that chorus, I was just like, "*Yeah!*" I was super-pumped.

Rogers Stevens: "Holy Man" is another song that I wrote most of and then brought to the band—I wrote most of the words. It was about my experiences as a child—some of the things I went through. My parents went through a bad divorce, where my mother ended up leaving my father for the guy who was the preacher of our church. The song's not specifically about that, but it definitely reflected the cynicism I had about being a church-going kid. I brought that in and we worked that up. I had really basic chord arrangements and that riff at the beginning, and the band filled it up. Shannon changed a few of the lyrics and made it work vocally for him.

Brad Smith: Rogers had a big hand in writing that. Shannon I think came up with the melody line.

Rogers Stevens: I think ["Seed to a Tree"] came from our get-together jams as a group. One of those things that we were rolling tape, heard something, and started working with it. We put it all together. I'm pretty sure those were all Shannon's lyrics. To me, that song is open for interpretation. I think it has to do with his relationship to his father. We didn't play that song a lot. I didn't really dig too deeply into that one, to be honest.

Brad Smith: "Seed to a Tree" was another funk attempt—on the heels of "Dear Ol' Dad." Maybe Rogers and I came up with that. Shannon wrote all the lyrics. By the time "Seed to a Tree" was written, we were functioning as a full band—the band members without Shannon would go down and work up pieces of music. And Shannon would come in later in the day, and he and I would stay down there and work on stuff. Or we would take a cassette to where he is, let him hang out in his bedroom, and listen to four-tracks.

Christopher Thorn: "Drive" was a finished song that I brought in, that Shannon sang over. I worked with this guy named Willie [at a second-hand clothing store called 'Jet Rag'], and he started to experiment with heroin, unfortunately. I was telling Shannon the story—Shannon was friends with William as well. One day, Shannon came down to visit me at work, and Willie hadn't had drugs, so he was detoxing—going through withdrawals. The song "Mother" came on from John Lennon, and he started crying—it was this really heavy moment. So Shannon wrote the lyrics about that—and the lyrics are about some other stuff that I wouldn't want to talk about, about some other experiences Shannon and I had.

Brad Smith: Shannon had a magnetism for people that were deviant. And this guy was definitely a deviant. He would always call Shannon for a ride to take him downtown to score some heroin. That's what the song was about. Christopher came up with that riff, and that song was pretty much about a story that happened to him and Shannon. You hear those songs and lyrics and it was really like whatever happened that day—in a strange way. Those were just real life stories that we were all telling each other at the time. That little spoken word thing in the middle of the song, "But the next day the phone will ring and it will be him. Can you drive?" The guy would call him at really strange or inopportune times—it might be 3:00 in the morning, it might be 2:00 in the afternoon.

Rogers Stevens: "Time" I remember specifically, because when we left California, we had one big U-Haul truck and a couple of cars. We all caravanned it across the country. We got crystal meth, and I remember we were all doing this—I had never done it before, and I don't know if anybody else had either. But we were going to do it, the old 'trucker's little helper,' to help get us across the country. We ended up driving all the way to Texas from Los Angeles without stopping. We were really happy to be driving. Got to Texas and somewhere along the way we decided, "We better try and get some sleep." So we got a hotel room and we all were in one room—sleeping end-to-end. I remember lying in bed for like an hour and somebody asked if anyone else was sleeping. Of course, nobody was, so we just got up and left again. Drove the rest of the way to Mississippi, which was where we were going to stop off for a little while. So we got there—I remember pulling up to my dad's house with all this stuff, and people just being on a 'different planet.' It was strange to see the family in that situation.

"Time" came from that experience a little bit, and a lot of it from being in Mississippi at that time. My dad had owned a piece of property that was formerly a bar. It was empty, so we went in there and set up, to do some writing. We had the basics of the song, and Christopher started playing that whole opening part. I think Brad and Shannon put the basics of the song together over that, and the lyrics are about being in Columbus [and] West Point. And then we just filled in as a band. I really liked that song because it had so much energy—it was fun to play live. [The ending] was one of those things—it was so open. It was just a little simple two-chord thing, and we could move around with it. Some audiences you would lose with it—sometimes it would be good. As we went along with it, we started settling into it and doing that on some other songs. Sometimes it was out of boredom and sometimes it was out of inspiration. It was hit or miss.

Brad Smith: We probably wrote that song in the amount of time it took to play it. Shannon was 'Johnny on the spot' with those lyrics.

Shannon Hoon: I hope people can find something on the album that they can relate to. And I think that's possible. We're not the only group of guys from small towns—there's a lot of people who come from repressed environments.

Owen Orzack: I thought ['Blind Melon'] was a very interesting mixing of genres. It was like the Allman Brothers meet Jane's Addiction. They looked retro, but they had a unique sound.

Shannon Hoon: Someone who tags our band as like a Jane's Addiction or puts us in the Seattle sound category has obviously just listened to one song. Or maybe part of a song. But if you listen to the record as a whole—we rip off everybody! And the unifying force may have nothing to do with music. Just points of view. We get everybody at our shows—the groovers, the stage divers and blah, blah, blah, all that stuff.

Glen Graham: When we were in Mississippi, on the way to North Carolina, Christopher was upstairs at my parents' house—we were walking around looking at what's known as 'the playroom.' Where all the family pictures are—a couple of hundred family pictures. He saw [a picture], and said, "Oh my God, that's the cover!" Just like that. And I looked at him like, "O.K., great—that sounds fine to me." Georgia [Glen's sister] will be thrilled. It took a lot of convincing. I think Shannon went for it immediately, I can't remember Rogers' reaction, and Brad was totally against it. That was funny, because he wrote "No Rain"—that was the thing that helped "No Rain" sell [laughs]. I'm sure he was glad in retrospect. It's a dance recital. It was 'Mrs. Betty Lott's English School of Dance.' Which is ridiculous—I don't know what kind of English dancing requires a bee costume. I think they were doing a dance to "Be My Little Baby Bumble Bee." It was like little girls do—jazz, tap, and ballet.

Tim Devine: It was about handwritten lyrics—not pre-printed lyrics. Keeping it rough around the edges. Not making it anti-commercial per se, but keeping it 'homegrown.' A lot of that came from [Shannon]. The back cover of the first album with the marijuana seeds definitely came from him. I don't know what the rest [of the image] is, but it's definitely pot seeds.

Lyle Eaves: It's something with candle wax that Shannon did.

Rogers Stevens: [The original 'Tones of Home' video] was one of those things that was foisted upon us. We were basically given an unproven director to do something—his name was Cronenweth. His father was nominated for an award for 'Blade Runner.' So this kid was trying to make a [video], and we were probably pretty uncooperative and difficult to deal with at that point. We ended up not liking the video for whatever reason and canning it. Which is amazing, because they probably spent a fair amount of money on that. This was the second thing [the band shelved]—the label was still allowing us to do these things. I don't know if anybody would get away with that kind of thing these days. Which I think is an indication of how much Capitol was willing to stick with us and indulge these sort of failures. Hale really knew what was going on. Just being able to green light stuff like that—to allow us to make mistakes and blow money. I mean, it's all our money in the end—we end up paying and recouping—but still, they laid out some risks for us, and I think it was much appreciated by the band. And realized later about Hale.

Jena Kraus: Rogers and Shannon [in August of '92] were coming to New York for a record company meeting. I came to see them—it was me, Domenique, Rogers, and Shannon. We were hanging out one night and we were in Shannon's hotel room. He had bought all these colored candles and tin foil. He covered his windows in tin foil, at the Mayflower Hotel. I stayed over that night, and the next day, they were at meetings. I was walking and I looked over at the side of the building—hundreds of windows—and I saw this one window that was shining brighter than the other ones, because the sun was reflecting on the tin foil of his window. I felt like that was really symbolic and metaphoric—there was this one brighter window there. When we were in his hotel room, he was playing songs. It was so amazing—I don't think even the recordings did him justice. Just to sit and listen to this guy sing. As a singer, it was really inspiring to hear someone that just...I don't know, it was just unreal. His voice and his songs were amazing—the melodies, the lyrics. Everything. I always remember sitting there like, *"Oh my God."* I couldn't believe the amount of talent he had. And just a fun person to be around—always joking and laughing. Making everybody laugh. And really smart.

Shannon Hoon: When you hear someone come up and say, "Man, I know what you're talking about"—that's the best. That's all you ever want, for someone to know what in the hell you're talking about. You bleed what is sometimes a frustrating point of view, you bleed it through writing it—and playing it. And to have someone interpret what you had to write down, because you couldn't find anybody else to comprehend what you were trying to say, to have someone you've never even met before come up and say, "I know what you're talking about," that's who you're looking for. I mean, it's just the best.

Crammed in a Van Tour

*After the release of 'Blind Melon' on September 22, 1992, the band
hits the tour trail, headlining their own gigs on what's dubbed the
'Crammed in a Van Tour,' as well as playing with some of rock's biggest
names—Ozzy Osbourne, Alice in Chains, Stone Temple Pilots, John
Mellencamp, their old pals Guns N' Roses, and almost, Bob Dylan.*

Brad Smith: That period where we're in a van, sharing doobies, playing clubs,
and just not giving a damn about anything—that was one of the best periods
of Blind Melon's history in my mind. I look back at that period with a lot
of fondness, because that was right before we got so successful that the band
came apart at the seams on a personal level. We named one of our t-shirts
'Crammed in a Van Tour.' We knew we were making an impact, because we'd
come around to the same city the second time, and the crowd had doubled
or tripled, and the word was getting out. That was probably the most roman-
tic period of my musical career—coming back to a city you'd been to once
before, and people flocked to see the shows. It's one of the best, most honest,
real types of marketing and appeal that I've ever been involved in. It was such
a great feeling; at that point, I was successful in my mind. We still wanted to
sell records at that point—that's why were out on the road—but you felt like
you'd made a mark.

Paul Cummings: I worked with them for three years, and I thought that was
the best they ever were. They weren't jaded, they hadn't had enough of being
on the road at that point, and they were still hungry. The record was *just*
starting to kick in around that time. It was still new and fresh to them. [Shan-
non] was pretty quiet, originally. In the early days, everybody shared rooms. I
would room with Shannon, and he was an actually pretty good roommate—

he was neat. In those days, they didn't get in as much trouble, because we didn't have a tour bus. You don't sleep very well in a van, so everybody was tired most of the time. When you're tired, you get in less trouble. I think the manager was smart—a lot of bands take tour support and get buses, that they end up having to pay back to the record company, or it comes off before they get any money. And he never wanted to do that. They tried to do as much as they could without paying for tour support—it probably worked out better for them in the long run. I would drive half the time, and the other band members would split the other 50% of the driving. We had one of those Ford Econoline vans—everybody had a seat to lay on, and somebody would sit shotgun. Shannon always seemed to take the far seat in the back of the van.

Lyle Eaves: The back [seat] was the longest one—Shannon felt he deserved that. There was a little minor squabble sometimes over Shannon feeling entitled to whatever the best stuff was. But that's the way it worked out—he usually got what he wanted. That's the way his personality was. If you ever made a bet with Shannon—flipped a quarter, drew straws—he was going to win every time.

Brooks Byrd Graham: [Shannon] always had his headphones on. Y'know, you sway a lot back there, and he would yell—"Man! What are you doing? Watch where you're driving!" And then when he would drive, he was a maniac driver.

Shannon Hoon: I annoy the holy shit out of these guys so bad!

Christopher Thorn: We were under the false assumption that our record was going to come out and be a giant hit. And then reality struck us—"Wow, this is really hard work." We were having a lot of fun, because we were playing and seeing the country, but we were a bit stressed out. We didn't realize that you actually had to work a record. Thank God we had a record company like Capitol, who knew it was going to be a slow build, and they were prepared to keep us on the road for a long time. If we didn't have that support, we wouldn't be having this conversation.

Bill Armstrong: I remember thinking, "They're going to have to take some time on the road." Certainly, the potential was there, but it didn't feel realized. Everything with them still felt premature. Even when they were playing these big shows—it was good, but I felt like they still hadn't clicked into their own. It felt early. It felt like exactly what it was—a group of guys who got together, wrote a lot of good songs, had a lot of potential, but still, you can't replace 'road time.'

Lyle Eaves: That was a time of them getting it together—still, not a lot of people knew who they were. The people that came to the shows liked them and got into them, but they weren't well known. They didn't have a hit, the album wasn't selling. I think they were still trying to find their way at that point—where they were headed. We did *a lot* of touring.

Jeremy Hammond: Shannon was very charismatic—he had this great chemistry with the audience. He always wanted to bring the audience into the performance with him. He came on stage with bare feet—he was a hippie.

John Fagot: When they went out live, they really had an effect on the audience. Shannon was a great on-stage performer, and he was *real.* He did it out of a 'hippie thing,' that was kind of a leftover from the '60s/peace and love thing. But it was real. And when you get something that's real like that, it effects people. And Shannon—not just through his on-stage performance, but his demeanor in interviews and on television and everything else, you really liked the guy.

Lisa Sinha: Shannon took every show very seriously—even if he was screwed up or drank. Every show, he put his heart and soul into it.

Jena Kraus: I saw them next in October—at Irving Plaza [in New York City]. The show was amazing. The crowd was totally into it. Later that night, we all went to a party at this guy Marlon's house. Shannon and I were the last people to leave. It was like 4:00 in the morning and we were walking around the streets of New York. He's like, "Are we going to sing together? We're going to sing together, aren't we? Somebody helped me, and I'm going to help you." And then we went and got poppy seed muffins.

Rogers Stevens: [The "I Wonder" video] was done in West Point, Mississippi. A friend of my younger brother's crowd was living in a trailer out there, in this place called Tibbee. It's a creek, Tibbee Creek, which runs through there. Same director that did the "Dear Ol' Dad" video, he came down. We went out in the woods, called a bunch of our friends and told them to bring people—"We're making a video." It was just local kids from our town. The idea was they were going to get everybody really muddy, which they did. We set up, played live on the porch, and they hosed this yard down. They just trashed it—we ruined a lot of stuff that day, that we didn't intend to ruin.

Denise Skinner: Out in the mud...it was outrageous. There was a bridge [Shannon] decided to walk across the high arch part. Everyone freaked out about that, because it's like, "Hey, if you fall and die—where does that leave the rest of the band?" He was always a risk taker out there.

Rogers Stevens: I remember that scaring the shit out of me. I'm really afraid of heights, and I also have a problem seeing someone do something like that—that makes me scared too. He climbed up—that's the Tibbee Bridge. We used to shoot guns off that thing when I was a kid. A really scary, rickety old bridge. It's gone now, but you can't believe it was still being used—really looks like it's going to collapse.

Lyle Eaves: I stayed away from most of the video shoot, because all I heard was how I was going to end up in the mud. So me and the first monitor guy finally went out there late, and they were pretty soaked in mud. Shannon was probably doing acid, which is what he did for most of the videos. So when we got there, he started chasing [us] around—he caught Chuck, tackled him, and cracked two of his ribs. I had to take him to the emergency room. That was about my extent of that video.

Paul Cummings: It looks pretty funny looking back on it. I guess I'm not surprised it wasn't a big hit.

Lisa Sinha: That was kind of a tame period—when they were getting big. People were chilling out—not being too crazy. I talked to him all the time. He was really general about all of that—"It's going good."

Christopher Thorn: I remember right around the time the album came out, we had an Ozzy tour. It was us, Alice in Chains, and Ozzy. That was a really fun tour, because I was a giant Ozzy fan. I remember playing bigger places and it was great. I think we had a little bit of fear walking into it, thinking, "We're not really metal—how are we gonna win over this Camaro/beer drinking crowd?" I think the fact that we had Shannon running around like a madman onstage helped win over a lot of audiences that would've been bored.

Mike Inez: I knew them when I was in the Ozzy band. They were on a van on the Ozzy tour—they were great guys. Me, Zakk Wylde, and Randy Castillo, we had our own bus—the three of us. And we just felt really bad for Blind Melon—in the back of this van. You could tell they were good at what they did. There are a lot of bands out there that you see play, and you go, "Oh man, *I don't want to be that person."* With Blind Melon, they had talent, the right attitude, and were super sweethearts. So we used to get them on the bus—let them stretch out a little bit and have a couple of beers. Certain bands you just pull for—they were certainly one of them.

Rogers Stevens: It was only a couple [of shows with Ozzy], or a couple of weeks or something. I met him a few times. He came into our dressing room the first night, and kept asking Brad some question that we couldn't understand. He was asking for the vodka! [Imitating Ozzy] *"Where's the vodka?"* And then one of his handlers came in, and said "No, no—these guys are the opening band." He said, "Oh O.K., have a good show!" Then Sharon [Osbourne] came out on the road and everything got totally whipped into shape. Clearly, he was saved by her in a lot of ways. People in his band were lifting weights backstage. Kind of intimidating. We didn't see [Ozzy] a lot, but the one time

I did see him backstage, he definitely seemed to be more of the 'Mr. Hyde' type.

Alice in Chains was on the bill. That was a pretty strange billing in a way, but it seemed to work. We never got booed—which is the benchmark of success at that point. It was fun for us. I remember Alice in Chains—seeing them a couple of times and being impressed with their show. One time—this is a fucked thing—they had a bass player [Mike Starr], who I guess was their original bass player. He came in and their second album had just come out—he was all hyped about it. I guess he was bragging about that it was high up in the Billboard charts. He was pretty stoked. And then about three days later, he was canned.

Lyle Eaves: We had a good time on it—being around Ozzy was a trip. But the audience could care less about them. They weren't really having a good time on that tour because of that. They played real early, and nobody knew who they were. I think they hung out a little bit with [Alice in Chains]—I know Shannon really liked Layne [Staley]. He talked about him a lot.

Lisa Sinha: [Shannon] and I drove the LTD—this car—to St. Louis or something. I had to drive back. That's when he met Layne. I know those two had partied some. He liked Layne, thought he was a cool guy, a good singer. I didn't know Layne that well.

Shannon Hoon: Our strength is in our live shows, and it's not like we're too good to play anywhere. If the offer is feasible and we can work it out, we'll be there. It's not as if we're 'above' anything.

Buz Zoller: It just seemed like Shannon was 'on his own' a little bit. It was always 'Shannon and then the band.' It wasn't like an animosity where they hated each other—but it was a little bit of a separation. I don't think they ever argued or anything like that, but it was always kind of 'them and him.' They seemed like they were a band…and it seemed like they were a little bit of just his backing band. Maybe there was some animosity as time went on about that.

Kim Smith: You *knew* big things were going to happen. And the shows were great—they were getting packed. People knew already about Shannon at that point. Even though they weren't selling a lot of albums right in the beginning, still, the shows were packed. They were great shows—Shannon was a little out of control, but it was fun [laughs]. He was out of control in a good way. He was really excited to be on stage and doing the stuff with Blind Melon at that point. He was a great frontman.

Shannon Hoon: Going back through that mental Rolodex at a thousand miles an hour...you flip into an untouchable state of mind. It's healthy, whatever it looks like.

Marlon Stoltzman: He was just an absolutely outstanding performer. Real, real special live talent. It was like the minute anybody saw Blind Melon, they were converted.

Denise Skinner: Shannon was different at every performance. What always impressed me about the whole band was no matter where Shannon was mentally or emotionally that evening, they would all rally. And were very cognizant of making sure it came off as a band. Rogers and Christopher were awesome—and Glen too—when it came to stepping up to the plate and doing things that needed to be done. What I loved about the live thing was that these guys would really win the audience over—even if the audience was hostile and not there particularly to see them. These guys would just go out there and work their asses off. Shannon was all over the place—physically, he was all over the stage. And there were times he would come out with the strangest hairdos [laughs]. I always marveled at that—that they could get out there, play their hearts out, and no matter what the crowd was, by the end of the gig, people wanted more.

Jena Kraus: The thing about Blind Melon shows—the crowds...there was a different vibe. It wasn't just a normal rock show—it seemed like people were really cool. Everybody was into it and having a good time. I mean, it was aggressive in a certain way, but in another way, people were cool to each other.

To me, it was what the Grateful Dead wanted to be. I'm sorry to the Grateful Dead, but I've been to Grateful Dead shows, and I feel that a lot of people there are kind of bad. This vibe—people would smile at you and you would feel the music. It was amazing.

Buz Zoller: They were really true to their instruments. I don't even think they used effects or anything—they just plugged their guitars into their amps and played. It was kind of the opposite of [Flowerhead]—wanting it to be louder and more distorted. *More.* But it had that same kind of vibe—'60s, groovy, psychedelic. Just in a different way. So we had that 'kindred spirit' with them. And they were small—they toured with two people I think. They had the road manager and one guy who was a tech. Very nice and humble—they knew they were nobody's at that point. It didn't bother them—they went about their business and didn't have big heads at all.

John Fagot: I saw them once in L.A. at a club—it might have been the Troubadour. There was a show they did, where it was almost just an industry crowd. It was all the label people, and people from radio, other labels. Normally with an industry show, you get a lot people talking, doing business in the back. It's not the greatest crowd. But this crowd was screaming, right on the stage, and dancing. I was upstairs looking down on it—it was odd to me to see all these industry people who normally don't get affected. I've probably been to over 4,000 live shows in my life—so when you do that, you can be a pretty harsh critic, because you've seen everybody. That's the kind of audience it was, and they were just singing and dancing—it looked like a damn hippie free-for-all [laughs].

Barbara Prisament: Since I was based in New York, I'd see shows all the time. Every once in a while, there would be a show that you just had that sense that a band was going to break—they were on the verge of something big. Everyone in that audience [at the Wetlands] could feel it—there was just something palpable in the air. The rest of the country didn't know yet—it hadn't broken wide open, it wasn't on MTV yet, it wasn't all over the radio yet...*but the kids knew.* The reaction to "No Rain" that night at the show was unbelievable. I called L.A. the next day, and said, "You guys don't understand—the Blind Melon show last night was telltale, this band is going to be huge! Something is happening here."

Kim Smith: It was like a family—we became a family. All the girls got along really good. We were out on tour a lot together, actually. We'd even stop during the tour and go skiing —the whole crew, when we were in Colorado, we went to Winter Park one year. Even the crew people were family.

Heather Thorn: We had a rule, where [Heather and Christopher] never spent more than a month apart—that was the limit we would go. But in all honesty, I feel like the wives and the girlfriends had the best of both worlds. We were all really close—all the wives were really close and all the guys were really close. You hear a lot of in-fighting amongst bands, and it wasn't like that—we as a whole were truly like a big family together. All the girls got to show up at the good places, and when they went to the bad places, we left [laughs]. I was out on the road a lot though, it wasn't too bad. And since Christopher and I were together for so long, there was not that 'jealousy' thing. I'm sure if I had met him two weeks before he went out on the road, it would have been a whole different scenario. It was hard, but I got to see the world, meet tons of people, and have a great time with my best friends doing it. I wouldn't trade it—for sure.

Brooks Byrd Graham: It was kind of grueling. What was fun about that time—we would go bowling. We were really into bowling for a long time. Shannon was the most enthusiastic bowler—everything he did was with such force and energy. He would get that ball and he would *swing it around*—it was almost like he was throwing a baseball. He was real competitive, always wanting to do something. Like, he got rollerblades at some point in the tour, and he would go out and rollerblade all the time.

Buz Zoller: I remember shows where people would pass [Shannon] joints, and he would take them. Brad would [too]—they would pass them around, so it wasn't just Shannon being the oddball. They smoked a lot of pot—they were 'open minded' to lots of things. I'm sure whatever Shannon's personality was, he was probably way open to everything. But at that point, if there was anything, it was well hidden.

Brad Smith: After a while on the road, we didn't have to buy any weed, because people would give us tons. We had so much weed back in the day—nobody bought weed for years. Fans and people wanting to hang out with you would come up and give you a quarter bag for the trip home. But if you do four or five shows in a week, you've got at least an ounce on you at all time.

George Nunes: Every show I saw was great—depending on obviously Shannon's consumption of whatever he was taking that day would make it interesting. But I never got the vibe that they were out of it or out of control. Every time I saw them play, they were dead on. It was a lot like jazz—you never know how it's going to turn out, and certainly, expect the unexpected.

Buz Zoller: We did this one show with them in New Orleans, with Stone Temple Pilots as a last minute addition. This was when "Sex Type Thing" was their first [hit]. I remember how weird that was—how this band from nowhere got to butt in and get in on our show.

Rogers Stevens: We were playing some place in New Orleans with [Stone Temple Pilots]—a one-off show. [Shannon and Scott Weiland] had words with each other or something—I don't know what happened. I do know that Shannon took a dump on their deli tray! I know the two brothers [Dean and Robert DeLeo]—those guys are super-cool, really nice guys. I didn't have any problems with them. I remember sitting there listening to Scott telling stories backstage—one of those 'all about him' kind of scenarios.

Paul Cummings: New Orleans always seemed to be bad news. Stone Temple Pilots played on the same show, and they were late getting there—everything ran late. At the end of the night, we were taking the van back to the hotel, and Shannon said, "I'm going to stay." I said, "Are you going to get back O.K.?" And he said, "Don't worry, I won't get in any trouble. *I have too much respect* *for you.*" I thought it was weird that he said that, but I go back to the hotel and about an hour and a half later, Brad comes to my room, and tells me [Shannon] has been arrested. He'd been drinking, which was always bad news for him. He basically picks up whatever vibe's going and goes with it—if it's a happy vibe, he's a happy drunk. If something gets out of hand, then it just escalates.

What happened apparently the cops got involved where they were, he ended up running away, the cops are running after him, and I think he ducked behind a car or something. When the cop came, he punched him—he was arrested for 'battery on a police officer,' 'disturbing the peace,' and there was one other thing. He spent the night in jail. Luckily, I had enough money to bail him out, and we had a show in Baton Rouge the next day. I remember it wasn't just him—it was three or four other kids that were arrested at that thing. I don't know why, but I sat at the jail all night. In the morning, I bought a bunch of donuts and coffee for all the other kids that were waiting for somebody to come and get them out of jail. So I bailed him out, and he was very apologetic. We did the gig in Baton Rogue, then him and I went back to New Orleans, because he had to appear the next morning. He stood there and had the charges read to him—he had to appear at a later date. I don't know whatever happened with that one—I know he didn't do any time, and I don't think he did any service there.

Eva Pfaff: I remember them being tired one day—and taking them to the doctor. I was worried about them. I felt a little 'motherly' toward them. I remember at least arranging that—whether it happened, I don't remember. But I remember them being very grateful, that they felt somebody was looking out for them a little bit.

Paul Cummings: Once when we were sharing rooms, we got a call from one of the record company guys. And Shannon didn't feel like talking to him. I think he said something like "I'll be right back," got up, and went out for a couple of hours. I was out, came back an hour later maybe, *and the guy was still holding on the phone.*

Mike Osterfeld: I met with Lyle, and he said, "I've got an opportunity that you're not going to get somewhere else. There's this band, Blind Melon—we're going to open up for Guns N' Roses." The minute he said, "We're going to do stadium shows," I was in. It was like being thrown into the lions—it was amazing.

Glen Graham: Then we got the Guns N' Roses thing. We went out with those guys, and that was amazing. That was sort of life changing. You felt a lot better about the whole plan. We got pretty good responses on the Guns N' Roses [dates].

Gilby Clarke: Riki goes, "I can't believe Shannon's band is doing so well." I'm like, "God, *that's right!*" I didn't even put two and two together—Riki reminded me. He looked much different from the Cathouse days to the Blind Melon days.

Lyle Eaves: [Shannon] loved to grab people and tackle them. When we opened for Guns N' Roses, I go into the production office to meet these big time road guys—who at the time, were heroes of mine. Y'know, this is what I want to do—the same thing these guys are doing. I go in the office to meet these guys, and as I'm sticking my hand out to shake the hand of Opie, their production manager, Shannon comes through the door and tackles me—in the production office. Lays me out on the floor. *A great first impression.* It was always something with him. He definitely acted first and thought later.

Tim Devine: I flew into Detroit to see them on the Guns N' Roses tour at the Palace of Auburn Hills, the arena where the Detroit Pistons play. Axl was nowhere to be found at 10:00/11:00 pm. I don't think it was until midnight that he showed up. Blind Melon had played their set from 8:00 to 9:00, then for the next three hours the crowd just milled around the smoke-filled hall hoping that they were going to see their idols at some point in the evening. This was in the days when Axl would keep the audiences waiting all night.

Mike Osterfeld: Watching the stage manager for Axl try and jump in front of a limo to keep Axl there, because he felt like he was having some déjà vu and didn't want to play a show. It was watching *real* rock star problems.

Christopher Thorn: I hated waiting around for Axl every night—that kind of sucked. I saw what I *didn't* want to be—that's one thing that that tour taught me. People stepping aside because Axl was walking down the hallway. It's like, "What the fuck? He's just *a guy*." I'll never forget people playing ping-pong in this big hallway, and then suddenly they stopped playing and moved to the side. I was like, "What's going on? Why would you stop in the middle of the game?" Everyone's sort of winking, like, "Look who's coming down the hallway." It was like, "Oh O.K., it's Axl. Why are you guys stopping? Are you afraid he's going to get hit with a ping-pong [ball]?" It was so pathetic. I thought, "I never want to be like that—you're still human, *you're still a fucking punk*." We used to have to wait, because he would fly in and out on a helicopter. In the States, we weren't flying around with them—we were in a van, trying to keep up with them on tour. There were times when we would want to leave to get to the next show, and we would have to *wait* for Axl to fly in on the helicopter. It was just always this 'waiting on Axl thing.' It would drive me crazy. But I'm so grateful that we got to open up for them and play to that many people.

Shannon Hoon: I think the big rock shows are for certain people, but not for us. It was a good tour, and we got to play to a lot of people, but as far as what kind of environment we feel comfortable in and what kind of vibe we create, it's definitely realized better in a smaller, sweatier, stinkier place than a 60,000 seat venue that's sold out.

Rogers Stevens: Airplane! We toured on the MGM Grand [when Blind Melon played in Mexico with G n' R]—that was really fun. It was full-on rock star treatment. We went from touring in a van to getting on their plane. And they were in their full-on decadent collapse at the time. So that was sad to watch, because I was a big fan—they still played great. You learned a lot from them—they were one of those bands that could really fill up a stadium.

They would play on stage at a stadium, and you'd think, "Wow, I don't know if I have that sorta 'outside personality' to do that." But they could really pull it off.

Mike Osterfeld: The MGM Grand, we would sit on the tarmac and wait for hours for Axl to decide he felt like flying. We would be on the MGM eating chilled shrimp and drinking whatever we wanted—with the doors open, smoking cigarettes. I would sit in the farthest back seat of the plane—while Shannon and Slash would be up front partying their brains out. That was another good story—having to carry him off the plane one time. Slash's guy—who looked just like Slash—had to carry Slash off the plane when we showed up in Guadalajara. They both popped pills, so they passed out on the flight, and they couldn't wake them up. So he's carrying him out, and I'm carrying Shannon out. They're coming running to the tarmac with wheelchairs for us. Paul Cummings had to spend that night making sure Shannon kept breathing. He had to keep checking on him in his hotel room, because we were real worried he wasn't going to wake up.

Gilby Clarke: Our tour bus was a plane. One of the times, Shannon came with us. He ended up sitting beside me, because we hadn't spent a lot of time together. Sometimes at shows—especially with G n' R—we were in and out. I would try to go early to watch Blind Melon or Faith No More—'cause I hated sitting in my hotel room. I'd rather be at the show, watching the bands, and getting into the groove. On one of the plane rides, [Shannon] sat next to me, and we hung out and talked about what was going on. But man, he was getting so liquored up, so fast. I kept saying to him, "Dude, *pace yourself!*" Shannon was always 'in the moment.' Whether that moment lasted five minutes or twelve hours, he had to get to that moment quickly. That was wild, because we were just hanging, having a couple of cocktails, and I remember him going faster. I always liked Shannon because he didn't buy into the whole 'rock star' thing. It wasn't just because at that time grunge was fashionable—to not care. He was just cool. He loved being in his band and touring. He was on a plane with Guns N' Roses—he was having the time of his life.

Mike Osterfeld: I'd sit in the back of the plane—away from everyone—and frickin' Axl would come on with his ten entourage people. His masseuse, food therapist—all these people—and he'd sit in the last seat in the plane! Even though he's got his V.I.P. room in the front, he'd come sit next to me. I'd immediately get up and try to get the hell out of his way.

Glen Graham: We went to Mexico with them—that was kind of odd. Played stadiums and a bullring. One Guns N' Roses show in Mexico—we used to start our set with "I Wonder." This is an outdoor show, daytime. Someone tuned Brad's bass incorrectly and when we started the song, everybody's looking around trying to figure out the source of the problem and it was a total train wreck. We're all looking at the guitar tech, and when something like this would happen, Shannon would typically get pissed—something's not right, it's your fault, fix it. I remember trying to play the first verse, and maybe the first chorus. Everybody's freaking out. Nobody knew whose guitar was out of tune. Then finally, *we ground to a halt.* 60,000 people booed, just consistent. That was pretty good.

Mike Osterfeld: By this point, the guitar techs for Guns N' Roses figured out what was going on, and came running to my rescue. *The band walked off stage!* Left Shannon out there, and he can't talk to these kids. Well, as far as I'm concerned, I'm fired, I'm on the next plane home, I'm done. [After the show] I'm packing up the gear—I just want to bury my head in the sand, it's over, I just destroyed their show. And Shannon comes up to me with a drink, and says, "Dude, I just want you to know that I don't blame you for any of that. That can happen—that's a mistake. But the band walking off stage and leaving me out there by myself in front of those kids that I can't talk to is absolutely unacceptable." That was one of the things that endeared me to Shannon.

Paul Cummings: I remember when we did the shows in Mexico, we did Guadalajara, Monterrey, and two nights in Mexico City. Shannon wanted to say something to the crowd, so we got somebody to write out what he wanted to say, and stick it on the stage. It seemed like a good idea, but it got to be a bit too verbose for him. The crowd in Mexico City—in an arena—was probably one of the most responsive and best rock crowds I've ever seen. They did the thing where you light the lighters, and for an opening act that they hadn't even heard, the place was lit up with lighters. I was near the stage—Shannon turned around and his jaw dropped.

Christopher Thorn: I have really intense memories of opening up for Guns N' Roses in Mexico. They didn't know any better down there—they thought we were giant rock stars in the States, so they treated us like we had sold millions of records. So we're in Mexico with a bunch of people that don't speak our language and they're chasing us around. It was the first time we felt like, "Wow, this is cool!" People showing up at the hotel and asking for autographs—they had *no idea* who we were. I think just the fact that we were American and opening up for Guns N' Roses. My one super intense memory of those shows, in "Deserted," we used to go into this long, extended jam. And I've never seen this before—we're playing in front of like 80,000 people in some giant place in Mexico City. They were turning on and off their lighters to the beat of the song, at the end of the song. And I've never seen that since—it was so unbelievable to look out and see 80,000 people doing this. I'll never forget that moment.

Rogers Stevens: The show in Mexico City, we were in a van or limousine going underneath the stadium, to go to the backdoor to get there to play the show. I remember hundreds of people just smashed up against the chain link fences, trying to see—thinking we were Guns N' Roses. It was like freaking Beatlemania there.

Gilby Clarke: We used to do an acoustic set. There was a part of I think "I Used to Love Her"—every day we would have somebody different come out and play bongos. Normally it would be crew guys—the lighting director, one of the backline guys. We always had a Domino's Pizza outfit for this person—a Domino's Pizza shirt and hat—and what they would come out and deliver us a real pizza. Because our set was so long—it was like a three hour set—we always got hungry halfway through! Every day it was someone different, and every day—I would sit next to Axl on the couch—he would turn to me and go, "Who is that guy?" "Axl, that's Phil—*that's been our lighting guy for the last five years.*" And then one day, Shannon came out—naked!

Shannon Hoon: Since it was the last show we were doing with them, I decided to do it, so I took [Axl] his pizza wearing nothing but a horned Viking helmet. Then I sat down and played the congas. Axl was very shocked.

Nel Hoon: I never went over a week without talking to him. When he was in Europe with Guns N' Roses, he made so many calls home that I think Axl got mad at him—*because this was on Axl's bill.*

Shannon Hoon: The best shows I've ever had were shows where the club was so full that there was that element of danger, where you really didn't know whether you were gonna make it to the next song. I mean, there was a lot of energy in some rooms where there was no way security was going to be able to handle what was going to start, and everybody knew that at the same time. When everybody knows that, all that has to happen is that the curtain just needs to be pulled open. On the stages we're playing now, that's a big element that I miss. I like those shows where you wondered if you were gonna make it to the end. And even if things do explode, it's not because people don't want to hear the music; it's just because the energy in the room got a little bit too much for everybody, and we all kind of had a nervous breakdown together.

Charles Raggio: The first night [Inclined toured with Blind Melon], the promoter of the show was a deputized sheriff in the city. It was the first show of my career and only one of two that I settled with a gun on the table. There was no reason why this gun was on the table, nor was it mentioned why there needed to be a gun on the table. What had gone down that night was the security guards were being ruthlessly violent all night long. The crowd was doing just what a general admission crowd does—a little bit of crowd surfing. There wasn't anything over-the-top.

But these bouncers were huge and viciously violent—and Shannon got fed up with this one cat that we had noticed early on in the evening. He was guarding the pit, [the barrier] was two feet from the edge of the stage. Just large enough for these giant bouncers to sit in the middle. And one thing led to another, and this guy really roughed up this girl, and this young, scrawny boyfriend jumped in to try and protect his girlfriend. Apparently, the bouncer beat the shit out of this poor kid. Shannon at that point, towards the end of the show, had enough, and came running forward from the drum riser. Swung his mic stand—with the mic on it—and clocked the security guard on the top of the hand. He broke his hand.

So this turned into a huge ordeal between the promoter and the group. It turned into this whole drama on the first night. We're like, "What's this tour going to be like?" But it was a quiet, intense Shannon [that] had enough and jumped in to defend a fan. It sounds like a simple story, but when you were there, there was something really noble and cool about it. Of course, violence is never cool, but it had to go down like that that night, and he handled it. The promoter threatened that they were going to file charges and arrest Shannon, the tour wasn't going to go on, blah blah blah. It was idle threats—it was literally, trying to take a bribe. Basically a big tip to the security guard. But everybody stood their ground, and no money changed hands. We just moved on to the next city. It came down to the fan was going to press charges as well—that was the leverage.

Lyle Eaves: The bouncer started hitting this little skinny kid, and knocking him six feet every time he hit him. And Shannon hit him with his mic stand. We found out it was a cop, Shannon takes off. We end up in this shouting match—Shannon's hiding in the walk-in freezer in the basement of this place. And I didn't know where he was—threatening to arrest me if we didn't get him out. But the kids were coming out of the balcony in the truss that was holding the ceiling up—they were hanging from them and dropping into the mosh pit. Like 16 feet. It was pretty freaky. You get that feeling in the crowd like things could explode at any minute. After that fight, security was suddenly not on our side any more—*at all*. He hit more than one security guard with the mic stand—I know it happened in Kansas City, and it seemed like he got into it in New York at the Ritz. If he saw a security guard man-handling a kid, he would stop the show—he didn't think twice about it. Shannon ran on emotion all the time—he didn't think about anything he did. So, stuff like that happened more times than I can remember.

Paul Cummings: Sometimes he would grab the top of the mic stand and start swinging it, so the base was swinging around. It always worried me, because I thought that thing was going to come off and clock somebody. But he never actually lost that part of it. He'd start spinning it, and the band members would give him as much room as they could.

Shannon Hoon: Tiptoeing between sanity and insanity. It's such a rush that you don't know how to control it. You never know what you're going to be feeling from one minute to the next.

Charles Raggio: The show in Jackson, Mississippi, which is strange enough anyway—in 1993, it's still a very divided place. Very strange crowd. Outdoor show, a hundred and something degrees, 80% humidity. Jackson in the summer. It was a small outdoor show, and there wasn't an air-conditioned green room—everybody was really miserable, and Shannon was trying to warm up for the show. We're like, "Go on the tour bus, man—the generator's running, the air conditioner's on, just go in there and chill. Go in the back lounge and do your warm-up's." You know Shannon's voice—very throaty, very raspy— it sounded like it hurt sometimes. He went on our bus and we didn't tell our bus driver, and our bus driver was the quintessential old guard—a white southern bus driver named Tarzan. Tarzan was a handful and had a mouth on him. He was this 72 year-old man—more or less harmless. One thing leads to another, Shannon's back there warming up, [Tarzan] hears this, goes storming to the back lounge, and starts screaming at Shannon. Something along the line, like, "Jesus Christ boy, it sounds like somebody's skinning a cat back here!" It started this thing for the rest of the tour, about Shannon skinning a cat. We got 2,000 miles of touring out of that one.

Miles Tackett: Shannon was the most colorful character of the troupe, for sure. Just how he carried himself and expressed himself—in his own way, as far as an entertainer or a one-man show. He had a lot of passion. He was very warm—the energy that he put off was very warm. Unless you crossed him…

Charles Raggio: Some quiet, smart, intellectual, humble guys. Shannon particularly, had a real 'southern charm' to him. But Shannon was also... there was an intensity that went with the quiet thing. It was impressive and intense—particularly at first. It's like, "What's this cat about?" But he was always very sweet. And the tour immediately from the first day was...it was never a opening group/headlining group at all. It was always, "Let's eat dinner together." There was some fun after-show stuff immediately. They had clearly been doing it a little bit longer than Inclined, in that it wasn't as new and exciting—they always had a work ethic about them. But really humble, down-to-earth, sweet guys. Immediately they asked Miles to hang out in their dressing room—Brad was wanting cello lessons, so they were always sitting playing bass and cello together before the shows.

Tim Devine: In the summer of 1993, there was tremendous flooding along the Mississippi River leaving large sections of the Midwest underwater. There was a charity concert hastily organized called 'Flood Aid' to help bring awareness and donations to the residents of the severely distressed area. The performers were to be Bob Dylan, John Mellencamp, and Blind Melon. Tour schedules were rearranged and we all flew to St. Louis to be part of this event.

Rogers Stevens: Driving through to go to that show—through the Midwest—I remember the water being up to the road, on both sides. Miles at a time. And you'd see nothing but rooftops out off the highway. We got put on that right at the end. We met [Mellencamp]—I just said, "Hi." He's got that really hot wife, *I remember her* [laughs].

Tim Devine: We got in the night before and hung out at the hotel watching the weather forecasts rather closely. The next morning, conditions worsened. While waiting to leave for the show, we suddenly got word that another big storm was moving in and that the show may be cancelled. Moments later came the word that the airport was preparing to close. The concert was cancelled and we jumped in vans to catch the last TWA flight that was going back to L.A. before the airport shut down. I ended up sitting next to Dylan on the flight home where I remarked that it was ironic that 'Flood Aid' had to be cancelled due to flooding. He responded by saying, "Yeah, man, what a bummer," then immediately pulled his leather coat up above his head and buttoned it up high leaving only a tuft of hair protruding out from the top. I guess he had had enough conversation for one day.

Buz Zoller: Shannon always had a video camera with him. Always videoing everything. There's probably some creepy tapes floating around. I remember this one show, I think it was in Canada or someplace up north—it was in a gymnasium. We had to do our soundchecks really quickly, so everyone was in the same room. We used to carry a football with us, and we were playing football with them—Shannon had his camera.

Owen Orzack: He had his little man-purse bag—that was his video camera and whatever else was in there. I'm sure there's miles and miles of footage someplace.

Brooks Byrd Graham: He was really attached to his video camera. He used it as a friend to talk to, and he wanted to videotape everything. I was one of the trusted people—"You hold the camera for a while." He was just walking around with it all the time. He held it out in front of him to talk to it—"Here were are, going into the store, we're going to do this in-store now, look, here are these people. Let's put the camera in this guy's face."

Domenique Johansson: He had a real interest in documentation. The 'collector' kind of attitude, when you're discovering bands and you have to have everything the band did—every rare outtake and bootleg. It was like that—that kind of child-like thrill. He also used to record stuff—even himself when he would write songs, tape them, and then play them for you. He just wanted to share everything—it was like a learning discovery kind of thing. He would watch them over and over. Sometimes when you'd get back to the hotel, he'd watch and play them. A couple of the other guys had their [cameras], but they didn't use it the same way Shannon did. Shannon seemed to bring it with him when he would go to other concerts—he'd go backstage. He just documented everything. I think it was also an expression of him—this is how he was experiencing life. I think at some point, he would share this with his family, with friends—people that weren't necessarily around. I think he had designs some day that he would do stuff with this—even just remembering things for himself when he got old. "This is what I went through, I'll show it to my kids."

Marlon Stoltzman: One of [Shannon's] famous comments was, it was a Friday night, and he said, "Marlon, I feel so good that I want to stay up 'til Wednesday."

Nel Hoon: After they started getting big, it was different. All of a sudden, Shannon realized that this is really hard work—"I maybe would rather stay home and plant flowers or whatever." But at that time, it was too late for him to do those things.

"No Rain"

Already on the road for nearly a year, three videos under their belt, and album sales of 'Blind Melon' having thought peaked by many at Capitol, it's suggested that the band start thinking about 'album number two.' But due to some crafty maneuvers by label employees, Blind Melon is granted one more video from the album, "No Rain."

Tim Devine: There were people at the company that thought, "Enough already. We had put this band on the road for nine months, we had done three videos, we were only at 150,000 albums—maybe it was time for the band to go back and record a new album." Certainly, nobody thought there were millions of records left to be sold on this one. I remember a few of us having to fight for the possibility of a fourth single, and particularly, a fourth video—because it was unheard of to go and spend more money shooting a fourth video, after you had shot three videos and only sold 150,000 albums. But we felt in some kind of internal compass that enough groundwork had been laid—there was enough foundation—that if we could lay one more song on top of that foundation, that we had a chance to take this record to a point where the band's career would be cemented at least to the degree of being solidly on first base in preparation for a new album. In those days, that number was probably somewhere around the 250,000 range—that was a good showing for a debut. I don't think anyone anticipated what was going to happen next.

John Fagot: They did three videos, but what happened, this one song kept sticking in people's brains. And there was another fellow, Jeremy Hammond, he was a product manager. Jeremy fell in love with the band and the song. The company was looking at the economics of it, and saying, "Look how much money we spent on this band trying to break three singles, making three videos—it just doesn't make sense to go this deep in a fourth single. And if it was such a great song, why didn't it come up before?" So Jeremy and I were the two guys that argued, "*This* is the song that's going to break this band. For whatever reason, it doesn't hit you immediately, but once you listen to it for a while, it really sticks in your head."

Jeremy Hammond: We made videos and clawed away at trying to get some traction with these tracks at radio and MTV. But nothing really gelled. The press wasn't incredible either—I think they were getting some O.K. reviews. We totally over-spent—we spent too much money on videos and marketing— but this band needed tour support. We had this undying belief that if we persevered, something might happen. And it got to a point where the company wanted to shut down the project, because we had spent too much money. We had spent about $20 a unit, I think—it was probably a couple of million bucks by the time we sold 100,000 records. Which is an astronomical amount of money for that amount of sales. But we were hell bent on breaking the band.

Domenique Johansson: There was always the timing issue. It's rare that a band gets development and money the way that it happened with them. I do remember there being a lot of discussions on that being the single. The label I think wanted it more than the band. The band didn't want it—I think they were looking to develop a few other songs before they put out something that they thought might hit more commercially like that. It was the one [the label] wanted to start with. They focused immediately on that as the song they thought would drive the sales of the record. The band wanted to push ["No Rain" as a single] as late as they could in the development of the record.

Tim Devine: A lot of people that had been to the shows were noticing that the two songs that stood out in the live setting were "Change" and "No Rain." We noticed in different cities people started singing along to both songs—yet neither had been a single. So we talked about it back and forth—we had a number of meetings about it. Everybody chimed in. And we basically decided to go with "No Rain," because it seemed to be receiving the strongest reaction at the live shows—particularly the "*Oh, oh, oh, oh*" part.

Jeremy Hammond: I'll never forget it—two of the people in the company that were big fans of the band sent me a photograph. They set themselves down on a street corner with a sign, saying, *"Will work for 'No Rain'."* That was the message to me loud and clear—that was the clincher. So "No Rain" became the single. I went to the head of promotion, John Fagot, and said, "We're going to come out with another track." And frankly, he was resistant—we had failed to have any hits off the band. So after some rather heated discussion about it, I convinced him that we should at least take it to alternative radio and see if we could get something going—but on the condition that I produced a video for him. So I had to get a video. This discussion on the video came up in one of our V.P. meetings, and it didn't really go anywhere. I could see it was going in the wrong direction—the C.F.O. said, "We're not spending any more money on this project." So I followed him out of that meeting up to his office with the video producer, and we sat in the office. I said, "Look, this is it—*we've got to do this video.*" I made an impassioned plea, and at the end, [Capitol] crumbled and said, "O.K." So I got $75,000 to make a video for "No Rain."

Tim Devine: So we decided to shoot a video and that the concept should basically mirror the album cover. We were under no pressure…only that *everything* was riding on this. So, we decided to shoot 'the bee girl video.' Now, the bee girl was originally Graham's sister, but it was an older photo so we had to go out and find 'the new bee girl.' There were a number of young actresses submitted, but we didn't want anyone too pretty. In fact, the whole premise of the bee girl video was that this was a girl that didn't fit in. She was a little awkward. That's what we set about to find when we were making the video. We settled on a girl named Heather DeLoach. We went out to a field north of L.A.—in a wide opened area that turned out to be near the Ronald Reagan Presidential Library. I don't remember if it was a one-day or two-day shoot—I seem to remember it was a one-day. I think we knew the day of the video shoot that this was going to be something different.

Lyle Eaves: [Shannon] had a real thick, heavy beard before they did "No Rain," and Chris talked him into shaving. I've got pictures of him—we were in a hotel room, he would go and shave part of it and come in, and Chris would say, "No." I've got like four pictures in a row with the beard disappearing.

Rogers Stevens: I remember thinking, "O.K., they're spending some money on this." There was a much larger crew, and it really seemed like the label was thinking, "We can make this song a hit." But who knew the video was going to be what it was? I just said, "Let's use that image from the album cover." That's all we said to [director Sam Bayer]. And came up with a whole concept and everything. Even though there is a high production value to it, it still comes off as being homegrown in a way—because of the way we looked. We made zero concessions to being in a video—fashion-wise or anything else. It just looks like a bunch of degenerates in the middle of a field. It was done out in the Simi Valley somewhere. You can see the landscape—it's really beautiful. There were wild horses there. At that point, we're out there smoking pot and I think Shannon was taking acid. I mean, why not? It's a video, it's all day, you've got to be out there—you might as well enjoy it. And then all those people—I guess they put out a casting call, hired extras, and dressed them up like that. It was a surreal day. The way the video looks—that's the way it felt out there.

Mike Osterfeld: I show up without a hi-hat stand! You know how I made Glen's hi-hat stand? I busted conduit off the wall, put the bass drum pedal on the conduit, and basically tacked it to the side of the hill. If he really had to hit that hi-hat stand during that video, it would have collapsed.

Marlon Stoltzman: On the "No Rain" video, [Shannon] arrived on acid. I said to him, "Why do you do that? It's a big day." [Shannon said] "It was such a beautiful day." It came from such a naivety in a sense.

Paul Cummings: If you ever see the picture of [Shannon] urinating up in the big arc, that was taken there too—there's a bootleg CD that has that as a cover. I remember it was a really hot day—a lot of us got sunburns. It's a lot of 'hurry up and wait' when it comes to those things. They'd already done a lot of the conceptual stuff with the little girl—they shot a bit of it in downtown L.A.

Glen Graham: A video shoot is not 'show up, shoot a video, go home.' It's like it's a mini-movie, and it takes days of shooting. The first video, "Dear Ol' Dad," I still think is our best. But the "No Rain" video shoot was just this huge production. Samuel Bayer was great—he took the thing and spun it in a way that it resonated with people. I certainly wouldn't have done it that way—I don't think any of us would have.

John Fagot: It was tough to work the song, because it wasn't the kind of music that fit into the pigeonholing format that radio has. It's like; radio has alternative, active rock, classic rock, top 40—all these formats. And the music, even if it's great music, if it doesn't fit exactly into what they usually play, it's hard to get it played on the radio. So we worked it really hard. The kind of president that Hale was—he was one of the last guys that believed in 'artist development.' Nowadays, there's not a lot of artist development going on- just singles and people that have a hit album and then you never hear from them again. Hale was from the era and the idea that you developed artists, and then your artists stay with you a long time—that's the way you built a really great label. So he stuck with them.

Tim Devine: I remember having a rough cut of the video and taking it around the offices to show people. There was no question in people's minds when they saw that clip that they were seeing something big. People could barely contain their excitement. We watched it over and over again. We realized that once we had a cut of the video that our aspirations of selling another 100,000 records were probably *too low*. Anyone that saw this clip was immediately excited. This was going to clear our pathway to breaking this band big. After almost a year into the project, we had finally found the key that unlocks the magic kingdom.

Glen Graham: We were really leery of the whole 'bee girl idea.' But when we saw it...I mean, I remember having a copy of it at my parents' house on break, and showing it to them. It was like, "Wow, this is very appealing." Of course, MTV put it in brainwash rotation...for which we are eternally grateful.

Success of "No Rain"

By late summer of 1993, "No Rain" is an official smash hit—played heavily by both MTV and radio (peaking at #20 on the Billboard Hot 100), which sends 'Blind Melon' up towards the top of the charts, as well (by September, it is certified platinum, and peaks at #3 on the Billboard 200). But just as they break through, Capitol Records experiences a significant change in their ranks.

Brad Smith: MTV started playing the shit out of it. They played the video to hell and high water. The formula at that time was to get MTV to play the shit out of your song, and you're going to sell millions of records. That's exactly what happened. We were getting great tours, as well. When you connect to the audience, and they're singing the songs back to you and you're *the opening act*, you're like, "O.K.—we're making a bigger mark here."

Glen Graham: Song on MTV equals people show up. And for the rest of the first go around—before the 'Soup' record—it was 'the "No Rain" show.' They want to hear you play the song, and that's when they perk up. When I got the demo in North Carolina, the one that was supposed to entice me to relocate, "No Rain" wasn't on it. I first heard the song after I had been in L.A. a couple of weeks. I didn't know it would be a hit, but it was certainly my favorite song. I thought, "That's the one—my mom would like that song. That's probably the only place where your taste and my parents' taste cross over." People started showing up, paying attention, and singing the words. Wanting to get backstage, hanging around, and wanting things from you. I remember a lot of 'gifts' shall we say—lots of throwing of little marijuana presents at the time. A lot more press. You go from trying to figure out what we're doing wrong, why is this not working, why are we driving around in a van forever, to going, "I wish this would slow down a little. Is it really this important to go this fast?" And the answer is yes. It got really hectic, but it was really exciting.

Rogers Stevens: I remember very specifically where I realized it—playing this club, Mississippi Nights, in St. Louis. We were staying in a hotel right near the club, and we were looking out the window, seeing a line of people around the block, and thinking, "I wonder what those guys are doing?" *They were coming to our show.*

Charles Raggio: By the end of the short run of dates that we did with them, every single club was sold out with a line around the corner. I remember Indianapolis was absolutely jam-packed. It felt like within ten dates of the beginning of the tour. It didn't feel like you were going through markets that had better promotion or better radio support or anything else. Those were the conversations each day—how much things were actually evolving on a daily basis, as the single blew up.

Shannon Hoon: This record's been out a year, and people are coming up and going, "Oh, the new album's great." And we're like, "If you only knew." You have to go back to the starting point with a lot of people. But I guess it just keeps your feet on the ground.

Jon Plum: I never saw the potential hits with them. All the songs I thought would be big, weren't big. I had no idea. When you're working on records like this, trying to perceive which songs are going to be big—it's nearly impossible. Maybe it gives some attributes to A&R guys, that are able to hear these singles.

Shelley Shaw: They had a hit with 'the bee girl song,' and I remember they didn't feel that was representative of them. As I recall, that was a 'Brad song'— he wrote the music and words. They were like, "That's really not us," and were annoyed because it was associated with this 'cartoon.' Again, the band had this thing that they had shame around—that they had to try and get away from. There was a lot of that with them. First the G n' R thing, and then the bee girl thing. They were always trying to get away from something that had worked in their favor on one level.

Nel Hoon: [Shannon] was surprised, because it was his least favorite song. He said he had sung that song so much that he hated it. I think that that's why they did so many different versions of it. It had been played so much on MTV and it was like the world's favorite song. I'm sure that's why people went out and bought the album—when in fact; there are so many beautiful songs on the album. I think they probably all learned to hate "No Rain."

Shannon Hoon: I don't like the fact that some people like "No Rain" only because of the video. It needs to be the other way around. If it's not, then don't buy our record.

Shelley Shaw: The bee girl got an agent and got on Leno—so it kept getting worse [laughs].

Domenique Johansson: People started to focus on the bee girl herself. She had her own publicity person and they were smart and savvy enough to take advantage of this for her, too. I can't blame them. But when [Rolling Stone] came to me and wanted to do a 'Random Note' on the bee girl, I thought the band was going to flip a wig [laughs]. They had this thing for the bee girl—that this was the marketing image of Blind Melon. It's exactly what Blind Melon didn't want, and Rolling Stone was really the only major outlet that was very persistent on that. And we ended up giving them access to the bee girl, because we wanted to make it known that anything you do on Blind Melon has to come through us. You can't go out and do interviews with the band—it has to be coordinated or done through us when it goes into the music press.

Hale Milgrim: This is going to sound really strange—it's almost like the kiss of death when you have that type of success on your first record. In fact, I'm sure if I sat down with the group and/or management at any early time, I never would have said, "Well, I hope we sell two, three, or four million."

That's just not my style—it's not the attitude that I take. I believe you have to build a real, true base. If you build a real, true base, then you don't have to be concerned about whether you have the radio hit or not. That's probably one of the problems that transpired. I'm just speaking of purely from a natural way to build an artist, is by letting them go out there, and if they're really as good as they pretend to be, then they will build their own fanbase. And if they build their own fanbase, it doesn't matter whether the press people are excited about it or not. You may not be able to sell a lot of albums, but at least you can go out and tour.

Bill Armstrong: The guys in general in the band were really humble about their success. They had a lot of opportunities to turn into jerks because it happened fairly quickly for them, and they were really cool. I always felt like they wanted to reach out and share their success with their friends.

Nel Hoon: Shannon never felt like he was a rock star, but everybody else looked at him in that way—especially here in Lafayette. I remember he and I would go to the grocery store together and the grocer clerk would ask for his autograph. Shannon thought that was so funny—he said, "I'll give you mine if you give me yours." His little nephew came home—I think he was maybe in the second or third grade—and he said, "Everybody in my class wants your autograph, Shannon." Shannon wrote his name 23 times on this notebook page for my grandson to take back to school with him the next day. He was very caring and giving.

Denise Skinner: I remember Shannon going, "This is just too weird. Where I come from, people didn't like me—people thought I was weird and an outcast. Now that we have a hit record, everybody wants to know me, everybody thinks I'm cool." He had a hard time with that. That put him in an emotional quandary about himself, that I think had a lot to do with his insecurities and what led him on that 'destructive path.'

Eva Pfaff: In the course of what was probably less than two years—when the band got super huge—I remember him in not so many words saying he really wished that he could walk down the street like a normal person. He definitely had that 180 degree realization that as great as it was, there was something to be said about having your privacy and your space. It made him really treasure the ordinary life. It was like, "This is great, but boy, do I miss every once in a while having an ordinary day."

Shannon Hoon: People chip away at all of the sacred things I believe in. All these meet n' greets. Ugh. I have to hold my vomit back. As soon as I get off stage, there's a record company guy dragging me off to meet some local D.J. I don't need that to get by. I wake up in a different pair of shoes everyday. I look in the mirror and think, "Yeah, I'll be that guy today."

Hale Milgrim: There was a change in the management structure. Joe Smith, at the end of '92, left Capitol Records and Charlie Koppelman came in as the new chairman. There was a difference of opinion in the direction of the company, the artists on the label, and the number of employees that were working for me—and what I believed should be there. Just a difference in leadership. He was my boss, and it's probably smart not to have a difference in leadership with your boss. And we had just come out of—in '92—the best year Capitol Records had ever had.

I left the company not under my own will. I have probably blocked out so many things—because it was sad to me. I felt that Blind Melon and Radio-head—there were a number of artists that I was fortunate enough to sign, or give the approval to sign, that I never got to really follow it through. When I was at Capitol Records for Blind Melon, we never had the great success. I'd seen the video for "No Rain," I knew we had a great video that had fabulous potential, but I was then out of the company. Usually, what happens with [record] companies that change management often is the existing artists that are on a label, the new management team comes in and decides if they feel if there's any potential in it. And then over the course of two/three years, they start signing their own new acts. Generally speaking, the first 18 to 24 months is the previous management's signings and vision, and then your vision and signings take place.

Denise Skinner: To be quite honest, I didn't see Gary [Gersh, Hale Milgrim's replacement] supporting any of the earlier artists—even the established ones like Bob Seger or Bonnie Raitt. When it came to do things creatively with the catalog, Bruce Kirkland, who was his head of marketing, was the guy that came up with all these ideas, and the staff implemented them. I wouldn't regard Gary as any sort of 'idea guy.' He pretty much struck me as a schmoozer. He will take credit for a lot of stuff he's never participated in.

George Nunes: I don't know that it really changed a lot. Gary had a completely different sensibility than Hale did. Hale was very much 'artist friendly'—he would hang with these guys and it was how he was. I think Gary coming into the position...it wasn't 'his band.' No matter who comes in, you always have that, "This isn't my band." But Gary's a smart guy and he got the idea that this is an important act at Capitol. The commitment that I saw stayed the same—it was a different time, he's a different guy, and like I said, it wasn't his band. But as far as the resources and the push, I didn't see any change.

Denise Skinner: It's night and day. Hale Milgrim is an 'artist person.' In the sense that he sees the good in any artist. He doesn't treat them like a commodity. And he also doesn't take credit for things that he didn't participate in. Hale was awesome, because if I found myself hitting walls at sales or promotion, Hale was accessible. I could grab Tim Devine or Simon and say, "We've got to go talk to Hale and get blah blah blah to pay attention." To be quite honest, I'm not a fan of Gary Gersh's. I didn't like working for him. He's not an honest person, and to be quite honest with you, he's an out-and-out liar. When we were having problems with Shannon with regards to the drug thing, Gersh claims that he reached out to him, but he never really did. Had Hale been there, I think things would have been a little different.

Domenique Johansson: The 'Hale Milgrim regime'—when he ran Capitol—it was such an incredibly artistically welcomed place. Most artists that I know loved it, they loved Hale. He was about the music, he was a cool guy, he gave people what they needed to work records, he had time for you. They had a great rapport with him—Hale was very special to them. He got fired—it was after a six-month freefall. It created a lot of tension in the label—every band feels that when that stuff goes down. We had Radiohead, we had all this great stuff going—but a lot of it wasn't big, mega commercial sellers. I think that was one of the reasons why they had their issues with Hale. But the band, they felt it as severely as any of us that worked at that label that were 'Hale people.' And in comes this other regime, and it's supposed to be God's answer to all the problems in the music industry—Gary Gersh signed Nirvana and this and that—and it's going to be great. All of a sudden, some key people brought in a really nasty vibe.

Shannon Hoon: Sure there's a lot going on right now. But as quickly as it is to come by, it can be gone that quickly, too. A lot of this is just a little too god-damn serious. It's something that you have to keep at arm's length. You can't let it affect you, because it's just a time frame.

Neil Young and Lenny Kravitz Tours/Rolling Stone Cover

As one of the top breakthrough artists of 1993, Blind Melon land two prime tour opening spots—Neil Young and Lenny Kravitz. Additionally, the group grace the cover of Rolling Stone Magazine...naked.

Paul Cummings: The Neil Young tour was one of those dream tours they wanted—they obviously had a lot of respect for Neil Young. They were the opening act, there was a middle act—it was either Soundgarden, Stone Temple Pilots, Social Distortion. [And] Pearl Jam did three shows. That was great for them to be on that. The first time they were called to meet Neil Young, they were all standing there like they were at the principal's office—"Yes sir, no sir, very happy to be here." That was a big deal for them. Neil Young likes an hour between when he goes on and the act before him, so a lot of the time, they were going on about the posted door time.

Lyle Eaves: That was a weird transition—you could watch it happen day-to-day when that video took off. Neil Young's crowd, you could imagine, could care less who Blind Melon was. Plus, being the first band on a three-band bill, they were going on [when] it was daylight. I mean, there was *no one* there. Half the time they played, there would be 125 people in a 33,000 seat outdoor shed. The crowd didn't care. And then all of a sudden, the video starts taking off, and there would be like seven teenage girls standing by the stage screaming. It was the first thing that hit me—"What the hell is going on here?" And then the next night, there's 200 of them. Within a week, there was actually a crowd showing up to see them. You could literally watch it happen.

Glen Graham: I've been a Neil Young fan since I was very young. Just getting to see six weeks worth of shows was amazing. He had the oddest choice of a backing band possibly ever for Neil Young—Booker T & the MG's. Booker T & the MG's are fantastic...but as Neil Young's backing band? And they had Jim Keltner as the drummer—it was a thrill to meet him. My memories of that tour, like most tours, have nothing to do with playing. Neil was touring with his kids, one of whom had severe Cerebral Palsy. He was in a wheel chair—Ben, the model train guy. He was on the side of stage the whole time watching and loving it. And his other son, Zeke, who was about 18 or at the time, I think he had Cerebral Palsy—but extremely mild. I remember at Bill Graham Amphitheater, Neil giving him a Bronco or something for a birthday present. It was casual. It was like, these are adults—people who have done this 50 times. It was just nice to see what you could grow into eventually. Also, David Briggs was on that tour. David had a monitor on the side of the stage—I think he was next to Ben—and he would stand there and do the same thing that he did in the room when we were recording 'Sippin' Time.' He would dance and conduct—it was incredible. They might as well have put lights on him.

I remember [Neil] knocking on the dressing room door one time, looking in, and going, "Hey guys, do you mind if I borrow a guitar?" We're like, "Uh...*sure!*" He looked at us with this little impish grin, like, "O.K., these guys are scared to death," and ducked out, real quick. That was really it. I remember Lyle, who was a motorcycle guy, was really impressed because Neil carries his motorcycles with him. And he, his guitar tech, and possibly his soundman, structure the tour so they end up away from San Francisco as far away as possible, and then they ride home. That's so cool—you're finished with the tour, it's not, "Fly home, you're in your house, and you can't sleep." These guys have a decompression time. I also remember Neil Young's bus—which burned. This old Buffalo Springfield bus, that he had decked out—it looked like a hippie boat inside. The coolest stained glass windows, and he had the tops of two Hudsons welded over the holes in the roof so you could sit up there like you were driving one of those Hudsons down the freeway, twelve feet off the ground.

Rogers Stevens: The audience was somewhat older than what we were used to playing for. And he was a really kind man. I mean, I've heard things about him, that he can be cantankerous. But he's a great songwriter and he has to deal with a lot in his life, I'm sure. The first night we were there, he invited us to his dressing room for a party for his son. That was really nice.

Shannon Hoon: Sometimes I think of being on the same stage as Neil Young, and it makes my knees buckle.

Nel Hoon: I think what he loved the most about that was getting to meet people like Neil Young. I went to either Cleveland or Cincinnati. My son, Tim, and I drove there because Tim was a huge Neil Young fan. He had been since he was a little kid. It was just unreal. I think [Shannon] enjoyed the bands he opened for so much more than he enjoyed playing to the big crowds. It was just so great to meet those people that he had listened to all of his life.

Susan Silver: They called it a, not a hurricane, but a gale-force storm, or some crazy thing [when Blind Melon/Soundgarden/Neil Young played the outdoor Jones Beach Theater in New York]. Blind Melon played and it was raining *incredibly hard.* By the time Soundgarden got on the stage, there was an inch of water—the wind was blowing the rain horizontal and stuff was starting to rip off the facades of the stage. I just remember after that, the huddle in the Jones Beach dressing room—both bands had just been through something that was otherworldly. It was really fun to experience that with them.

Kim Thayil: I remember Chris [Cornell] saying, "We'd like to thank God for the light show."

Danny Clinch: When they did the Neil Young/Soundgarden tour, I was hanging out and photographing them. That was the first time that Shannon asked me to play harmonica with them, which I did. It was in New Jersey, at the P.N.C. Arts Center. I told Shannon I played harmonica, and he said, "Oh, well then you'll come out and play harmonica with us." I was like, "No, no, no—my mom saw me play and I played once at a barbeque." He was like, "Come on Danny, *it's all a big barbeque.* Come out and play." I figured by the time the show starts, he's going to forget and they're going to go on. Sure enough, he's like, "Come on Danny, you've got your harmonica? This is what we're going to do—we're going to play 'Change,' you're going to come in, we're going to bust into 'Dear Mr. Fantasy,' and you're going to play with us." And you know what? If he never said that to me...I play harmonica all the time now—I've played with the Foo Fighters, Cracker, and I play in a blues band. I play all the time out and about. If it wasn't for him egging me on, I definitely wouldn't be enjoying that part of my life right now that I really enjoy.

Hale Milgrim: One show in particular will always stand out—Costa Mesa at the Pacific Amphitheater. Because there was terrible traffic, I was late. They were in the middle of their first song. I'm walking down the aisle towards my seat and I'm just beaming, because here's my band playing in front of Neil Young and Soundgarden. All of a sudden, I realize out of the P.A. in the middle of the song, Shannon is singing my name as I'm walking to my seat! He noticed me walking down and starts singing to me and looking at me as I'm walking. It was exactly what that band was about—this improvisational moment. My wife and I sat down, and I remember beaming throughout their entire set—feeling so great that I had been fortunate enough to be there at the right place at the right time to sign them. I felt that they had taken a giant leap both in their performance, stage presence, and working together as a group. I felt that *anything* could happen for them. I saw them after the set, and I remember wanting to hug them so much—I was so proud of what they had been achieving at that stage of the game.

Shannon Hoon: It was worth it to see Neil play every night.

Danny Clinch: I think Neil Young was really fond of Shannon, and knew he had what was 'special.' I think Neil gave him a harmonica once—because Shannon was sitting by the edge of the stage.

Nel Hoon: One of the shows—it may have been a Neil Young show—[Shannon] had just had a birthday and I hadn't given him his birthday present. So I had bought an antique jukebox, and researched and found everything that was a hit in 1967 when Shannon was born. I had all of those hits put on this old jukebox. And that's what I gave Shannon for his 24th birthday or something like that. The band even thought that was the coolest thing they'd ever seen.

Brooks Byrd Graham: We drove that tour, and so did Christopher and Heather—we didn't ride on the bus. We were free from the restraints of where the bus was going. They played well, I think they were happy doing it; it was a pretty 'no frills' tour. When they toured with Lenny Kravitz, he had *excellent* catering [laughs]. And Neil Young's like throwing out some spaghetti. They just got better playing.

Mike Osterfeld: We'd been out with Neil Young all year it feels like. We're playing the L.A. Sports Arena, and you've got everybody coming in the back door. Gene Simmons is not being allowed in, and I'm walking in from the bus going, "You know who that is, right?" And they're like, "Yeah, he's not on the list." "Well, he's my guest"—and I walked Gene Simmons in. I always had a problem with shmoozers sitting on our road boxes—putting drinks on our road boxes. I'd get alcohol dumped all over the boxes, and I'd have sticky shit the next day. So we come off stage, I take the gear, pack it up, and moved it halfway down the hallway. Glen wanted to get into his box because he wanted something. So we're walking around the corner, there's my road boxes, and there's two guys sitting on them. *And it just pisses me off.* I walk over, come up from behind them, tap them on the shoulder. I'm like, "Excuse me." All of a sudden, *Jack Nicholson* jumps up and goes, "Oh, I'm sorry!" and runs away! Runs away in a white three-piece suit, with blue suede shoes on. The manager for Neil Young—who was there with him—says, "You see that guy right there? *He's got the best weed in this town.*"

Paul Cummings: On the Neil Young tour, we had the Rolling Stone cover shoot. They found out that there was a possibility that they were going to get on the cover of Rolling Stone, so they sent a photographer, Mark Seliger. We had a day off in Austin, so they did the shoot in Austin. They did what ended up on the cover—them naked. But before that, the band said, "Let's dress up for it." So we went to this costume shop—I remember it was called 'Lucy in Disguise with Diamonds.' We got a bunch of white tuxedos and top hats, and they all dressed up. I remember they took a bunch of pictures, but I don't know what happened to that—I've never seen them anywhere.

Brad Smith: We almost got thrown off the Neil Young tour—there was a big fight backstage, and it was about the cover of Rolling Stone. For some reason—and I don't even know if any of this is true, to tell you the truth, we were all out of our minds back then—someone said something about, "It's just going to be Shannon on the cover." And then the whole band was in a fight about it—whether it should just be Shannon or the band. At that point, I just had it. I wrote "No Rain," that became a hit and put us on the map. That song came from someone else in the band other than Shannon. It was such a unified effort to make that song a hit—Shannon made it a hit, Blind Melon made it a hit—but *I* wrote it. That was my angle of argument—whether Shannon should be on the cover himself or we should be as a band. I don't even know why it came to that, but I was so fucking pissed off at this stupid conversation we were having—it was so black and white to me—that at soundcheck, I snapped and smashed my bass into my Ampeg head. Shannon said later that I threw the bass at him, and I didn't—I think a piece of the bass went over by him just by accident. Shannon thought it was hilarious—the next day, it was all good. Shannon had so much fun telling everybody that I smashed the bass and threw it at him. He thrived on that kind of stuff.

Domenique Johansson: Shannon, just to show how behind he was it being a band, said, "We're just not going to be separated. He's not going to be able to do separate shots of each of us—we're not going to go for it." We did a number of different things—the things in the water, in this creek outside of Austin. It was an all-day thing. They got Shannon up front, but not quite separated. He was getting frustrated. At one point, he wanted to talk to me, and Shannon turned around, he goes, "Let me talk to them." And I said, "No—you can't be the bad guy. I'll talk to him." I go out to talk to him, and he comes bouncing out of the bus—he takes the photographer by the arm, and he's like, "I know Domenique wants to tell you this but I really want to." The photographer got mad, but Shannon charmed him. "That's my assignment, I have to do it." "No you can't, because then they'll use it—it's not us. We're a band and that's what this is on." It was very courageous. He was a really good person—I think the photographer related to that. We ended up at this inside studio, and [the photographer] was like, "O.K., well then you have to work with me on giving me some awesome shots." So that's how the naked shots came up [laughs].

Rogers Stevens: The cover date of the issue we found out was going to be Halloween, so we thought it would be a good idea to do…there's an old Beatles record cover ['Yesterday and Today'], where they take these baby dolls and dismembered them. It's really strange. It was pulled from the shelves and what they did was they pasted over the cover with a more benign cover. People can still find those—where you can pull off the old cover and reveal the old scary cover. So we thought that would be great—to do a knock-off on that. And we could do a little bee girl thing—we could just chop up the bee girl and ha ha, it's a joke. But that was not gotten by people. We tried the picture, but they did this weird thing where they painted us different primary colors, and it looked terrible. It ended up just going horribly wrong. So now there's these ridiculous pictures of us floating around, looking like the Blue Man Group.

The naked picture was kind of an off-the-cuff thing. Mark Seliger was like, "Let's try this." So we did—we all had to get stripped down in this studio, full of attractive production assistants. So we're walking around with our fucking gear tackle out, and ended up being like that for a couple of hours! We had to do the shot a bunch of times, because somebody's dangling bits were hanging out. It was tough to get it right. I remember when the magazine came out, we were in New Orleans on tour. I got the magazine, and I just couldn't believe it. I was so embarrassed. I thought we were going to be something totally different, and then that picture was there—I really hated it. But now it doesn't bother me. Another thing is we went out to this weird artist colony in Austin—the pictures that are shot in the water that on the inside [of the article]. That's all done out there—it's a really beautiful country out there. We got into this natural spring water thing—it was *fucking freezing*. We were out there for a long time and were really starting to get ornery.

Mike Osterfeld: It was such a big deal to do this gold record party. The management and the lawyers wanted to have the party at Joss, because it was such a hot place at the time. Everyone's been working their ass off to get to this gold record level, and to be able to have this gold record party. And it was such a letdown—they went from gold to platinum *in a week*.

Brad Smith: When we got the gold record, we weren't making any money—that just means we recouped. We *might* make some money—that's all that meant. We were still making $500 a month—we were in poverty, really. Had gold records on the wall and no real money.

Rogers Stevens: That was a crazy party. That was one of those nights that a lot of good things happened, and some things that ultimately turned out to be bad. We all got hammered. Shannon got up and said some things—that were probably best left unsaid—to some of the label people. Shannon thanked Hale—who wasn't there—and didn't thank the new guy [Gary Gersh], who was there. They had a contentious relationship. So it was a bit of a slap. You just don't know—you're 23/24, trying to navigate this treacherous business. When people are 'yesing' you all the time, you start to think that that's just the way it is. But it's only later that you realize that there's much greater forces at work—as far as the finances and all that stuff. You just don't get that at that age. We were completely green, naïve, and dumb to the whole game, really.

Denise Skinner: There used to be a term when you got lied to by Gary, it was called 'being Gershed.' I think when Shannon did what he did at the party, he 'Gershed Gersh.'

Domenique Johansson: That's a typical 'you never know what Shannon's going to do' kind of thing. That night, he was on this roll. He would come up to you with this big smile on his face—like he was your little brother. He went into the bathroom, and in this place, right across from the toilet is this Henry Miller sketch. It was a bunch of sketches that were signed—it was an original. And he was upset that they would put a Henry Miller sketch in the bathroom—that you couldn't even look at it unless you were taking a dump! He was on this roll, that the picture shouldn't be there. They were all presented with platinum records, and we were all there for a long time. The tour bus was outside, a lot of us were going off to the hotel. We all go out to the bus, and as we're leaving, Shannon has this funny look on his face. They're all carrying out their records—except Shannon—who was carrying out that Henry Miller picture!

Rogers Stevens: So we go back to the hotel and continue on with that night, which got even crazier. That night there was a journalist from Rolling Stone there, that was doing our cover story, and she wrote about me smashing a bunch of tables—which was really embarrassing. The restaurant figured it out [who stole the drawing] and called the cops. They showed up at our hotel in the morning. Luckily, Chris Jones took it to a Kinko's and made a laser copy of it—we all have a lovely, framed Henry Miller drawing, with a picture of the band. It was no big deal—they just came and took it, and said, "You guys were drunk, you're idiots. Give it to us."

Shelley Shaw: Lenny Kravitz had a real old school agent, who was stringing us along. We were so excited, and then we were like, "Oh my God, he didn't make the offer—he's talking about somebody else." Then he made the offer, and everybody was just flipping out.

Mike Osterfeld: The Lenny tour was 'it' for Blind Melon. When we showed up for the Lenny tour, we had already opened up for everybody. We went from an 'opening act/support band' to being 'the headliner.' People actually came to Lenny Kravitz to see Blind Melon. Watching Shannon and Lenny interact was amazing—they loved each other.

Owen Orzack: [Shannon] would tape himself naked all the time [on his video camera]—he didn't have a problem getting naked. I remember we had gotten a new bus in Pittsburgh—that was the big deal. It was like, "Holy cow, we made it—we've got a new bus!" It had a little emergency hatch that you could open up to let air in the roof, and you could open it up all the way and go up on the roof. I remember at the show in Pittsburgh, he took off all his clothes, jumped on the roof, and there was this huge crowd outside the bus. He was running around filming them. He threw the camera down to me, I threw it to Paul, and Paul ran out and took pictures. There was a lot of that. I remember we stayed at a hotel in Seattle called the Edgewater Inn, which is a famous 'rock hotel.' It hangs out over the Sound. You could literally fish out you window. The windows were all open—Lyle and I were in my room, and for some reason, Shannon was there. This ferry was coming into the slip next to the hotel—it was pulling in, and Shannon ran to the window and mooned everybody on the ferry!

Shannon Hoon: You're brought into the world naked; there shouldn't be anything wrong with it.

Lyle Eaves: Shannon rode on the tour bus with Lenny—not every day—but I know he spent more than one night, when they'd go show-to-show with Lenny, hanging out with him. Shannon got on the stage one night...he went into Lenny's wardrobe and got a pair of Lenny's big high-heel boots, platform boots. Put those on, didn't have another damn stitch on, and put a piece of bread over his dick. A long piece of French bread. Walked out on the stage, got behind Lenny, and was acting like he was humping him with the French bread. The crowd starts reacting to it, and Lenny doesn't even know he's behind him! Lenny finally sees him and plays it off like it's a joke, Shannon turns around, starts walking off stage—he broke the French bread in half and threw it in the audience. Which Lenny was all pissed about, because it took attention away from him. He's a spoiled brat—big time. He was kind of hard to deal with—as being an opening act, sometimes he didn't let us soundcheck. But I think that was a good experience for them, because they got a different crowd to see them.

Craig Ross: They were really laid back and cool people. Especially Shannon. He was a really great guy. We hung out a little bit—mostly it was after shows. Of all the people in the band, it was Rogers and Shannon who I became mostly close with. There was a lot of after-show hanging out and drinking.

Glen Graham: I thought [Lenny] was great, because it was *a show*. He was doing shtick, and doing it really well. That tour, to me, was like, we've got members of Led Zeppelin and members of Parliament-Funkadelic, with a hybrid of let's say, Paul Stanley meets Sly Stone, as the frontman. He rehearsed those guys every fucking day. I'd walk in, in the afternoon, hoping to get a soundcheck, and he'd be up there drilling these people. And these people were all kick ass, fantastic, super players. Several of them were jazz players—Cindy

Blackman is an amazing jazz drummer. And he's up there trying to get it just perfect. He's doing the 'James Brown thing.' It took me a long to realize that it wasn't that they were fucking up, it was that he wanted it to be completely in his control. I always thought it would have been better if he'd let them go loose a little bit, because they were all motherfuckers. But it was his show.

Lisa Sinha: On Halloween [in Vancouver] when he got in all the trouble, I know [Shannon] had my underwear on [laughs]. I specifically remember that. I remember Christopher had one of my dresses on that night. It was Rogers' birthday.

Paul Cummings: It was the trifecta of it being the last show on the tour, it was Halloween, and it was Rogers' birthday. I think everyone in the band was drunk when they went on stage. Shannon had on one of those hotel robes, he was painted silver and wearing girl's panties when he came on stage. I was in the offices backstage, getting paid I think by the promoters, and somebody came and said, "He's up there on stage, *naked.*" Didn't think much of it. And then he said, "He's pissing off the P.A. stack! They're going to arrest him!"

Brooks Byrd Graham: I remember we were staying at the edge of the stage, watching. We knew he was going to do *something*. So we called Lenny and his band over to watch whatever was going to happen. It was like, "Oh, well… maybe this isn't such a great idea!" All Lenny could do was just shake his head.

Craig Ross: The night that sticks out is Vancouver, when [Shannon] went nuts. At the end of the tour, you do a prank on the other band. I remember us convincing our guitar tech to dress like a bee, and go out dancing during their last song. It took a lot of coaxing to get him in the bee costume. By the time we pushed our 'bee' out on stage, Shannon was already—I think—naked. And I don't know what was all over the stage, beer or what, it was quite slippery. Our 'bee' slipped, and I remember Shannon jumping on top of him naked.

Glen Graham: Rogers was annihilated, Shannon was beyond the beyond, and Christopher and Brad were a little drunk. I don't remember at what point in the set this happened, but it seemed to happen really quickly. It went from a dress, to an Iggy Pop underwear deal, to berating the crowd, standing on the speakers on stage left, to pissing on the crowd. You can't exaggerate this—*an arch 20 feet.* You saw people get up…I mean, chairs, just scramble back. They're looking at like, "Wow, he's got his dick out, that's interesting. Wow, he's taking a piss, it's coming…whoa!" You've got the Canadian police that are around, and you know this is going to be bad. I think it might have even been the last show of that leg of the tour. We had this bus driver, Ron Mooney, which everyone used to call 'round man.' This poor guy had a gun pulled on him—he was used to traveling with gospel acts. But yeah, Shannon hosed the crowd, and it was not cool at all. I think the show was shortened somewhat. I remember when we were going back, passing [Lenny and his band], they were like, "There's no way to top that!"

Paul Cummings: Upon completion of the performance [police arrived]— they weren't going to chase him around the stage. So we're starting to think, "O.K., maybe this *is* getting serious." I go out there, they're finishing the last few songs of the set, and we come up with this plan. The plan was the Lenny Kravitz crew were going to try and get him dressed, get him off the stage, and get him to the bus. And from about a hundred yards away, I looked enough like him—I had about the same length hair at the time. When he came off stage, I put the robe on that he went stage with, and went running off in the other direction towards the dressing room. I get to the dressing room, and a few of the cops have run after me and chased me. I get to the dressing room, and I think, "Alright, we pulled this off." Eventually the cops figure out I'm not him and they're a little pissed at me.

Shannon actually made it to the bus. That probably would have been O.K. at that point, but then he wound up somehow on the roof of the bus— naked. So he's arrested at that point. So me and a record company guy—it was a Friday night, I think—are driving down to the police station. He's trying to get the lawyer on the phone, and they say, "Well, it's a Friday night, she's not going to get in probably until Monday." So I go down to the police station to get him, and strangely enough, all I had to do was sign for him, and they released him to me. But they said, "If he goes back to the Coliseum, he'll be arrested." Since this was the last show on the tour and they were going to fly out of Seattle to fly home anyway, we just arranged to meet the bus at a certain spot, put him on the bus, and we're out of town. Obviously, he had to appear at a later date as a result of his activities. I think the newspaper up there called it the '21 beer salute.' And it did make the front page of the paper up there—the record was really selling up there at that point. It gave him a little notoriety—not the good kind.

Shannon Hoon: Customs is very hard for me. They're always like, "Oh, you're that 'pissing guy'." They always have something funny to say about my underwear.

Owen Orzack: We did a bunch of North American dates, and then we flew straight to Europe. Doing big gigs in Europe, because Lenny was really big in Europe. We did Wembley and all the big European venues—and a couple small ones.

Craig Ross: I remember having a good night with Shannon in London—but that was basically at the gig. That kind of feeling that you think that you're doing something really good, people are going for it. And I remember the Lenny thing was going really good in England at the time, and being back-stage with Shannon, and sharing that vibe of when things are going good. It was at Wembley.

Glen Graham: I remember [Lenny] freaking out a couple of times. A Gibson rep came one time with a Flying V, showed it to him, and he was pissed off that day. I think we were in London. David Bowie was supposed to come to the show, and they were supposed to do "Fame." He'd been rehearsing "Fame" with the band for days. The story was from our monitor guy, "David does not want to do 'Fame,' David wants to do something from his new material." And Lenny basically told him, "This is my show, and we're going to do 'Fame'." And David said, "Well, I guess I won't be playing." He was furious about that, and probably other things too. I think maybe they were filming the show—that may have been why Bowie was coming—and the whole arena was lit red. Lenny left the stage mid-set in a sort of mock pout thing, implying, "If you people aren't going to give me anything back, I'm outta here!" They booed and it was terrible. This little road manager guy is back there, pushing him up the ramp, going, "Come on, you cannot fucking do this!" He walked past that Gibson rep, picked up that Flying V, went out, and smashed it to bits. Looked at her and shot her a big "Fuck You" smile. I thought it was pretty entertaining. I mean, only people in the entertainment industry can get away with acting like it's always 1973.

Paul Cummings: The last show of the tour I think was Birmingham—Shannon wanted to do another one of his 'naked bits.' He was told in no uncertain terms that in England, you *do* get arrested for this. It's not maybe, it's *definitely*. He actually listened that time. And instead of being completely naked, he had a baguette gaffer taped around him strategically. Lenny liked them and the crew liked them. I remember the Lenny Kravitz crew—the band didn't show up, but all our band was there—they went go-kart racing. Shannon won— even though he was slightly inebriated. After the Lenny Kravitz European tour, we did a run through Canada—a headline tour—because the record was really selling up there. Because of the 'naked incident' in Vancouver, there was at least one show where we had a couple of undercover cops up in the balcony, keeping an eye on things. There was never any problem on that tour.

Brooks Byrd Graham: [Lenny Kravitz] came over to our house after the tour. It was where we were living in New Orleans—Rogers was there—and Lenny came, the tour manager, and the guitar player was with them. They had these big motorcycles—they roared uptown to our house. [Lenny] was in 'full outfit'—leather vest, leather pants that laced up the side…with kind of gap between them.

Saturday Night Live/Japan Tour/"Change"/ American Music Awards/Headlining Tour/ Kurt Cobain's Death

Already burnt out from nearly two years of touring, in early 1994, Blind Melon experience the good (an appearance on 'Saturday Night Live,' their first Japanese tour, Grammy nominations for 'Best Rock Performance' and 'Best New Artist,' a headlining U.S. trek) and the bad (the surefire hit "Change" not breaking through, a violent altercation at the American Music Awards, Shannon becoming unglued due to drugs, Kurt Cobain's suicide).

Shelley Shaw: They did 'Saturday Night Live,' which was fun and really huge for them. I did come east for the 'Saturday Night Live' thing. I remember Shannon said that he really connected with Chris Farley. I think that he said that he found some sort of kinship there and he loved him so much. I don't know if they kept up or hung out or anything after that, but I remember them 'clicking.'

Rogers Stevens: [Chris Farley] was a great guy. My impression of him was that he was just like his T.V. personality—really funny. We had no idea he was going to do that bee girl costume thing—totally surprised us.

Shelley Shaw: Shannon's family was there—his mom and dad. Before they went on air, Shannon was talking to the audience. He was like, "This is a monumental day people, because I actually have my mother and father in the same room, sitting next to each other for the first time in years!"

Rogers Stevens: I remember that was one of the shows that I got really nervous for. Because it is live. T.V. is weird—you spend all day waiting around for this moment. There's a lot of anxiety about what it's going to be like. You only have three or four minutes to nail it, and then you're off. You don't get another song to redeem yourself. A lot of attention is put on this one little moment. So I spent the whole day drinking. By the time the show came around, I was definitely a bit more 'relaxed.' But I thought Shannon was great. It's not too bad, I thought the performance was O.K. He sang pretty well. I remember the show was totally unfunny. They had a lot of good cast members on the show at that point—they have a cast party after the show. We went to that and hung out with all those guys. Jason Patric [was the host], who's a really good actor—you should see 'Geronimo'...I don't know if he's very funny.

Paul Cummings: They did the Zeppelin cover, "Out on the Tiles" [for the Zep tribute album, 'Encomium'], right after 'Saturday Night Live.' We drove up to Woodstock—they enjoyed that. [Producer] Eddie Kramer played them some Hendrix outtakes he had. It was someone they respected. I remember Glen was really happy with the drum sound—he's usually not. They ran through the song a few times. The arrangement they ended up putting on the record changed the song a little bit. A couple of the verses and stuff. They were pretty fresh because they'd been off the road a little bit. The worst thing for me was that we drove up there in a van. It was a diesel van and I didn't notice when I filled it up with [regular] gas—that cost me some money.

Brad Smith: We got asked to do that thing—we were totally honored. We all knew the song [hums the song's riff]. We were touring with Lenny Kravitz at the time. Jack [Daley, bassist] from Lenny Kravitz's band, I was playing it backstage one time, and he was like, "You know what's weird? I was in a Led Zeppelin cover band for five years." He showed me a couple of things that the line did that I didn't pick off the tape. He was really helpful. We would rehearse it backstage, because we knew that we had this recording coming up. We got in there with Eddie Kramer—Eddie is just a sweet old soul. A lot of great stories—just a really great guy.

It was a super half-assed version at the time. I remember thinking, "This doesn't feel right, is this what they want?" So we went back in to listen in the control room, and Eddie says, "You guys have got to listen to the original version." So he put it on in the control room. And that's when all the switches went off. It was more in terms of attitude—it wasn't the notes so much. I remember Eddie making us listen to it in a way that we hadn't listened to it before. It was a good move—he pitted us against the original composers right there in the studio. And it made us raise our game to a great level—that's one of best tracks on 'Encomium.' We smoked it and cooked it, and I attribute that to Eddie playing the right card—pitting us directly against Led Zeppelin in the studio.

Rogers Stevens: We went up to Bearsville [Studios]—I ended up living near there for a while. It's now closed—it was a studio built by Albert Grossman, who was the manager of Bob Dylan and the Band. So a lot of people worked up there. We had always talked about how we were into Led Zeppelin, and then found out that Robert Plant liked the band. He came to a show or two in England. I was kind of disappointed in the way it came out, but it was cool. It was a hard song to do—there's a lot of tough, deceptively difficult rhythmic things in that song. We kind of glossed over them and didn't do them. I think it was a high song [to sing]. I remember [Shannon] having a hard time getting the vocal, and that was before the days of auto-tune—when you could go in, fake it, and then fix it. He actually had to sing it and it was a struggle—but we got it. I remember Eddie Kramer pulling out all these photographs—the guy worked on the Hendrix records, he engineered the original Zeppelin recording of that song. He has loads of photographs—intimate studio pictures of everyone from Zeppelin to Hendrix. Killer stuff that you've never seen before.

Paul Cummings: They did five dates in Japan.

Owen Orzack: We were on our way to do a series of shows in Japan, and at the time, Shannon and Lisa were living in Chicago—I was from the Washington D.C. area at the time. We were all going to meet in L.A., and then the band, the crew, and everybody fly together to Japan. It was actually the day after the Northridge earthquake in L.A. We were worried that the airport was going to be closed, and then Paul called us—"The flights are on, *go!*" My flight was delayed because of ice and Shannon's flight had mechanical trouble—both him and I missed the connection to Japan. Lisa was with him, too. We ended up having to spend the night in L.A.—we were at the Marriot right next to the airport. We were on the top floor of the hotel, and they had a big aftershock, at 5:00 in the morning. It was like somebody was shaking the bed to wake you up. My phone rings, and it's Shannon on the other end. He's like, "*DUDE, DID YOU FEEL THAT?!*"

It was freaky, because we had to take this international flight. I can pretty much safely say that Shannon never crossed a border without 'holding' something. And we were on our way to Japan, I was like, "This is not good." So we connected in Portland—L.A. to Portland, and it was Portland to Osaka. We got to Portland, made our gate change and were just hanging out. We literally walked into the gangway to get on the plane, and there was like six customs guys standing there with dogs. I was like, "Hmmm, O.K., *this is going to be interesting.*" So they went through everybody's stuff. In Lisa's purse—all the way at the bottom of her purse—was this bud. Tiny, dried up—it obviously had fallen out a year ago or something. It was like the nth degree. You would have thought it was the end of the world. She managed to sob her way out of it, I bullshit the hell out of them, like, "Hey, she doesn't normally tour with us. She's got a brand new passport. Take her, not us—*we've got a show!*" Then finally when we got on the plane, it was a little lighthearted. We get to Japan, get off the plane, and we're going through the customs line there, and they pick me out. Shannon was laughing. He's like, "Of all the people they pick, they pick you!" I had to open up everything, stick my tongue up—everything short of them slapping on the rubber gloves. He was laughing his ass off.

Lyle Eaves: The very first show, we were running behind, which Shannon thought was hilarious. I'm like, "Do you remember what happened to Paul McCartney when he came to Japan with pot?" Stuff like that didn't bother him at all—he hollowed out the heel of his shoe and filled it up with hash, and brought it back from the Netherlands. I didn't know about it until we got through security back in the States. He's like, "Can you smell that? I've got a whole block of hash in my shoe!" "Oh man...just shut up. Don't tell me this until we get out of this airport."

Owen Orzack: We got there, and by the time I got out of customs, we drove straight from the airport to the gig, and Shannon was on stage ten minutes later. We were late—they were almost going to cancel the gig. I had to reset all the stuff, because Lyle tried to do it, and it wasn't right. The first show was at the Blue Note, or some weird club. And it was fine—a cool show. I do remember that one because I think Duff and Slash were at that show. We played a bunch of smaller clubs, but in Japan, that's not uncommon for bands to play smaller places. But they were very cool places—good crowds. The weird thing in Japan is that they come to the hotel—all the girls and all the fans—they hang out in the hotel lobby. They'll sit all politely, and then when the band members come out, they'll all ask for autographs and give gifts. We were laughing because Christopher was the most popular band member in Japan. And Shannon loved it—he was taking videos the whole time, and they were all taking videos of him. [Shannon] was usually the center of attention, and he wasn't in Japan, which we were laughing about. We couldn't figure it, we were like, "Well, he's short and he's got dark hair—*maybe that's why the Japanese girls like him.*"

Christopher Thorn: I don't know why—I think maybe because I was their size or something [laughs]! Japan's great man—they treat you so differently. We traveled using the Bullet Train, so you'd go to the train station, and there would be all these fans waiting on you. As you're pulling away, you have that little 'Beatles moment,' where their faces are up against the train as you're leaving. Really different audiences there. I don't remember the shows as much as them giving you gifts. And the only people there that are American are either models or rock stars. So you'd go to like 'the American bar,' and there would be beautiful girls and guys that were in bands that came over to be on tour. They're really different fans, and they have this 'respect thing' for you. When you leave your hotel, they wouldn't bother you, but they would follow you. So wherever you walked around town, they would be ten feet behind you. We traveled a lot with an interpreter who would show us around, and he would bark at them if they got too close. We'd be eating at a restaurant, and they'd be peering in the windows, looking at us—giggling, laughing, and pointing. And the other weird thing from that tour I remember—compared to the States or anywhere else in the world—you play a show, they clap and go crazy, and then get really quiet. And I never saw anybody leave a show in single file [before]—they're very organized. They treat you so good over there.

Rogers Stevens: We were out at this restaurant with the promoters in Japan. We were with the top guys—just drinking lots of sake and having a good time. I remember going in, and everyone took their shoes off when we got there. [Shannon] put squid in a bunch of people's shoes—in mine, I think one of the guys we were with. I remember—or barely remember—putting your shoes on and being drunk enough to take a few steps in it before you realized that it was full of squid.

Barbara Prisament: I remember being concerned a little bit after "No Rain," wanting to make sure we didn't wait too long to come with the [follow-up] single. I wanted to make sure we didn't miss the momentum. I remember being backstage and telling Chris Jones—"Don't wait too long on the next single. Stay on them out there in L.A., make sure you get your next single going and everything in place."

Glen Graham: There was some disagreement about how we wanted to be represented. Since "No Rain" was a hit, that was sort of the lightest thing on the album. We put out "Tones of Home" [for which a new video was shot] in between "No Rain" and "Change," which was a mistake. We should have just done "Change" and built up from there. The video for "Change" was abysmal. I don't even understand what it is. I have no memory doing it. I saw it the other day, and I just thought, "Wow, when was this?"

Brooks Byrd Graham: It should have been [a hit]. It was really because of the change in the record company—that was really disappointing to everybody.

Nicholas Bechtel: I had been touring for a while, doing different stuff with the Black Crowes—as a general assistant. Owen Orzack was out doing monitors for a band called Gutterball, that opened up for the Crowes. Owen told them about me. At the time, periodically, Shannon would find himself in trouble.

And Paul was being stretched thin. Lyle called me from Japan one night when I was kicking back at the house. He told me the possibility of them wanting to bring someone on, that would take care of the band and look after Shannon. Owen had highly recommended me. I had tentatively had the gig, and then at the last moment—this is just before the American Music Awards in '94—I got word that Chris Jones had decided to just keep it the way it was.

Rogers Stevens: Just Shannon and I went to [the A.M.A.'s]. For some reason, we got a bunch of beer—it was a recipe for disaster. We went and we sat down—we were sitting right by the front of the stage. We were like, "Eh, I'm not going to sit here and watch the whole show"—the taping of it takes forever, and they're doing performances by people we really didn't want to see. Went back, and we started hanging out with Tony Hawk, the skater, who's a really nice guy. We were sitting back there talking to him and his wife. Drinking, which turned into more drinking—it just went on and on. Someone came and told us that we had to go back out, because they were going to announce the award we were up for. So we went out there and sat down. I think we were watching Michael Bolton or somebody—we were heckling him, which was stupid. Basically showing zero class [laughs]. We didn't get the award, which is neither here nor there, we really didn't care about that.

At one point—I was kind of drunk—I remember looking over and seeing Shannon standing up in the aisle talking to Scott Weiland, saying something to him. They had a contentious relationship—a clash of egos or whatever. He did something, and then the security guards came down the aisle. So I stood up and went over to try to get him to sit down. The show was going on—if you were watching it and they panned back, we were right in the second or third row in the center aisle. It would have been on television. So they came down, grabbed us, and 'chicken-winged' us all the way down the aisle—in front of everybody. Took us out on the sidewalk. I wasn't fighting back—Shannon was fighting back with them. They slammed me down, I think Shannon saw that, and he hauled off and hit one of those cops—it was one of the most perfect sucker punches I've ever seen in my life. It started down below his ankles, and came all the way up like an upper cut. *Just nailed that guy.* We didn't know they were cops, because they were in plain clothes. So they took him to jail in Compton. I don't remember how many days he spent there, maybe he got out over night. They for some reason let me go...he went to jail *in Compton!* It was like, "Whoa!"

Nicholas Bechtel: That night, Shannon and Rogers got arrested by the police, and the next day I got a phone call from their girl in the office—I was down in Florida on my way home—saying, "Would you please call Chris Jones about this position." He and I talked, and they brought me on. Man, we clicked right away. He said Shannon needed a friend and keep an eye on him. Be there and be an interceptor of problems or be able to intervene—be there watching him, whatever should go on. Somebody that can step in and monitor the situation, because at that time, the band was really escalating, and they had just started their headlining tour. Paul Cummings, his hands were pretty busy with dealing with everything. That is where I came from—doing that for the Crowes. I was their personal assistant and assistant tour manager.

It was really unique with all those guys. It was just like we were either brothers or cousins—like we were family. Within the first half hour on the bus, I was all excited—listening to what they wanted to do and Shannon was telling me his ideas about he wanted to paint something. I was coming up with these ideas—"We can find some paint here." I jumped right in with them, as if I knew them forever, and it was easy because of his personality. He reminded me of one of my cousins that I had grown up with. So we clicked right off. After the first week or so, even Glen came up to me and goes, "I was really skeptical about who they were going to hire and what was going on." When you see me, I'm the least intimidating person you could ever see [laughs]. And he goes, "I expected this big, gruffy security guy. All of a sudden, I look over and there you are—this baby face and long black hair." Shannon was really receptive to it.

Shannon—I was completely surprised. When I got hired on with the Black Crowes, the first thing I was warned about was Chris and Rich [Robinson] were notorious for knock out, drag out fistfights. When I got hired with them, that was one of the things that I was warned about. They said, "Watch out for that. Let it go on for a little while—if it gets serious, break it up." Never happened. Same thing with Shannon. They said, "Watch out for

Shannon—he's a loose canon." I think it was the alcohol thing that would really put Shannon into the 'danger realm.' When I was out with them, there was really nothing—it was just mostly smoking a lot of pot. I had heard about the stories, and I think after the incident at the American Music Awards, he had settled down for a while.

Brad Smith: The pitfall of keeping the band on the road is, 'idle hands are the devil's workshop,' and Shannon took that proverb to heart. He got deeper and deeper—he'd made a mess of himself on the road after a certain point, after about the two-year mark. We should have gotten off the road sooner. Hindsight is 20/20.

Rogers Stevens: We got totally burnt out. Nobody could tell us to do anything we didn't want to do, but we shouldn't have agreed to tour as much as we did. We should have not done that last tour—that tour with the Meat Puppets. It was just too much. We had been out for so long and it was time to circle the wagons and make another record, and we ended up going back out on the road for another three months. So that was more of a negative experience then anything.

Marlon Stoltzman: The other thing that wore on Shannon was that they definitely should have gone back into the studio after touring the first album. But then the hit broke just as they were coming off the road, and the record company kept them on the road for another year. It was just too monotonous and too much. The first tour helped the spiral. They had *one album*—you try playing one album for two years. I'm not saying he wouldn't have gotten more involved in drugs—it just bored him, the monotony. He didn't like the record company, which is a normal thing for a lot of bands. But I would always say, "Well then, play on your street corner. Do you want to make money?" It's a business—you don't have to be on a record label, you can just jam in your garage. This is when they really peaked. He said, "We're going to go to dinner tonight [with the label]. I'm going to tell the worst jokes and watch everybody laugh."

Heather Thorn: I think they were all burnt out and all could have used more time [off], but that is just the nature of the beast, and you've got to do what you've got to do when things are going well. But at that point, I'm sure they were all like, "I can't stand you. Get me off the road—I just want to veg out in my house."

Paul Cummings: It's an old story—you take a bunch of kids that have never been on the road, put them on the road for 18 months, and they just never want to do it again. They were so burnt out by the end of it, so tired of playing those songs. They did that last tour and it actually sold pretty well—they sold out Roseland. We had a band bus and a crew bus at that point. There were no soundchecks I don't think anywhere on that tour—maybe the first show. The band would show up, do the show, go right off the stage into the bus, and gone. Didn't hang out, didn't soundcheck. The crew were loving it, because they never got to see the band—the band would come, do the show, and then they were gone. Quite pleasant for them.

Glen Graham: That was our 'headline tour.' I remember this—and this no one will ever believe, I don't even think the Meat Puppets know this—I was in a band, Café Des Moines, years ago, that would warm up for those guys. Nobody came to see them, and we knew about them—we were fans from early on. When I got in Blind Melon, I was the person who turned people on to those types of bands. I didn't watch MTV, I didn't pay any attention to it. I didn't have it growing up—it didn't interest me. So I had no idea that Nirvana had done that 'Unplugged' thing with the Kirkwood's—not a clue. Only years after that, did I realize that those guys probably thought that the only reason why we got them was because we were going to try and play off the success of that little, "Oh people know who you are, so more people will come and see you." Absolutely untrue. I had no idea that was the case.

I begged for that band to open for us—how, I don't know, but they said, "O.K." And Shannon's [pick] was Alice Donut. I thought they were some of the coolest, most laid back, funniest people we ever toured with. But the Meat Puppets—I love them. The 'Too High' to whatever thing...I'm like, *'Up on the Sun.'* I remember one thing they did. It was Gene Simmons' birthday—

they wore jockstraps on the outside of their pants as a 'codpiece tribute to Gene Simmons.' I thought that was pretty funny—totally lost on our fans. Two brothers that had been together for a really long time, and Derrick [Bostrom, drummer]. Alice Donut, my God, they did "War Pigs." Steve [Moses], the drummer, would play trombone with delay on it—I thought that was the coolest thing ever. I think people really responded to those guys. I don't have any concept of what Alice Donut's following was, but I thought they were pretty cool. I thought they were smart. But that tour was great—there you are, you're playing headline shows. When you're doing that, you feel like you're where you were trying to get all along. That's the goal—headlining your own thing and not playing to 150 people.

Nicholas Bechtel: Shannon *loved* Alice Donut. He used to hang out with them—we'd smoke out on the bus. And then hanging out with the Meat Puppets, who were just legendary, and listening to Cris' rock n' roll stories—they were just one after another. I remember Shannon even commenting, "I can't believe *they're* opening for *us*."

Curt Kirkwood: They were all really nice, easygoing guys, and Shannon was a lot of fun. Just always 'up,' and loved to have a good time. [There were] people around trying to keep him from having a good time. We'd have to sneak off and have a good time—it seemed he'd do anything for a good time. A lot like vandals I grew up with in Phoenix. He was a lot more mellow—he wasn't a vandal. He had that very Midwestern, sort of '*yeah*' attitude. The rest of the guys were quiet. Super laid back guys. I know [Shannon] told our rhythm guitar player to take a pee on the floor of a bar they were in one night, so Troy [Meiss] did it! They all got thrown out because he immediately whipped it out in a crowded bar and started peeing. So that's the kind of frivolity that would happen. Sometimes for sure he'd become a little obtuse, because God, if not if for people smoking weed and shit, who knows? You kind of forget what happens show to show. I'll tell you one—we dodged his keeper in a college gymnasium, between these rows of lockers, where we'd slip over to one locker. We'd hear him say, "Hey Shannon, are you in here?"

Stephen Moses: It was a strange combination of bands. It was us, and the Meat Puppets were on there for half the tour, and then Dig. Blind Melon's fans didn't know what to make of us. Another interesting thing about Blind Melon fans—after Blind Melon played "No Rain," *a lot* of people left. They would stay to hear that song. Maybe their mommies and daddies were outside waiting to pick them up. But the band still had a bunch of really cool songs. I got to really like the band. One of the things on the tour was that alcohol was not permitted anywhere backstage—I guess Shannon had a little run-in with the law before this tour. Actually, the law was not going to let him out, but then they said they had to make sure that none of the bands had any alcohol backstage. No alcohol on the premises. Of course, we had our riders, where we were going to get a couple of cases of beer and a bottle of this and that. We'd have to bring it out to our van. That was so Shannon wouldn't lose it. But then on the bus, he'd drink a beer—it was no big deal. He was totally in control of that.

Tomas Antona: Before the tour, we were told to keep our booze in the van. I think I had beers with Rogers and other members, but I don't remember ever seeing Shannon drunk or wasted at all. I remember him being upset once because he found out—this is much later, towards the end—he was pissed that the booze was being hidden from him. Like he was a child or something.

Sissi Schulmeister: Before the shows, they'd have a room where they would have incense and candles—kind of set the mood—and they would jam a little before they'd go on stage.

Tomas Antona: I remember talking about the Butthole Surfers and Rage Against the Machine. We'd talk a lot about music with Rogers. Rogers said they were the 'young pups,' and all of us had toured a boatload. We broke down in the winter up in Rochester of something, and they got their manager to come and hand us 500 bucks. They did shit like that—very cool. We couldn't make one show—I think it was in Utah—because Sissi [Schulmeister, bassist] got sick. So Shannon would go and give Sissy some Ensure every day, because she wasn't getting enough iron. Also, Shannon's [girlfriend], Lisa—

really sweet, really cool people. It was down to earth, no bullshit conversations about what was going on. On our last show, Shannon came on stage with us and did "My Best Friend's Wife."

Sissi Schulmeister: He and his girlfriend were a really great couple. They really fit perfectly together.

Stephen Moses: Before we got to San Francisco, we called our record label, and had them make us 'bee costumes.' When they started playing ["No Rain"]—the band didn't know we were going to do this—we went out in our bee costumes. Alice Donut in bee costumes, like the bee girl. We came out in a conga line dancing, freaking them out, kinda pushing them around—messing with them. And they loved it. I still have that bee costume in fact—I use it on Halloween.

Danny Clinch: I remember [Shannon] one time coming down to the hotel front desk, checking out. And they were like, "You watched all these movies." "What movies?" "Porn movies." He's like, "Man, I will tell you—I am a law-abiding, good Christian man. I would *never* watch anything like that!" He was trying to talk his way out of it.

Marlon Stoltzman: I remember hanging out at the Paramount Hotel, and we went down to the street, because [Shannon] loved walking around the streets—he really loved 'experiencing.' There were about eight taxis lined up outside the hotel, and he just walked over all the taxis. He started at the back of the trunk of one, walked on the roof over, and all the guys were screaming at him.

Jena Kraus: There was all these weird coincidences that would happen between me and them. Me and my friend were going up to New York to see them—they were playing Roseland. They didn't know I was coming—I couldn't get in touch with them. Our plan was to get a hotel room, and then try and get tickets for the show. We get in this cab, I didn't know what to say, because I didn't know exactly where we were going. I just made up two streets that

I knew would intersect. We get there, and Shannon's standing there on the corner! Later that night, Christopher came up to me, and said, "Jena, I know you have some songs, and I have this traveling little A-DAT studio with me. If you want, I'll record a demo for you, and at the least, you'll have a demo you can show to people." I could never find people I had chemistry with beside Blind Melon—and they had their own thing happening. So we planned the next week I was going to go to Baltimore. I went down there—we did a bunch of songs. That was amazing—after their show, in a hotel room. Brad and Shannon were there, and I'm singing through their mics. Everything was just like, "Wow, I'm playing with my favorite band!" I was there for two or three days—I was so grateful and happy with the way everything went. And I hoped deep in my heart that Christopher would call and say that he wanted to work with me more. And then he did call. He was like, "I believe in you—you can do this." He said he wanted to help me, and that we were going to be partners in my little venture in the music industry.

Paul Cummings: The last show was in Austin—it was an outdoor gig. They weren't headlining—it was them and Smashing Pumpkins. There were like 20,000 people there—Smashing Pumpkins were pretty big at that point.

Marlon Stoltzman: They played Letterman when Kurt Cobain died, and [Shannon] had a question mark on his forehead. I went to see him in the hotel, and he smashed the TV in the corner. He was devastated. He's like, "This guy was such a good guy, there was so much going for him. Why, why, why?" It's kind of ironic. He was so upset—that whole night and for a while. That was quite a heavy night for him—trying to come to terms with that.

Paul Cummings: Whenever they broke something in hotels, I would always tell the front desk—in a vain attempt that if they kept having to pay for stuff, it would break the habit of doing it. So I told the front desk that the television was broken, just put it on our bill. So Shannon had the idea of, "Let's box it up, put it on the plane, and pretend it got damaged by the airport baggage people." They actually did box it up—I don't remember if it ever made it to the plane. We never did end up getting billed for the T.V., oddly enough.

Glen Graham: [Cobain's death] freaked him out badly. I think he knew—"If that guy can succumb to the pressures of what's going on inside his brain, then I know I can." I don't know that he was thinking those thoughts, but I think something resonated in him, like "Oh shit—*uh oh*." I don't think they ever met—but I don't know. Kurt Cobain at the time was the focal point of youth culture—unfortunately for him.

Jena Kraus: In April, they were up in Mammoth. I flew up over Mammoth Mountain—it was so cool being up in the mountains. The air was so fresh. And I remember him playing the songs they had recorded. It was amazing. I heard a lot of the stuff that ended up being re-recorded on 'Soup.' Just hanging out with them in this cabin. I brought my guitar with me—the last day they were there, they recorded "The Pusher," and Shannon played my guitar. It was such a trip. There was a song called "Shivering" or "Shattered" that was pretty good. "Tickled Pink" was there—that was at Mammoth. Then Shannon and Rogers left, and Christopher and I stayed on for another two days and we recorded more songs. They wanted me to cover Bob Dylan's song, "She Belongs to Me," and I remember Shannon telling me the lyrics, as I was writing them in my journal. It meant so much that they thought of me when they wanted me to cover this song.

Rogers Stevens: I think it was just me, Christopher, and Shannon—hanging out with some recording gear set up, working on some things. I remember doing "The Pusher" up there, but it was just me playing guitar and Shannon singing. When we did the 'Nico' record, Christopher put the banjo on it, and I put guitar solos on it, drums, and bass, and it was done. But I think we did that out on the porch of that house—it was fucking freezing. We were doing snowboarding, smoking pot, and writing songs—some were good, some weren't. I don't remember what songs exactly were done up there. But it was cool—we were feeling it out. I don't remember any hard drugs being done in Mammoth—just a lot of pot smoking. He was doing lots of snowboarding during the daytime—learning how to do it. He was doing crazy jumps—pretty funny. Shannon and I took this little airplane—it had two seats in the back—out of there. It is one of those airports where the approach is scary, because there's a mountain there. I remember just massive turbulence and him turning green. We thought that was it.

Brad Smith: The record company and management never wanted us to come off of the road. They were already driving the band into the fucking ground with tours and shows—we had to beg to get off the road and to write another record. They would have kept milking "No Rain" until the band would have disintegrated. We had to put our foot down at a certain point, and go, "No more touring—this is the last one." We did that tour, got home, and everybody got to decompress. I moved to New Orleans, Glen and Rogers lived in New Orleans, Shannon lived in Chicago, Christopher stayed in Seattle. But we didn't talk to each other for months after we got off the road. We were like, "*Fuck this.*"

Rehab/Euro Tour

Shannon's drug use spirals out of control, resulting in his first stab at rehab. A string of European festival dates are set for the summer, which ends earlier than expected, at the request of Shannon.

Nel Hoon: I don't know what time Shannon started doing drugs—the hard drugs.

Rogers Stevens: Shannon was...his drug use, that was from day one. That wasn't a new thing. He went through phases—he was always game for whatever. I think he had a lot of problems back when he was living in Indiana, and he got out. Coke was the problem—heroin was never the problem. We tried to deal with it—got him into treatment a few times.

Glen Graham: I knew he was a 'coke guy' the day I met him. I didn't realize how bad it was...he hid the coke in L.A. quite a bit. I don't think anybody really knew he was doing it—he wasn't doing it as much as he was later, by any stretch of the imagination. His biggest problem in L.A. was drinking. He was the worst drunk you ever saw in your life. Shannon died every day—that's the truth. When he was having a hard time mentally, he would just go out and blow out. He was one of these guys that had the stamina to keep going for days and days. Until he's breaking down Christopher and Heather's door, and they're having to have him arrested—that kind of stuff. You feel sorry for him—there's just nothing you can do.

Bill Armstrong: Shannon was an extreme guy—in whatever he did. Like, if he's going to do music, he's going to do it 130%. If he's going to go out and drink beer, he's not going to drink one, he'll drink a twelve pack. He was extreme in every single aspect of his life—and that also included drugs. See,

I never really thought of Shannon as a drug addict. I thought of him as, "If he's going to smoke pot, he's going to smoke a bag of pot. And if he decided to go sober for a while, he'd go totally stone cold sober." He's what in A.A. they call 'a gobbler.' Shannon's going to do whatever's around, and a lot of it. When I think of drug addicts, I think of people that are reclusive, in their hotel room, lights drawn, shooting heroin all by themselves. And Shannon wasn't that type of a guy. He's the kind of guy who would probably drink a lot of beer and do a lot of whatever else is around. If there's nothing around, then there's nothing around. But you know how guys like that are—he's incredibly charismatic, and he attracted those kind of people to him.

Domenique Johansson: It did escalate and get out of control. Through the troubles of dealing with the success, the pressures that had developed within the band—no matter how close the band is, there's always dynamics that go on between them. There's all this stuff that you're always managing. A lot of hangers-on in your life. A lot of people that aren't a good influence. And Shannon wasn't really good about keeping those people away. These people, the way they get an 'in' with the band—you know what women inevitably get to a band with. Well, men couldn't get to a band the same way, so frequently their 'in' is to give them things. Whether they manage to give them some rare guitar, an unusual harmonica—something they know that he might be into. Or most frequently, drugs. So they'd end up being their drug slugs. In every town, you'd have one or two of these guys that would bring something. And every time you went through there, it seemed to escalate—they would bring more. Then because they were supplying something, they would bring people with them, and then it would become a bigger scene of this drug crowd. He was thrilled that people were interested in him—he was generally a nice guy. He was really susceptible to those people that gave him drugs. Especially when they went through California down into Texas.

Heather Thorn: Shannon was that guy that if you met him one time, he was your best friend...or so you thought. He had that wonderful ability to make you feel that way, so everybody always wanted to hook him up and make him happy.

Tim Devine: His biggest vice that I was aware of was pot. He was a big marijuana proponent and never too far away from his bong. But it seemed to be relatively harmless. Obviously, later that didn't turn out to be the case. I never saw him do coke. I think the band would tend to be on their good behavior around the record label people. I spent many times on the road with them—Shannon always showed up for the shows, unlike his counterpart, Axl Rose, at the time.

Shannon Hoon: You know, I'd rather have a gold bong than a gold record.

John Fagot: When I met him—at this point in time in the music industry, a lot of people were doing cocaine and drugs. It wasn't that unusual to run into people that were doing drugs. But I would never have thought that Shannon was one of the guys that would be doing drugs—because he was so gentle, and such a nice, good person. He wasn't a real 'rock n' roll star'—he wasn't interested in that. He just wanted to do his music, have a good time, and enjoy it. It didn't even occur to me.

Lisa Sinha: I dealt with him and his drugs—was he open with me? Very open with me about it. Once it got out of hand, he was all freaked out and upset. But when he was first starting, he was just, "I'm going to have fun." Basically, "I'm going to do what I'm going to do." I wasn't going to stop him—there was no way. Once it got bad, he really wanted to sober up. But I think when you're a drug addict, it's very hard to make the commitment. For him, he was doing it off and on. Things are really happy-go-lucky, all fun when you're doing it, but then when he would come down from it, it was all, "*Ugh.* Life stinks." Everything was really negative. So it was lots of mood swings with him.

Paul Cummings: They were all potheads. A lot of the time, it was just that—as far as I could tell. It never bothered me so much—being the tour manager, it made [Shannon] quieter, so it was fine with me. At least it kept him quiet. I could never understand why they had to do that as much as they did, but it's better than him drinking. It made it easier for me—I guess that's selfish, but…

Shannon Hoon: I feel more internal when I'm high. It's just comfortable. It's like, why do you take a shower in the morning? And on a tour like this, you don't have a lot time to sit down and think. But when you're high, you find the time. You make the time. And then you realize that the time was there.

Jena Kraus: I think his real problem was alcohol. Once he started to drink, then he would do coke. So coke and alcohol were his real things. But honestly, when we were in Mammoth Mountain, I brought pot, and everyday I would be like, "Shannon, do you want to smoke with me?" And he wouldn't smoke until late at night—they were working. When I was in Mammoth Mountain, he wasn't doing drugs a lot. He was really focused. I mean, yeah, he did party, but at that point, he didn't seem that bad. I've seen people on drugs that are junkies—looking to get high. He wasn't really like that. I didn't see him passed out or anything like that. I mean, I did kind of worry about him.

Shannon Hoon: I'm a terrible drunk. I can't even pass out, because my friggin' hyperactive state won't permit me to. But I like to drink. There's nothing worse than when you wake up with all your clothes still on, like today. I mean, when you can't even kick your boots off, how good was your sleep, really?

Lyle Eaves: Obviously, a super-addictive personality. Always would try anything, do anything. Loved to do acid, smoked weed non-stop—all-day, every day. I had a little bit different view of that because I don't even smoke pot—I never have. People that do, kind of not shy away, but turn their back on you when they're doing that kind of stuff. There was a lot of times when he was doing drugs that I wasn't that aware of—he would keep it away from me. He didn't think I was cool with it—not that I ever judged him on it or lectured him—but people that are doing drugs stay away from people that aren't.

Marlon Stoltzman: In the beginning, it was definitely much more recreational and fun. He would party with anyone—he was a very open person. He wasn't like the 'dark closeted drug addict.' It was very fun—let's have fun, let's party. I never saw the 'monster side,' which apparently there were moments, which if I suppose you do that amount of drugs, you're going to have your moments.

But he was just a teddy bear. Just wanted love—all the good things in the world, people, and all embracing. It's possibly an early period where it helps with their creativity, but that goes very quickly, and then all you are is a desperate drug addict. There were times also when I guess he was embarrassed about it, and he didn't want to even see me. Where he came, went home, and called me the next day, and said, "I'm sorry—I'm embarrassed, and I don't want to be that sort of Shannon."

Glen Graham: It's not just the drugs—it's that he was terribly depressed, or he was terribly manic. There was very little in between with him. I was the same way—but I don't have the same personality that he does. I don't have the same sort of background, of robbing liquor stores or convenience stores, and getting into knife fights like he did. Perhaps if I did, I'd be just like him. But he and I shared the extreme ups and downs, and we talked about it many, many times. Late night phone calls from Lafayette to New Orleans, with him in tears talking about being sick, and not knowing what to do about it. And of course, I was in no position to help him, because I wasn't under psychiatric care at that time, and should have been. I would have had a lot better time. But he came from a background that frowned on the psychiatric community, or at least he thought they did.

Brooks Byrd Graham: Without a doubt, he had some sort of chemical imbalance in his brain. It probably would have been called manic depression. There's varying degrees of manic depression, and it manifests itself in different ways and different people. He came from such an unstable background, that he didn't have a lot of tools for coping with things. And plus, on top of his mental condition, there's a lot of pressure on him, and it made it very difficult. But maybe he could have been helped with some psychiatric medicine. He knew that he couldn't drink a whole lot. Because if he drank a lot, he got belligerent, and would wind up getting into a fight with somebody, and possibly going to jail. [If] he drank a little bit, he could control himself in that way—but not all the time. Sometimes he couldn't sing very well because he had overdone drugs. Or he had been doing something for so long that he had gotten sick. He would come off and be really mad. That was what was so scary about him.

So many people have all these really lovable memories—which is true. But when you were around him all the time, he would get really angry—because he had so much energy and forcefulness. He could be really scary. I remember every couple of days, he would get really angry and yell at somebody—and stomp off. And a lot of times, it was because he was frustrated with himself—he just took it out on everybody.

Glen Graham: He would get very upset—'tears/crying' upset. For all I know, he might have been having a similar conversation with everybody he ever met. But I certainly had those conversations with him. It freaked him out badly. I would tell him about my situation, how I felt—and it would just stop him cold. Without any distractions or other people to entertain, he would pay attention. I think it really got him, but there was no helping him at all. You could have gotten him out of rock band mode and got him to a point that he wasn't interested in doing it—he might have been a person who could have really benefited from psychiatric care. I mean, serious, long-term psychiatric care. Gotten the addictions under control and gotten on medication that could have helped him. He just had too many things working against him. From the outside, I suppose if you don't know the guy, he looks like a barrel of laughs. But he was a very, very dark guy—who got through life by being the class clown/life of the party.

Shannon Hoon: I don't know what it does to your mind. Man, you know what it does, it makes your mind...you have input overload, man. You're so caught up going down this one street so fast that you fail to realize that, wow, that was a cool street. But the one thing that frustrates me the most is, I like to do a lot of other things. I like writing music, doing things like this, but at the time, it's like there's other things that I have just as much enthusiasm in doing, and when I can't equally give the same amount of time to each one of them, I feel like telling one of my identities that this one's better than that one. And that's not true. So I'm on my way to the Frolic Room.

Rogers Stevens: People were talking to him to try to help. I got to know Steven Tyler a little bit in the last couple of years—I was talking to him about it, and he said that he called him at some point. I don't remember the specifics about what he told him.

Lisa Sinha: Mike [McCready] from Pearl Jam was real supportive of him getting sober. I know that he called our house a couple of times.

Brian Whitus: One of the first or second times he'd come home, I knew he was home, and I knocked on his door. Kept knocking, kept knocking. He looked out the window, and said, "Oh shit Whitey, I didn't know that was you!" He was acting kinda funny. I'd gone in the kitchen, and he had a spoon with something in it, and he was lighting the spoon up—I assumed it was crack. At that point, it seemed like he was doing it ever 20 minutes. He'd come to my house with me, and he did it down the bathroom. I remember him telling me—I believe—he spent ten grand in the last month on it. At that point, I was thinking, "*Holy Toledo.*" Then I knew he had a problem. That was a topic all the time. I'd tell him, "Goddamn it Shannon, you need to quit this shit. I've been around you before when you've passed out on stuff." "Oh, I don't have a problem—I can deal with it. I'm invincible."

Danny Clinch: Some people just have no fear. And he definitely had no fear—he would mix this, that and the other thing.

Riki Rachtman: It was like, here's a guy that I would see every single day, five days a week, eight hours a day for months. And in no time, it was like, "It's only a matter of time before Shannon dies."

Shannon Hoon: You just don't see it coming, right when you think you're starting to enjoy it...and the thing is that people don't realize the physical aspect of it—the physical addiction of it. It goes to a point where even when you don't want to do it, your body wants it. Addiction of any sort is not an enjoyable thing. I by no means am a Christian—I have my bouts with a lot of different things and my life would probably be a lot happier, I know it would be a lot happier, without these obstacles that drugs and alcohol have set in front of me. There's been a lot of time that I've wasted, there's been a lot of energy wasted, and there's probably been a lot of creative parts of my life that have been completely dissolved because of it.

Jena Kraus: Shannon had gone to rehab right after he left Mammoth Mountain. I think he went to Indiana for a few days, and then he was going to rehab. That's the first time he went.

Brad Smith: He was in a place in California, STEPS, and that in my mind, I'd imagine is like a prison or school. You have this structured environment that you're not used to, it's not your comfort zone, and you have to deal with a lot of really heavy issues.

Nel Hoon: I know this is going to sound strange, but over these years, those are things that I have put outside my head. I can barely even remember the time—maybe it's because I wanted to forget about the rehab thing or about him being on the drugs.

Brooks Byrd Graham: I remember thinking, "There's no way it's going to help—he doesn't want help." I don't think he would have ever gotten help, because that's not who he was. His mind was out of control, and that's the way he liked to live.

Kim Smith: I remember it was a tense time—mostly with him and Lisa. She was glad he was in rehab, but it was a big deal because he was trying to get clean—she was upset, wondering if it was going to work.

Lisa Sinha: It was terrible. We lived in Chicago at the time, and he was just a total monster. We were not getting along at all while he was in rehab. It was weird. They have you go through all these steps—religious stuff. Kind of try to convince you to dump all your friends. But it was really hard on him and I. I just don't know if he fit the whole 'rehab.' He was not himself at all. When he went in—he wasn't so hardcore into it. He'd call me and say, "Oh, so and so is in here, and so and so is in here." It's like, everybody sits there and brags about their drug problem. And who's the worst and who's done the most. For me, it was a really weird thing, because it was almost this glamorous thing—"Y'know, Johnny O.D.'d *ten times.*" It was all these stories about who was the biggest drug addict. For me, it was just stupid. Heather and I were talking about this once—in the 'grunge era,' it was cool to be a drug addict. Shannon truly had a drug issue—absolutely no doubt—and an anger management problem. As far as all this rehabilitation stuff, I don't think he took it serious. And everybody still is treating you special, and you get attention from it.

Paul Cummings: I visited him once—he seemed in good spirits. I remember I was oddly proud of him that he'd gone. He was not responsible most of the time, but he wasn't mean-spirited—he was just a big kid. So when he did something that was responsible, you felt good for him. And that was one of those times. I remember I went to a grocery store, and I saw him standing in the Vons there in rollerblades.

Brad Smith: Once you get home [from rehab], you're still digesting that information. Shannon probably went on the road a little bit too soon.

Nicholas Bechtel: Right when he got out of rehab, we bolted, and went to Europe to start a European tour. I remember the first stop—for this kid who just came out of rehab—was Amsterdam. We got into the hotel room and Shannon called me up, he said, "I understand if you don't want to go—but I'm going to go hit the coffee shop. I don't really want to go by myself." I said, "Dude, I am there right with you." I went with him. We smoked out and hung. I wasn't going to let the guy go alone and I wasn't going to encourage it, but you've got to look a little deeper into the 'human factor' of what was going on. We tried to get as far away from where everybody would be, and I remember we came out of this coffee place, just completely baked out of our heads. And who comes riding up on bicycles? Rogers and Christopher [laughs]. I remember Shannon looked at me real sheepishly, and I just went, "*Oh, I'm in trouble.*"

Robert Plant: I've never seen them before, but they're just amazing. They take the music off into uncharted places. They really have what it takes. Are they playing anywhere else while they're over here? I think they're so good I have to catch them again.

Rogers Stevens: I think we were at a festival in Holland, and [Shannon] went into one of those [port-a-potty's]. When he got in it, I started rocking it back and forth—it's sloshing around. I might as well have kicked a hornet's nest—he came out and he was ready to kill me! He was one of those guys when he lost his temper, it was really staggering. He totally went after me—I just ran. He almost killed me for that.

Nicholas Bechtel: Approximately ten days into it, [the tour] got cancelled.

Lyle Eaves: Shannon was in *bad shape* over there. The European show performances were not together—Shannon was just not 'in it.' I don't know how much relapsing he did over there. But obviously he did some, because it was all of a sudden, "We're going back—we're stopping right here." We turned around and came home.

Brooks Byrd Graham: It was Shannon's state of mind, definitely. His mind was out of control, and he was always trying to control it—his energy, passion—with drugs. That only works for so long, and then you fall apart. He was falling apart. And of course, he was exhausted. He pushed himself way too much.

Paul Cummings: It got cut short because [Shannon] just wasn't up to it. But we did Glastonbury and I think we did the Forum—it was a headline show at the Forum. A 1,500-2,000 seater in London. That went really well. And then they did go-kart racing again, because they liked it on [the Lenny Kravitz tour]. But even at that point, they knew they were going home. [Shannon] didn't really give a reason—he just didn't want to do it. I put them on the plane, and I stayed for a few days.

Kim Smith: I remember Brad coming up to the room and telling me that Shannon left—he went home. It was just too soon for him to be on tour after that rehab stint. He just couldn't handle it. So he went home, and we stayed in London for a few days. Then me, Brad, Rogers, and his girlfriend at the time flew to Paris, stayed in Paris for a few days, and came home.

Owen Orzack: I remember the crew, we were all pissed off, because we basically didn't get paid for the time we were supposed to be working. I remember I had to take another tour and I didn't get to do the Woodstock show, which was very disappointing to me. They were upset 'cause I wasn't there, and I was pissed. It was just a bad taste. At the time, I had a wife and a kid, and I needed to work—it was the middle of the summer, and I had a tour offer. I was out the door—I had to go do it.

Glen Graham: This is what really happened. We had all the girlfriends out. This was the big, "Let's take the girlfriends to Europe." We were playing all over—Spain, Italy, and places we'd never been before. It was very exciting. And very relaxed—it's festivals. I was feeling terrible, personally. [Shannon] was getting ready to have a nervous breakdown—there was no question about it. He came to me and said, "I don't know man, I don't feel good about this, I don't think I can do the shows." Y'know, stuttering, semi-coherent. And I was feeling the same way. I was like, "You know what? *I'm with you.* Let's go. Let's say, 'Fuck it.' I don't care that the girls are here." My wife was there. And I realize that this is a huge thing for us, but it's like, "Let's go home." And then I went to Chris Jones and told him that, and everybody was very upset about it. It wasn't about drugs—it was about his mental state. He was *freaking out.* The drugs weren't helping of course. If he'd just had the drugs, I think we would have played all those shows. We called it off. Management didn't want to do it and the girls were all pissed. If we hadn't gone home then, he probably would not have survived that tour. He would have done himself in one way or another.

Nicholas Bechtel: He went home, recuped, and got ready for the Woodstock thing.

The classic Blind Melon line-up at the Sleepyhouse in Durham, North Carolina, 1991
(L-R: Rogers Stevens, Christopher Thorn, Glen Graham, Shannon Hoon, Brad Smith)
[pic by Andy Martin Jr. – www.andymartinjr.com]

Shannon and his trusty can of bug spray
at the Sleepyhouse, 1991
[pic by Lyle Eaves]

Christopher, Rogers, and Brad embark on an all-night jam
at the Sleepyhouse, 1991
[pic by Lyle Eaves]

Shannon in Mesa, Arizona on the 120 Minutes Tour, 1992 [pic by Lyle Eaves]

Christopher, Glen, and Shannon (showing necklace his mother made) in Mesa, Arizona on the 120 Minutes Tour, 1992 [pic by Lyle Eaves]

Glen and Brooks Byrd Graham [pic by Lyle Eaves]

Shannon and Jena Kraus, October 1992
[pic by Marlon Stoltzman]

The boys unplugged (mostly) at an in-store, February 2, 1993
[pic by Brooks Byrd Graham]

This is a bust! California, 1993 [pic by Brooks Byrd Graham]

Shannon shaves off his beard for the "No Rain" video shoot, 1993
(note says "No Rain, No Beard") [pic by Lyle Eaves]

Live at Tipitina's in New Orleans, Louisiana, 1993 [pic by Brooks Byrd Graham]

Danny Clinch blowing a mean harmonica, 1993
[pic by Danny Clinch – www.dannyclinch.com]

Lisa Sinha and Heather Thorn
at Joss in Los Angeles, California,
September 11, 1993
[pic by Brooks Byrd Graham]

Shannon about to take a toke, 1993
[pic by Danny Clinch – www.dannyclinch.com]

Shannon contemplates playing or showering, 1993
[pic by Danny Clinch – www.dannyclinch.com]

Barefoot Shannon live, 1993
[pic by Danny Clinch – www.dannyclinch.com]

There's a full moon out—Shannon at the Edgewater Inn in Seattle, Washington, 1993
[pic by Lyle Eaves]

'Arrest night' in Canada,
Halloween 1993
[pic by Lyle Eaves]

Christopher and Shannon with the guru of fitness, Richard Simmons!
Backstage at Saturday Night Live in New York City, January 18, 1994
[pic by Danny Clinch – www.dannyclinch.com]

In limo on night of SNL performance
(L-R: Dick Hoon, Rogers' girlfriend at the time, Rogers, Lisa, Shannon, Nel Hoon)
[pic by Brooks Byrd Graham]

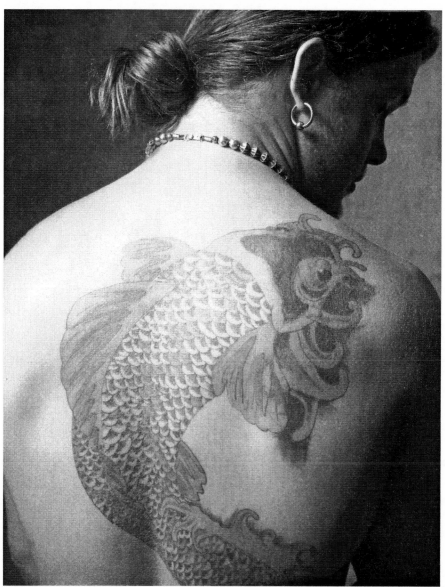
Shannon shows his back ink [pic by Danny Clinch – www.dannyclinch.com]

Shannon questions Kurt Cobain's suicide
before Melon's performance
on the Late Show with David Letterman,
April 8, 1994 [pic by Danny Clinch – www.dannyclinch.com]

Shannon in drag at Woodstock, New York, August 13, 1994
[pic by Danny Clinch – www.dannyclinch.com]

Shannon serenading the Woodstock nation
[pic by Danny Clinch – www.dannyclinch.com]

Shannon hugging the late/great Chris Farley—
post-performance at Woodstock
[pic by Nicholas Bechtel]

At Kingsway Studios in New Orleans, during 'Soup' recording
(Shannon on right with freshly shaven head), circa late 1994/early 1995
[pic by Danny Clinch – www.dannyclinch.com]

Taking a break from the wild 'Soup' sessions in New Orleans
[pic by Danny Clinch – www.dannyclinch.com]

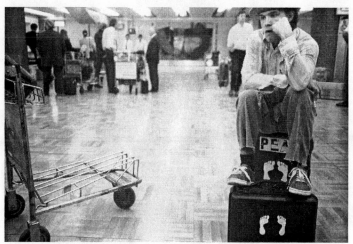

Shannon awaits his flight, 1995 [pic by Danny Clinch – www.dannyclinch.com]

Takin' it to the streets - Europe, 1995 [pic by Danny Clinch – www.dannyclinch.com]

Rockin' Europe, 1995 [pic by Danny Clinch – www.dannyclinch.com]

Classic mid-concert Shannon pose in Europe, 1995 [pic by Danny Clinch – www.dannyclinch.com]

Shannon strums backstage in Europe, 1995 (note 'cockroach necklace' tattoo)
[pic by Danny Clinch – www.dannyclinch.com]

Shannon stomps and sings – Europe, 1995
(message taped to Shannon's shirt says 'HELP')
[pic by Danny Clinch – www.dannyclinch.com]

Shannon Hoon, 1967-1995 [pic by Danny Clinch – www.dannyclinch.com]

Melon reborn! At Studio Wishbone in Hollywood, California, 2006
(L-R: Brad, Travis Warren, Christopher, Rogers, and Glen)
[pic by Danny Clinch – www.dannyclinch.com]

Travis Warren, live in Farmingdale, New York, June 21, 2008
[pic by Greg Prato]

Woodstock '94

Despite being off the road at the time—and Shannon doing his best to stay sober—Blind Melon accept an invite to perform as part of the mammoth 'Woodstock 94' festival. The result? One of the more memorable performances of the entire festival. But it comes with a price.

Glen Graham: I saw 'Woodstock' on television when I was ten—"The following is a CBS Special Presentation." This was in the midst of my total immersion in Kiss, so it was a real mind blower. I watched the whole movie and had no idea what it was or who these people were. I remember the Joe Cocker "With a Little Help from My Friends" segment and the Santana "Soul Sacrifice" performance most vividly—I knew I had to be a part of this sort of thing. Whatever they were doing, I wanted to do. But there was not a hint in my surroundings and upbringing that this was possible. I was in high school and college in the 80's in Mississippi. *Grim.*

Lisa Sinha: At first, it was one of those hokie things, like, "Is Woodstock a good thing to do?" Then a bunch of people started signing on, so then they signed on. He was really excited about it.

Shelley Shaw: I remember it was really hard to get the spot for them. We banged on the promoter about getting them on. And then he wanted them to do the shitty spot that they ended up having to do, and they were worried. But it ended up really positive for them. They really enjoyed it in the end. Back then, there was a lot of politics about, "What time are we going on? Who's before us? Who's after us?" And "That doesn't make sense to us." I remember getting a lot of hassle about that from management—they wanted a better spot. "My God, we have Guns N' Roses in our camp—we should be able to get John Scherr around the neck and get a better spot!" I think the band had a ball and were probably unaware of any of that kind of pressure. I think they just loved it.

Rogers Stevens: Just being really burnt out, because we went to Hawaii and did a show with Porno for Pyros [before Woodstock].

Glen Graham: I remember going [to Hawaii] and not having any sleep. We flew there and I don't think any of us got any sleep on the plane. We got off the plane, went up to the hotel room, came downstairs, our manager met us there. Immediately, it was 'down at the beach to go surfing.' Roasting alive. Met these people immediately—"Oh my God, Blind Melon! Holy shit!" With their fabulously beautiful and athletic girlfriends, who were doing this double-decker/stand-on-the-shoulders surfing stuff. We were in Waikiki—the biggest tourist/Brady Bunch beach. I remember spending the whole day out there, trying to learn how to surf—on adrenaline and probably pot. Rogers cut his foot surfing, took off in a jeep, rode around in pineapple fields. The show was in Kualoa Ranch—it was really cool. The stage was facing the mountains, the people were facing the ocean. I remember being in the bathroom before we went on, and Perry Farrell is standing there, doing his little eye make-up. Saying, "Hey man, how're you doing? Have a good show!" We did the show, I don't remember how many days we were there.

Marc Pollack: My memories of Woodstock were a few. One was the horrendous conditions of the concert itself—in the rain, in the mud, nowhere to sleep. It was a friggin' nightmare, quite frankly.

Paul Cummings: We all helicoptered in, and it was all very hush-hush—where you were supposed to meet up to go over to the festival. I think they didn't tell us 'til the night before—we were supposed to meet at this monastery over on the east side of the river. We met there—and I think the Cranberries were there, waiting as well—and we helicoptered in. As you came over the site, there were *a lot* of people there. It was pretty impressive.

Tim Devine: We arrived on the scene, and it was as if a whole city had been built out in a field in the middle of nowhere. Having been too young to be at the first Woodstock, I thought this was the closest I was ever going to come to this experience. We got in the night before and it was literally just a sea of people. They were on quite early. The show began with an homage to the original Woodstock by opening with Joe Cocker, who did his signature version of the Beatles' "With a Little Help from My Friends." That started the crowd going wild.

Nicholas Bechtel: Shannon being Shannon, he had somebody from Lafayette that was coming. He was going to sing "Soup," and he had this old rocking chair [that belonged to Shannon's grandmother, Vernie], that supposedly they were bringing to Woodstock. He tells me and Lisa that we've got to go out and find these guys that got that rocking chair, and they're sitting out near wherever the dinosaur was—some landmark within the campus of the Woodstock area. And this is not even an hour before show time. Me and Lisa are bolting, trying to get through the crowd, trying to find these people. And they're nowhere to be found. I'm panicking, I said, "They're going to go on stage and I've got to be there!" So Lisa goes, "I'll try and find them." So I'm having to cut back through this massive crowd. I get there, and Shannon's like, "Ah, *don't worry about it.*"

Christopher Thorn: I was really overwhelmed. You have those shows where you feel like you're really in control, you know what's happening, and you can feel it—you're taking it all in as you're playing. And for some reason, Woodstock was so overwhelming. I kinda felt shut down. There are two main memories—flying in on a helicopter, the first helicopter I've ever flown on, and you'd see as far as you can see, people. And right before going on, being backstage and being nervous. I'll never forget being backstage and seeing Peter Max, the famous artist, standing right behind Joe Cocker, who was opening the show. He goes on, and sings "Feeling Alright," and just being, "Oh my God, we have to follow this? The guy at the original Woodstock just played… give me a break!" I remember Shannon showing up in a dress, and going, "You're fucking nuts! What are you doing?" But that's what was great about him, he was never going to give you the same old shit—you didn't know what you were going to get from him. That's why he was such a great performer.

Lisa Sinha: Those are my clothes that he was wearing [laughs]. While we were in Hawaii, I had bought that white, stretchy dress. He hadn't figured out what he was going to wear. He was trying on all my clothes. "I'm just going to wear a dress, just to be different." Actually, I didn't want him to wear the dress—I had just bought it [laughs]. There was a fight over the dress. But I caved and let him wear the dress. It was a whim—"I don't know what I'm going to wear. I'll wear something of *yours*." He raided my suitcase and wore my clothes. I think it's on display at the Rock n' Roll Hall of Fame.

Shelley Shaw: [Shannon] told me he just *had* to drop acid before going on stage. And he told Chris Jones, "I had to drop acid man, this is what it is!" Everyone was just furious. I think he was sober for a little while, so that was kind of a nightmare. But I remember they were thrilled about the crowd and playing.

Marc Pollack: When I first saw Shannon before they went on—I saw him backstage—he was wasted. *Wasted.* It was obvious he was tripping. I think he took the whole 'Woodstock vibe' to another level [laughs]. He really wanted to live it. I don't think many people took it to the 'Woodstock extreme' as Shannon did.

Nel Hoon: He wouldn't let me go there. He said, "Mom, I won't be able to protect you, I don't want you to go to Woodstock." Later, I knew the reason why he didn't want me to go—he went off the wagon. But I think he really did enjoy Woodstock. That was the crowd that he really enjoyed performing [for]. I think that was the highlight of his entire life.

Shannon Hoon: When it was our turn to play, I was still on a complete high.

Miles Tackett: They kicked out the jams like they usually do.

Brad Smith: I remember being completely terrified, not wearing a shirt, and not hearing anybody on stage. The monitor system was horrible and everybody was so far apart, you couldn't physically hear Rogers' amp—I had to watch Glen's sticks move before I knew where the beat was. It was fun, but it frazzled you. You couldn't relax and enjoy it as much as you were trying not to fuck up the song. But it's emblazoned in my memory—looking out across this sea of people all the way back to the trees. You don't forget moments like that. It was awesome.

Glen Graham: I had no monitors for the first two songs. Our monitor guy, Owen, could not be there. Largest show you'll ever play in your entire life, and your monitor guy that you've been using for a year and a half is suddenly gone. We had a substitute guy, and I used ear monitors—I think Shannon did too—the rest of the guys didn't. When you use ear monitors—they're earplugs with speakers in them, basically. So if they are not turned on, not only do you not have any monitors but the additional challenge of overcoming earplugs designed to eliminate all external sound. Imagine an underwater monitor mix very far away.

There were no wedges or other monitors anywhere near me. So I click off the first song, and "Oh my God—I can't hear anything." Nothing. If you look at the video, there's panic on my face. I had a little microphone with a switch on it so I could communicate with the monitor guy, but of course, you can only do that between songs. So you'd have to play the first song, and after the first song, it's like, [speaks in a low voice] "*I don't have any monitors, I don't have any monitors.*" And then, "O.K., here we go—second song." Shannon's looking at you like, "I'm tripping on acid and it seems like a lot of time's passed. Please...*start the next song.*" Still no monitors.

Other than that though, once the monitors turned on, it was like, "This is fantastic." The enormity of the event scared the shit out of all of us. It's so weird, because when you're there, it feels like all eyes are on you. When you watch it on video, it's like, "Oh, I forgot—when you go to concerts like that, nobody is really paying any attention." There are scattered pockets of enthusiasm, but most everybody else is just standing there, waiting for another act to come on. But it was a great show—I'm glad I had the chance to do it.

Rogers Stevens: I remember thinking at the time that we didn't play very well, but I saw some of that when we did the 'Behind the Music' thing, and I thought it wasn't that bad. Shannon was amazing—he was on another stratosphere. It was just a lot of people, seeing a lot of people that you knew. This crowd situation was so overwhelming.

Kim Smith: Shannon got up there, did his thing, and people were going crazy. He was *amazing* that day. People were trying to grab at him and he was trying to touch people down in the audience—trying to get down in there.

Christopher Thorn: I remember him just going for it—giving 100%.

Tim Devine: Shannon was ever the magnetic spotlight—he pulled it all out that day. He grabbed the spotlight and captured the world's attention. Between the crowd, the press, and a live international video broadcast, literally the whole world was watching.

Paul Cummings: Since Shannon didn't like to use wireless mics, my job that [day] was to make sure his mic cord didn't get tangled up. When you throw those congas out there [Shannon threw conga drums out into the audience during "Time"], they have a pretty nasty spike sticking out of them—the part that attaches to the stand. You could do some real damage to people. It was kind of a joke between Shannon and Mike Osterfeld—I don't know if he bet him that he couldn't get them back or what, but I think Mike did end up getting them back. He's lucky someone didn't get their eye gouged out with that thing.

Miles Tackett: I guess because I played cello at certain parts with my own band, I got a call, and they asked me to come and play. [Shannon's] way of introducing me to the crowd was, "This is Miles—*Miles drinks Pepsi.*" I think it was a Coca Cola sponsored event.

Danny Clinch: I played harmonica with them at Woodstock. Shannon kissed me on the forehead afterwards.

Nicholas Bechtel: When he sang "Soup," and I don't know if it had to do with the wave of emotion of everything that was going on—between Kurt

Cobain and things that were going on with myself—that song is kind of a confession of, "I'd like to let this life go." I'd heard it before when we were in Europe—but when he started singing that, I stood there on the side of the stage and cried like a baby. I couldn't help it. I still get choked up when I hear that song. When he says, *"I'll close my eyes and make you all go away."*

Tim Devine: I remember we lucked out, because all of the news magazines were on a tight deadline, and the photographer from Time Magazine was standing there taking pictures. They were immediately taking their photos, getting in a van, and heading down to New York City, to get those photos all processed and laid out—this was in the days before digital. Basically, they put their article together that night—the first night of the festival. It was a Friday/Saturday/Sunday affair, and that magazine article, entitled 'Woodstock Nation,' came out the following Monday. It was on the stands across America with a big center spread lead photo of Shannon in his white dress, serenading the Woodstock nation. So this was a time when they had succeeded in capturing the media spotlight in a big way—from the 'naked cover' of Rolling Stone, Time Magazine, MTV, Letterman, etc.

Nicholas Bechtel: At Woodstock, I have the most incredible picture. We just came off the stage—Chris Farley used to show up all the time when we were in the area. Shannon jumps up into Chris Farley's arms, Chris is holding him, Shannon's legs are wrapped around his stomach and he's hugging the hell out of him. Chris looks up at me and gives me this big thumbs up. I've got that picture. We had Chris Farley's picture of when he dressed like the bee girl on our laminate. I remember the first time I met Chris, we played Roseland. We came offstage and there was Chris standing against the wall—that same, sweet personality, *"Hey, how are ya!?"* Just real happy.

Rogers Stevens: The backstage thing was a mess—a lot of pushing and shoving. It seemed like it was almost out of control. I remember Shannon and I went off stage, walked into this trailer right off the back of the stage to smoke a joint, and Henry Rollins was in there doing push ups! We were like, *"Please...don't...hurt...us!"*

Riki Rachtman: As a band, all of a sudden, Blind Melon got big, and then it was just totally different. The only thing to blame it on—pure and simple—was the drugs. *The drugs fucked Shannon up.* To the point that I saw him at Woodstock, he looked at me, and he didn't even know who I was. It was not the Shannon we all knew.

Paul Cummings: On those kind of shows, you get your dressing rooms, but you only get it between these hours and those hours. So you've got to vacate. It took quite a long time to get back—we had to do two loads in the helicopter, and I think the band got in the helicopter on the first load. The helicopter powered up to take off, came back down, the doors opened, and everybody ran out. Apparently, some light came on that wasn't supposed to come on, so the pilot shut it down and told everybody, "Get out, get out!" That was it for that helicopter—we had to wait another hour for another.

Brooks Byrd Graham: We didn't stay for the evening. Shannon did—he took a bunch of video and was really excited about it. He talked his way on the stage [for the Red Hot Chili Peppers' set] and filmed it.

Paul Cummings: I think that show went fairly well, actually. And then, they were kind of forgotten after the Nine Inch Nails thing—Nine Inch Nails seemed to steal the show, with the mud and all that.

Christopher Thorn: It's weird—we got mixed reviews. We got some bad reviews from that show, maybe I don't remember because I was kinda numb. I didn't think we sucked. Those shows are hard because you don't get a soundcheck and the stage is so gigantic, you can't hear anybody else—you feel disconnected in a sense. The audience was great. It was just afterwards, reading reviews—people saying we missed the mark.

Lyle Eaves: That was a miserable show for me—the sound system *sucked.* Joe Cocker got in the night before and did a soundcheck, and I think had his own console and stuff. They threw us in there with no soundcheck of any kind—it was just, "Hook up and go," which I don't even like doing at a damn club show. The sound guys there did not have it together at all. I was real unhappy with the live sound. As soon as I fought my way 45 minutes through the crowd to make it backstage, Glen's wife, Brooks, told the band that it sounded terrible. So that was the first thing I had to deal with coming off the show.

And Shannon's tripping on acid—so that was not a good conversation. I had to try to candycoat that. It's not [Brooks'] fault—she stood out there and watched, Joe Cocker started out sounding great, and then watched us, which started out as a giant train wreck, and then slowly started getting it together throughout the show. Going back and listening to the [recording], it was a good performance. But it was just a bad day personally for everybody.

Shannon Hoon: Yeah, it was a travesty. The thing I liked about Glastonbury was that there was a far less emphasis on corporate backing. In America, you can't put on a big show without a million lawyers firing lawsuits about. The reason the first Woodstock was such a success was because it was so disorganized, and came together naturally. This time, Woodstock was so organized that it ended up kinda chaotic. Any community spirit was suppressed by organization. But I do have fond memories of that gig.

Rolling Stones Tour

*After their Woodstock appearance, Blind Melon take some time off,
and hope to focus on writing their sophomore album in late 1994. But
instead of sticking closely to the plan, they accept an invitation to open a
string of outdoor stadium dates for their heroes, the Rolling Stones.*

Nicholas Bechtel: We came back from Woodstock, and got word that we
were going out with the Rolling Stones.

Rogers Stevens: When you're asked by the Stones, you must serve. It's like
being asked to be Secretary of State or something. I don't think we were particularly ready to go on tour from a personal standpoint, but it's one of those
things you can't turn down.

Paul Cummings: We get [to Mile High Stadium], and Mick Jagger's assistant
comes down, and says, "Mick would like to meet the band." They all went
down there to meet Mick Jagger. I wasn't there, but he said something about
it was nice to have them there, and if there's anything you need, blah blah
blah. They were nice to us. I remember those shows being weird for the fact
that they refused to play "No Rain" on that tour. They had become one of
those bands that hate their hit—at least at that point. I couldn't understand it,
but it's not my call. That probably would have been the only song that crowd
would have recognized. But it was very pleasant—we were treated well. The
catering was good, we got our little 'Voodoo Lounge' sticker set.

Glen Graham: The best playing we ever did, without question—and I hope
there are tapes of these shows—were the Rolling Stones opening [shows]. To
me, *that was it*. That was the pinnacle of our whole everything. I remember
standing there before the first show, Chris Jones looking at me, saying, "I
can see that you have the expression on your face like you're confident and

calm, but I know that you're freaking out inside." I was like, "You know what man? I feel totally at ease—I feel better than I've ever felt in my life." Mainly because we were staying at such nice hotels, most of which had lap pools. I was a swimmer when I was growing up, so I did laps in the afternoon before the shows, and was as clear headed as I ever got back then.

It was just incredible. One of my personal dreams. You could say, "This is your rock dream." There was a film called 'Let's Spend the Night Together'—it was an '80s Stones concert—and it's indoors some and outdoors some. And the outdoor thing at the very beginning, they had this curtain across the stage. The opening shot is behind Charlie Watts' drum riser, and they open the curtain. And as they open it, the guys come out. I used to watch that over and over again—"How cool would it be to be in the Rolling Stones?" And then to be in the situation where you walk out on the Rolling Stones' stage, and there's the Rolling Stones' crowd! It made no difference to us whatsoever that people could care less that we were there. We played much better than we played at that Metro show that was videotaped ['Live at the Metro']—far, far better.

Owen Orzack: It was great—huge, colossal stadium shows. We had a lot of days off, because we played every other day. The band did O.K. I never saw them get trounced or booed. For some reason, Shannon at those huge stadium shows did not want to use a wireless microphone. So he had this wired mic taped to the cable, with a hundred foot long cable. He'd run from side to side—hooking lights. Absolutely causing mayhem as usual.

Nicholas Bechtel: I had to be his 'cable page.' He would go blazing all the way as far as he could go, and I would be holding it—to the point that if he goes any further he's going to start yanking it possibly out of the snake. The band would just step back because they knew.

Danny Clinch: When they opened for the Stones, I remember them playing in the rain in Philly—going balls-to-the-wall, and Shannon going completely crazy. That was a great memory. The stage was wet, so he was running and just flying on the ground, and splashing in the puddles. Sliding all around.

Rogers stripped down to his underwear—he was wearing his boxers. Shannon fell to the ground, and Rogers went over and put his foot on top of him—like 'the conqueror.' He was up for that, for sure.

Nicholas Bechtel: It was pouring down rain—I mean *relentless*. Blind Melon put on one of the most incredible shows I've ever seen, and they got that entire stadium pumped. That was probably one of the most electric shows I'd ever seen in my life.

Glen Graham: One time, during "Time," in the mid-section where it breaks down—it's basically just Brad, Shannon, and me—I got up and ran down the right side ramp in front of the P.A. All the way down to the end, just to experience what a frontman experiences every night—realizing that fortunately, people aren't noticing me. On the way back, the wireless receiver for my ear monitors came unplugged and fell off. So somewhere on the long run back— and it was a hell of a lot farther than it seemed on the way out there—I realize I have no monitors. I barely made it back in time. All the while realizing, "I can't hear anything, *this is not good.*" Ran back, jumped in the seat, and kicked back into the song. I realized that being a frontman, that takes another kind of person. But it was a personal thrill for me!

Bill Armstrong: I remember going and eating dinner with the Rolling Stones with those guys. The whole thing is surreal. Like, here's your friends and then all of a sudden, you're sitting there a year or two later, talking to Mick Jagger. I'll tell you what my best memory of it is—it's not so much to do with the shows, but the band's ability to include the people who were friends of their's in those events. Rogers called me up and said, "You've got to come out—*we're opening for the Stones!*" Those guys had these real big career milestones, and as opposed to doing what some bands do—calling and telling you how great it is, and what life is like from the other side—Rogers especially went out of his way to include me in all of these things, that really weren't any of my business. All of those guys always made me feel like somehow, I was a part of it as well. And I think that they had that ability to do that with their fans. I really felt like I was a part of their success. Not in creating it or having anything to do with it, but I just felt like they allowed me to participate in it with them.

Rogers Stevens: When you do those kinds of things opening for a band like that, it's a big stadium that's half full. And there's very little feedback energy from the crowd—you just get into the fact that you're opening for the Stones...*and that there's a giant metal snake hanging over your head.* The stage is so big and you're so spread out. It's hard to really connect the dots in that way. But some of them were fun—it was really cool getting to hang with those guys.

I remember being in Memphis—we were staying at the Peabody. I had a bunch of family that came up for that show, and we'd been out—totally hammered after the show. So we end up in the bar of the Peabody at 2:00 or 3:00 in the morning, getting ready to call it a night, and Keith comes down with his bodyguard to the bar, from his room. And is just going out. We were like, "Fuck! There you go—*that's why he's him and we're us.*" But those guys were total gentlemen—no problems, no attitudes. They talked to us like we were actual human beings, which just made my life.

It's fucking great. Mick is running the show, tapping away on a laptop, and Keith and Ron are having very tall drinks by 3:00 in the afternoon. They have a snooker table, and Brad is playing snooker with Ron Wood. And Charlie's hanging out, totally dapper in his suit. Just really sweet people—really, really cool.

Christopher Thorn: Brad's a really good pool player, so he was playing pool with Ronnie Wood. We would go, hang out with Brad, and watch him play pool with Ron Wood. We got invited to their little lounge a couple of days into the tour. We weren't hanging out and high-fiving every time—it was so intimidating just to be around them. But they were all really nice. It wasn't that they were un-cool, it's just hard to exchange phone numbers with Keith Richards—you're in awe of being in the same room with him. But my memories of that tour were great. Although there was some drugs going on, the shows were fun. We felt like we were on top of the world—you're opening for the Stones, you're playing to shitloads of people. We were flying from show to show—we weren't even in a bus. To keep up with the Stones' schedule, we had to fly.

Lyle Eaves: When we were out with the Stones, Mick had this little section of stage, that was made out of—and I don't remember if this is B.S. or not—but they told me it was the floor out of his grandmother's house. It was inlayed into the stage. And it was the only thing wooden on the stage—it's where Mick stood. And Opie, who was Guns N' Roses' production manager, told me, "Whatever you do, *y'all cannot scratch, touch, or hurt this floor.* That's the only rule—you can do anything on stage you want, but don't mess with this floor. So make sure Shannon knows it." And I said, "There's no way in hell I'm telling Shannon not to touch the floor—because that's the first thing he's going to do."

So we got carpet padding and carpet, and taped it over this thing, so you couldn't even see it. Well about two shows into it, Opie takes it upon himself to tell Shannon what this floor is and to make sure he doesn't touch it. So guess what Shannon does that night? He puts his mic stand through it. *Completely through it.* They charged Shannon—I still have a copy of the invoice— $2,500.00, to overnight a new floor from England to the next show.

Glen Graham: We were doing bad, bad drugs on that tour. That was our, "We're touring with the Rolling Stones—let's experiment with heroin, *that would be fun.*" And when I say experiment, I mean literally, experiment. Unfortunately, for Shannon, this spiraled into a bad situation. We should have known better, and we didn't. Nobody got addicted to heroin...yet. Of course, Shannon was probably already. No one will ever know.

Nicholas Bechtel: I myself was a heroin user—I snorted. I knew then and there that you do that on your own time. You don't drop down with the band when they're doing it, because you're out there doing something else. I never will forget, I knew some stuff was going on—I think it started in Memphis. I remember the band went on, and Chris Jones turned to me, and he goes, "I got to ask you something. Shannon was on *something* last night—I don't know what it was, but it wasn't blow." I looked at him, and it was like a crystal light hit me. I love Shannon to death, but I ratted him out—I told him exactly what was going on. That thing definitely escalated real fast on that tour.

Christopher Thorn: This sounds like I should be in A.A., but I don't think us experimenting with drugs at that point was effecting the shows. We weren't doing drugs and playing the shows—we were playing the shows and then doing the drugs afterwards [laughs]. We were being stupid. It's hard when your heroes are doing those drugs, and you're like, "Wow, look at them playing to millions of people and having great careers." You just assume that there's no downfall to doing those drugs—even though there's plenty of stories. We all know a lot of people have died from those drugs. But when you're young, you think there are no consequences. I can't say that all of us in the band were doing them, but some of us were experimenting.

Paul Cummings: The last show was in Ames, Iowa—they had all their pictures taken together [with the Stones], although I never saw those pictures. I don't think even Chris Jones has a copy of that.

Rogers Stevens: There's a picture that I really wish I had, that's just us and them—the whole band line-up picture. I never saw it. I was arm-in-arm with Keith in the picture, and I remember when I put my arm around him, *he's built like a fucking rock.* You think, oh, you're going to break him in half. But when you grab him—he's totally hard.

Nicholas Bechtel: At the end of it, the very last night, I saw the monster that Shannon could turn into—that I was warned about when I got hired. We were in Ames, Iowa. We had finished the tour, and he had gotten belligerently drunk. I said I'd deal with it and I'll get him to the hotel. His hotel was a wreck—I got him packed and to the airport. You know that time when you're sobering up and you're going to have a serious hangover? By the time I got back to the hotel, Paul goes, "I just got a screaming fit from Shannon—his plane was postponed." So there he was in Ames, Iowa, completely drunk and coming out of his stupor, and his plane has been postponed. It wasn't a pretty scene.

Here's the thing that I saw that night. You know when you get the retarded kid to say cuss words and everybody laughs? It's like he was getting fueled [by] the drinks that night, and they were watching Shannon go into this mode.

From my perspective, I was like, "Dude...*what are you doing?*" It was something that everyone had been used to from the very beginning. I came from a different area of schooling—I mean, I went from kindergarten to college with the Black Crowes. When I saw Shannon turn into this person and everyone kind of laugh at it, it really pissed me off. That night was insane. He picked up a huge vase and threw it—tried to throw it out the window of the hotel, but it didn't hit. And it's the alcohol. The pot and everything, he's whatever—but when he's on the alcohol, that was a different story.

'Soup' Recording

Despite attempts to steer clear of alcohol and drugs, Shannon succumbs to temptation throughout the recording of Blind Melon's sophomore album, 'Soup.' Produced by Andy Wallace, the group records—and some members live—at a New Orleans studio, Kingsway, owned by renowned singer-songwriter/producer Daniel Lanois.

Christopher Thorn: By the second record we were all writing individually—more so than the first record, and bringing in more complete songs. The first record, we all lived in the house together, we had written the songs together. By the time we got to 'Soup,' everybody was living in different cities. So a lot of the writing happened separately—I was working on my own demos and would play all the instruments, show them to the band, and then we would work it up. We did write some songs together in the room. Shannon and I went to New Orleans and we rehearsed for about a month or so—we pulled together a lot of songs in about a month. Everybody came to the party with a bunch of songs. I lived in the back of Rogers' house in New Orleans, and we rehearsed there. I have great memories of that period of time, too—we knew how to work together, how to get the job done, and were really efficient at it. I think having time off after such a long tour, everybody was sorta refreshed. By the time we got together for 'Soup,' we were firing away.

Shannon Hoon: That was a testing time, I think, for all of us in a lot of ways. Making the new record and trying to alleviate the pressure of following up the first record, which surprised us. And I think that being in an environment where your willpower is definitely tested—some nights prevailing, some nights not—you were posed with a lot of different questions and scenarios. We were like, "O.K., here we go. Now, were we just lucky, or do we really know how to put together a record that is a record, as opposed to making a record with singles on it?" Whatever played a part in [that experience], I had to take home with me.

Rogers Stevens: There were songs that were written while [the first album's tour] was happening, and a lot of it was written afterwards. We were just sick of each other. I lived a block away from Brad and we didn't even see each other hardly. But that was over a period of a couple months, when everyone was trying to gather themselves and coming up with ideas. We found Kingsway, and were gearing up to go in there. We'd moved all of our stuff into my house, and started rehearsing and writing. We had a few things—I remember at one point we recorded in the basement of a hotel in St. Louis [during the first album's tour], they had some sorta ballroom down there. We had a few days, and just moved in there—we recorded "St. Andrews Hall" and "2x4," but they're demos.

Miles Tackett: I remember playing the Jeff Buckley album ['Grace'] on our way to Woodstock, if I'm not mistaken. We were all in a van together, and I played it for them. I was a big fan of Jeff Buckley's and was playing it for everyone I could. That might have been part of their introduction to working or talking with Andy Wallace.

Mike Napolitano: Andy Wallace was the producer—as far as the work, it was pretty regimented. Other than occasionally not being able to find Shannon, I think it went probably as most of his sessions go. He demands authority.

Shannon Hoon: Andy was a psychiatrist as well as a producer. There was an eight-foot groove in the floor behind his producer's chair where he would slide back and constantly go "Whoooah!" at some idea that one of us had. By the end, we all understood each other real well. *Real well.*

Brad Smith: Kingsway is a beautiful place—it's an old, turn of the century mansion in the French Quarter. Maybe 18th century—it was *old.*

Miles Tackett: It was an old Victorian house—really cool. They were living in rooms in this house—it was one of those really good 'live-in-studio' situations. It was a really beautiful environment to record.

Shannon Hoon: There was so much to do down there the main focus wasn't making the record. Which basically made the air about making the record more comfortable. The city has so much to corrupt you with, so much to distract you with. There's so many elements about that city that are dangerously entertaining.

Mike Napolitano: My first impression of Shannon was that he was off his rocker, which turned out to be dead on [laughs]. It was fairly obvious that Shannon had 'issues,' and they manifested themselves in the way of him just living on the edge—as he did. That was obvious in a minute-to-minute basis for him. As soon as you meet him, you can say, "Oh, you're *that guy.*"

Glen Graham: Chris was living in a hotel before the 'Soup' record, Rogers and I shared a house, basically—a block from Brad and Kim. Everybody was just sort of around. I'm assuming [Shannon] was staying at the Pontchartrain on Saint Charles, which used to be a really nice hotel. [Rogers and Glen] both had little mini-studios. He would record stuff, bring a tape to me, I would overdub drums, and give it back to him. Some of the stuff like "Lemonade" and "Swallowed" came about that way.

I had just moved into the house I purchased on Napoleon Avenue. Rogers then moved into the front part of the house I was renting on Constance Street and we used his vacated apartment in the back of the house as a rehearsal room, which basically meant we showed up and did coke. We worked out "The Duke," "Toes Across the Floor," and a few others. With tiny amps and in the dark. I remember just sitting in the dark, coked to the gills. We were not all coke people—I don't think Brad was doing coke. But the rest of us were. We were ripping our way through those songs. That was a coke-fueled album.

Mike Napolitano: I definitely would say it was a 'classic rock n' roll session.' Especially, you mix in the elements of decadence of the city—it was a New Orleans version of the classic rock n' roll situation. People going berserk.

Chris Smith: New Orleans was a fun and destructive time. Shannon and I had a really good time—we were out of control. We were into riding our bikes around New Orleans. Me and Shannon would leave on our bikes and be gone for a good 24-48 hours at a time. Stopping at every bar we saw, having two drinks at each one, and then moving on to the next. That usually would last until Shannon got arrested. I was right there when Shannon got arrested—sometimes, I think that was his goal. He'd get so drunk and so out of hand that he got arrested and would have a good excuse to fight with the police.

Shannon was a fun guy—people wanted to be around Shannon, and Shannon wanted to be around people. Shannon wanted to be around people that were ready to party. My brother was never into drugs—he smoked pot a couple of times and likes to consider himself a pothead, but I wouldn't say that he ever really was. And he certainly never tried anything beyond smoking pot. But Shannon wanted to be around those people that wanted to really party. By that stage, it was more destructive than anything—it wasn't so much fun as it might have appeared to be. People gravitated towards Shannon because he had money and drugs, was famous, and in a band. So it was easy for Shannon to pick up party people and bring them back to the studio.

Brad Smith: That was total mayhem. At the time, I had just come out of my 'pot haze'—I had stopped smoking weed—but the band wasn't finished with that kind of stuff yet. So there was a lot of cocaine, ecstasy, heroin, marijuana…whatever you want. It was at the studio all the time. And it was *fucking crazy man.* We didn't go into the studio until 2:00 or 4:00 in the afternoon, and nobody left until the sun was coming up. It was a total 'vampire existence,' laced with drugs, alcohol, and fucking craziness. People were there, that I had no idea why they were there. Looking back, it's amazing that we got a record done at all. But again, still, our chemistry was that we had our shit together—everybody in the band could play, and we had this crazy, unspoken telepathy. We finished songs so fast. We got together two months before the record, threw together everyone's ideas, had 26 pieces of music, and recorded 16 for the record. It was so fucking fast it was unbelievable. Bands don't do that these days—it's so over-calculated and over-thought out by all the major labels. It's one reason why they're losing, they're such fucking idiots.

Glen Graham: Fortunately for me I suppose, I had just bought a house in New Orleans—two weeks before we started recording in Kingsway. So I was moving, and there were only four main bedrooms in Kingsway. And we also had a cook for the session, who needed a room. So I decided, "I'm not living here during the recording, I'll just show up at 5:00 each day and stay until we finish." The biggest problem with Shannon and 'Soup' was that he really wasn't that involved. We wrote most of the songs without him and he added lyrics later. I don't know how much singing was actually done in Kingsway. We ran out of time there and Shannon had to finish at Ultrasonic Studios.

I'd show up there at 5:00. I'd get a little bagel sandwich, walk around the corner, walk into Kingsway, and there would be people there. "Who the fuck are these people? Why are they here?" It was coke dealers, basically. I mean, coke dealers don't come up and announce themselves as coke dealers. You think they're somebody's friend from out of town. The way we had it set up, the band was recording upstairs, and the downstairs was a control room situation. It was just a bad scene. Kingsway was good—it was fun, we had a good time recording. I missed out on most of the craziness, thank God. I mean, it was nuts when I was there, but it was apparently much worse when I wasn't there.

Brooks Byrd Graham: It seemed out of control. It was not good, in the fact that Glen was like, "I'm going to do my work and then I'm coming home. I don't want to hang out. [Shannon's] not in a good place—he's going out, finding coke dealers, and bringing them back to the studio. He shouldn't be doing that." It felt bad to be there. I just remember [Shannon] walking around with the bong, but he did that anyway. I think it was because we weren't staying there—I would only go down there when Glen was working. But I had a lot of anxiety then—I didn't want to be around what was going on.

Brad Smith: I remember coming down there and sometimes it would be eerily quiet—at like 2:00 in the afternoon. Nobody was awake, everybody was sleeping. And a couple of people that we had met in New Orleans were in the studio. I remember this one dude on his hands and knees, looking for pieces of cocaine and crack in the carpet. I found out later that there was a bunch of people there doing coke, and this guy was so fucking hooked and crazy that he stayed there the whole morning, looking for crumbs of coke in the carpet.

Lyle Eaves: I brought equipment down to them, because that's only a couple hours from where I live in Jackson, Mississippi. I would help them with a couple of things, but I did not stay with them. The band talked about it, like he was borderline out of control the whole time. I walked in the studio one day, and I didn't recognize [Shannon]—he had cut his hair and dyed it blonde. Super short. He walked up to the side of me and I didn't really look at him, because I didn't know who he was. He started talking, and I was like, *"Oh."*

Jena Kraus: When I came to New Orleans, when I first got there, I walked into the kitchen. And [Shannon] was eating a bowl of cereal. I did a double take—I wasn't expecting him to have a shaved head. When I went to Mammoth Mountain around April 1994, he had short hair then. Then around Woodstock, after that, he grew dreads. At some point he bleached his hair, and then shaved it.

Bill Armstrong: I don't do drugs, but I drank a lot at the time. But I remember thinking to myself, "Man, that's a crazy place to record your record—it feels like that's definitely the Devil's workshop down there." Knowing that Shannon's a 'man of extremes,' that certainly is an extreme place. *Extremely unhealthy.*

Domenique Johansson: It's weird that they picked New Orleans, but there was this 'thing' for New Orleans. Shannon was definitely in a pretty hazy state during that whole time.

Shelley Shaw: I went down to New Orleans during those sessions—in November of that year—and [Shannon] was a stranger to me. He was not bouncing off the walls so much, as it was like a 'lurking around in the shadows' kind of Shannon. We had always been close, been able to talk, and spend 'alone time'—and really hash things out. It was a really special thing. And he had a way of getting into these headspaces where he could be cruel and alienating—and just disappear. And that's who I found in New Orleans. It wasn't a very memorable or pleasant trip in that way. My history was with him, and I worked hard on knowing the rest of the guys and doing good work for them as a whole. But the divisiveness that was created by his behavior…in my alliance with him, there was always a little weirdness. Like, I come from his past and he's the problem right now, so we're a unit. It's not like they confided in me—it's not like I had that 'individual relationship' with the rest of them. So when he was 'off and gone,' it was very business-like and strange.

Shannon Hoon: Recording in New Orleans was an incredible experience. It's far more eccentric than L.A. Drugs are no less illegal than they are everywhere else, but they are readily available anyway. It led to some erratic behavior on our part. There was so much going on that it alleviated any pressure we might have felt. I sit and think of New Orleans, and I can't actually remember making this record.

Christopher Thorn: I remember one night we took ecstasy, and Shannon's just totally out of his mind. Shannon has this screwdriver, and he's claiming to stab himself in the stomach with this screwdriver. We're trying to get the screwdriver out of his hand. And then he cut himself with glass that same night—I think he broke a glass and ripped up his chest. The memories are so blurry because it was such a haze of craziness. There was so much drama going on. Shannon was so paranoid because he was doing way too much cocaine—he thought I was spying on him through his window. He came to my room, "Why have you been spying on me?" I'm like, "Man, I'm trying to go to sleep. I don't know what you're talking about." So much of our energy during the recording of that record was 'talking Shannon off the ledge'—just making sure he wasn't too nuts.

I have memories of waking up at 2:00 in the afternoon, going down and having breakfast in the kitchen, and seeing Shannon still up from the night before, cooking cocaine up on the stove. And me eating breakfast at the same time. And what's fucked up about it is me feeling like it was just another normal day in the life of Blind Melon. I mean, I should have been, "Hey, this is fucked up—*we're taking you to rehab today!*" At that point, we got so used to living in that insanity, it just became so normal for us to be like, "Oh, Shannon's on a bender." I regret not taking control of the situation and saying, "We're taking you to rehab today—that's fucked up. You're not supposed to be cooking cocaine on the stove as I'm eating breakfast." At a certain point, it got so exhausting—fighting about drugs and all that stuff—that you sort of gave up. Or at least I did.

Jena Kraus: When I went there, yes, he was doing drugs. He was out of control—worse than I had seen him. I remember some crazy things. One morning at 7:00, he came in with two strangers, and he's like, "Jena, break out the wine glasses!" We were at the top of the stairs—these big massive stairs, and he was drunk. He rolled down all of the stairs, hit the couch at the bottom of the stairs—moved the couch halfway across the room—and then popped up like a gymnast. Like nothing had happened. He did start doing drugs that he didn't normally, that I never knew him to do. He advanced to smoking crack. But even though he was doing that, he wasn't like a crackhead. I mean, seeing crackheads on the street—he wasn't like that. He wasn't doing it in that way. He did do it here and there—I think he was a guy that was experimenting. And being a little self-destructive...or a lot.

Miles Tackett: I remember they had a groovy hippie chef who was cooking up meals.

Rogers Stevens: I had a house there in New Orleans, so a lot of times, I left late at night, and I'd hear about stuff in the morning. I mean, *we were partying our asses off*—not in a productive way. It was fucking stupid. Really stupid—bad ideas all around. I had a high school friend, Jeff Clark, who was cooking for us at the time—he had gone to cooking school—and also partying with the band, unfortunately. One night I got a call from him, totally upset—in tears—because Shannon had gotten fucked up and smashed all of his CD's. He's one of these guys that really liked to collect music, and he had a massive CD collection. I think Shannon got hammered and smashed them as a joke. Stuff like that was happening all the time. It was destructive and a lot of it at the time probably seemed funny and cute, but looking back on it, it was just sad. That was really to me where everything went south. It became not recreational drug use anymore on an inconsistent level. It was consistent. Looking back, I really have a lot of guilt about it. I feel also bad for the people in the band that weren't doing it, and had to deal with it. Even if you did do it every now and then, it took the fun out of it—people doing it way more.

Jena Kraus: I remember there were two times in New Orleans that Shannon was sleeping, and I was there. He was like gurgling in his sleep and I was so freaked out—I got Christopher and I was like, "Oh my God, we've got to turn him over!" Him and I, we had to flip him over, and he was really heavy. Because we were worried that he was going to throw up in his sleep or something. We didn't know—he was making weird noises in his sleep, and he had stayed up for two days. He sort of got excited about things like that, which is really weird. You know how teenagers party and brag about it later? It was that kind of a thing—he thought it was kind of cool. He wasn't down about it, but maybe he didn't take it that seriously.

Shannon Hoon: When I think about the record, and making it, and all those stories, and nonmusical type things that went on there, I don't know how our album got made.

Danny Clinch: I remember him cutting up his belly or something, when they were recording 'Soup.' He was drinking a lot of wine. He definitely seemed to be indulging in a lot of drugs and stuff. I was down there way too short of a time—like three days. I documented a little bit down there, and then I left. He was in his own world at that point. He didn't really listen too much to anybody—he was just doing his thing. I remember him cutting up his belly, and when we took that photograph of him on the balcony [seen on the book cover]. That balcony was rotting away. He had no problem standing up there—hanging over the edge. I was scared for him, I said, "Let me just get this picture quick, so he'll step down."

I wanted to get an individual portrait of everybody in the band, so I took Glen, Rogers, Brad, and Christopher over there. I was trying to find Shannon, and I finally found him. It was a spot that was really visually cool up there in Kingsway—it was like this balcony that looked over Esplanade. There was this beautiful, old porch—with all that wrought iron. So I shot a picture of him hanging in that doorway, which is on the cover of my 'Discovery Inn' book. And then he climbed up there. He was like, "How about his, Danny?" I was like, "Oh, geez dude—I'm scared of heights. Stop that!" He's like, "Get this one, get this one!"

Mike Osterfeld: [Danny's photo] epitomizes Shannon Hoon. He had gone so far over the deep end for that album. He had taken himself into the darkest depths of his soul.

Rogers Stevens: It was doom and gloom in the Kingsway house when I went in there. Apparently [Shannon] was 'amusing' himself with a razor blade—freaking everybody out.

Jena Kraus: As for "Shannon versus the razor blade"—that was, well, during a night of *a lot* of ecstasy being consumed. Scary as it sounds, on x many things seem to feel quite good, even what normally produces pain somehow translates into chills of pleasure—such as dragging a razor blade across the skin in the shape of a tic-tac-toe board stretching the length of a bare chest. I wasn't actually there for that—I came there the next day. I remember him talking about it, and the cuts on his chest.

Lisa Sinha: I went down there a couple of times during the recording. I stayed away a little bit, but during that time, there was lots of drug use. I felt like he was not himself at all—just wild and crazy. I went down there, one night he was in the hospital—the first night I got there. They're like, "We didn't want to tell you," and I get there, and he's not even there—he's getting released from the hospital. *His kidneys were probably having a hard time processing the drugs.* He had shaved his head—he was just not himself. He was really raw—I was worried about him.

Shannon Hoon: New Orleans is just a city that enhances every kind of...madness. They say that the Devil was born there and I'm not too sure he wasn't born in the room I had to sleep in! It brought the werewolf out in me, man! That city will clean your pores, man.

Christopher Thorn: That was another night during the 'Soup' recording that blew my fucking mind. He pulled me aside—he had a really bad night, he was doing drugs. He told me that he was afraid to be in a room by himself, because he felt like his soul would attack him. He was saying crazy things to me—and I knew he was really out of his mind. And he told me he had a black heart. I was like, "Dude, *that's deep.* You need help—this is fucked up. What happened?" I think he had reached a real bottom. But I think we were all so in our own little world, that maybe we were all too fucked up to spend the energy to focus on him. "*You're* even more fucked up—we need to get you help." That night scared me though, because I'd never heard anybody say that before. That's one thing to do drugs and you're experimenting, but he definitely had a problem. He should have gone to rehab. I just thought, "God, to say that, that's so dark." Because for me, he had the opposite—*the biggest heart.* I'll never forget him saying that. And I didn't know what to do, I didn't know what to say to help him. I felt so helpless. What do you say when somebody says that? "You're a great guy Shannon, we love you?" You can't help somebody at that point.

Jena Kraus: During the 'Soup' thing, there was a time when he was eating a bowl of cereal—he was very emotional and crying, and saying that he didn't want to die. And he felt that his heart was black—I don't know why he felt that way.

Mike Napolitano: I do remember [Shannon] one time being upset about all the stuff that was going on, and how people were trying to think of ways to get more out of everything. And he goes, "*More is something I don't need any more of right now.*"

Jena Kraus: I know all about [Shannon] getting arrested. He was drunk. He may have been with Brad's brother, Chris.

Chris Smith: That was one of our 'tour of the bars' on bicycles. It had been me, Shannon, and Christopher all day. I think we started around 10:00 or 11:00 that morning, and went from the Garden District down to the French Quarter and back. We were at the last bar—about a block away from my house—called Le Bon Temps Roulette. We were off our heads by this point. There was a lot of drinks, probably a little cocaine, and we go to this bar. Christopher didn't stop at the last bar. Shannon went to close out his tab, and it was a ridiculous amount of money. He started to get out of control with the bartender—apparently, other people were putting their drinks on Shannon's tab. I'm standing at the other end of the bar watching. There are three guys sitting at the bar that were off-duty police officers—one of them was the bartender's boyfriend. So Shannon lunged at the bartender—he wasn't going to grab her or anything—he was drunk and out of his head, and was trying to figure out his bar tab and was agitated.

As soon as he leaned in her direction, those guys jumped on him. They saw it coming, and they didn't like the 'rock star guy' there. Before it even happened, they had already grabbed him, and they knew I was with him, because they sent somebody down there to grab me. Dragged us both outside—they handcuffed me to a fire hydrant and were kicking me. And two of them were over there [fighting with] Shannon. They were putting up a really good fight—it took two of them. Finally I told the cop, "I'm not even with this guy," and they let me go. So I go to unlock mine and Shannon's bikes. They finally get Shannon in the cop car. I looked at Shannon and motioned to him to calm down—he looked at me, rocked back with his handcuffs, and kicked the window out of the cop car. I just turned around and left. I went to Rogers' house, where Shannon's girlfriend, Brad, Kim, Heather, and Rogers' girlfriend all were. They immediately knew something was going on. They were like, "Where's Shannon?" I'm like, "He's in the back of a cop car—completely out of control."

Christopher Thorn: We get word that Shannon got himself in trouble. So we all run down there. They're putting him in handcuffs, he's spitting at cops, getting ready to kick the windshield out. Just being a total ass. I say to the cop, "Where are you taking him? I just need to know, so we can come bail him out." And the guys goes, "Oh, you're with him?" And the next thing I know, the cop punches me in the face. I'm handcuffed and I'm taken to jail with Shannon. It happened so fast. I remember I'd just smoked a little bit of pot—it was the end of the night, I was relaxing. I was getting ready to go to bed, and the next thing I know, I spend the night in jail. And the fucked up thing about this is, if you're such a mess, and if you're screaming, yelling, and being really obnoxious, you get your own cell! But if you're a nice, quiet guy like myself—you're in the jail with 50 brothers. And I'll never forget—the cell smelled *so fucking bad.* Like a bunch of socks and dirty underwear. I had a watch, and I used to put amber on it—for whatever reason—on the wrist-band. I remember sitting there all night, with my legs up, just sniffing my watch, so I could not smell the stench of this jail cell. And the other fucked up thing—Shannon had access to a phone! So he's in there making phone calls all night, and I'm stuck in a jail cell with a bunch of people. I spent the night in jail, all for saying, "I want to bail my friend out. Where are you taking him?"

Jena Kraus: [Christopher] had called me at like 3:00 in the morning and I talked to him for like six hours—the whole time he was in jail. He was really worried about Shannon—at one point, I heard this horrible banging noise. It sounded like metal hitting metal. Christopher was like, "Do you hear that noise? *That's Shannon's head hitting the bars.*"

Rogers Stevens: Shannon was in jail a long time for that one—two days or something. He was calling us collect every 15 minutes, telling us what was going on. I was on the phone with him once, and I hear a cop come in and say something, and I hear Shannon say, "Well, that would be hard to do if you had to look up from your donut!" And then you hear [mimics sounds of punches]—the phone hangs up. They beat the crap out of him. They let him out, we go and get him, and he's coming out arm-and-arm with these two other inmates that had been released. They're like, "Man, this guy totally entertained us for two days!" He looked like hell. It was terrible, but kind of funny in a way.

Kim Smith: He was bad at that point—*really bad.* To the point where he actually rented a hotel room down the street from the studio—just to get him out of that environment. Away from the studio, where all the weirdoes would come out to.

Mike Napolitano: When the sessions started, I didn't really know who Blind Melon was and I wasn't familiar with their music. But during the course of the session, I came to realize that this is a *really good band.* In the classic sense of a good rock band—they actually play together, and regardless of credits, definitely wrote together. They used each other's talents in the process of building the song.

Shannon Hoon: There's no way we could have made this record before now. It was the information overload we experienced together on tour that led to our having the intensity to create this record. Three years ago, we were too young to really know what direction we wanted to pursue. We were still getting to know each other as people, and this record is confirmation of how our friendship has grown. We've come to terms with how to use the friction in the band in a productive manner. You don't have to be getting along like best buddies to write a great song.

Christopher Thorn: I felt like we were making incredible music—like we were making our best work. Our record that was going to prove us to not be the band that was just the '"No Rain" band.' I still believe in that record. That is still my favorite record, and I was so proud of it. Even though it was crazy and insane—all that stuff fueled the creativity. I hate to say that, but it's the truth. All that craziness for me...I don't think you need that, but for whatever reason, at that time, it felt like it was adding to what was getting on tape.

Shannon Hoon: [Brad] wrote some lyrics on the first record, but on this record I wrote all the lyrics.

Brad Smith: I'd written lyrics for songs like "Galaxie," "Toes Across the Floor," and "New Life"—those were my pieces of music that I brought into the band. They did have lyrics, melody lines, and singing attached to them, but Shannon just threw those right out the window [laughs]! Shannon was a real artist—he didn't want to sing someone else's lyrics. That guy could write lyrics for days. In one breath, I don't blame him, but in another breath, what was a big part of Blind Melon's appeal was that these lyrics came from a bunch of different people, so you get a broader slice of American life and observation.

On the second record, Shannon wrote all the lyrics, and everybody brought in songs. Christopher brought in five or six pieces, I brought in five or six pieces, Glen brought in "Car Seat." That was the biggest hand he had had in any song in Blind Melon—it was great. Glen is always musical and he's a writer, but he would never write for the band, because he comes from more of a jazz/alternative background. He probably felt like nothing would fit. Shannon came in with songs like "Walk" and "St. Andrews Hall," Rogers came in with crazy stuff like "Lemonade," and "2x4" and "Wilt" were written by the band in a rehearsal hall together. It was a crazy time because it was so fast and we were so in tune with each other on a musical level. You look back on those days and how productive they were, and I remember at the time, complaining that we weren't getting enough done. Like, "What the fuck? We're not getting these songs finished, we're not getting them done in time." I was impatient, young, and probably much confused. I look back on it now, and I'm like, "Jesus man, *we were one of the most prolific bands around.*"

Shannon Hoon: We're not all best friends; there's a lot of friction in this band but we've productively learned how to use it. We all have a common denominator as far as respect for each other.

Rogers Stevens: There's things about it that I like, and there's things about it that I don't like. The production value…and this is not a knock on Andy, because he did a great job of getting that album made—the album doesn't sound as good as the rough mixes. Andy is amazing to watch in the studio, and the way he mixes. Obviously, he's one of the best, and he gets the call time and again, because he makes the shit sound huge on the radio. That's the way he did our thing, and maybe it was good for it, I don't know. It's just personally not my way of doing things. It's O.K. There's a couple of songs I'm not in love with, some I really like.

Brad Smith: It's too bad that we didn't challenge each other on lyrics, arrangements, and guitar lines—and even songs picked for the record. There are a few songs on 'Soup' that I fucking hate. And certain songs that didn't even make the record that should have been on the record, like [the song] "Soup." "Soup" isn't even on the 'Soup' record! It's just asinine. I think that's a testament to how bad our relationships had gotten in a way. It was functioning— we weren't dysfunctional. It just wasn't very healthy.

Rogers Stevens: That was at a point where we were at odds with each other over the direction of the band, and how we were doing things. It was a big fight over what songs and how the record should sound.

Jena Kraus: Before I left New Orleans, I had sung Shannon a couple of songs—we were in my room. I had to go get the plane, and he was like, "I'm going to pack up your guitar for you." He did, and when I got home, I take out my guitar, and he snuck a little note on my guitar. It said "Jena, you are one of a kind and love is all around you always. Shannon."

Rogers Stevens: I think the title and that [album cover] concept was Shannon's. I remember having a 'whatever' attitude about it. It didn't particularly impress me as an idea—I just wasn't really feeling it. I didn't hate it, so it happened. Y'know, "Hey Andy, do this" [Andy Wallace appears on the album cover]. Danny Clinch came down, they set it up—I think it was done at a diner in New Orleans.

Chris Smith: 'Soup' still blows my mind. It's such an elaborate piece of artwork—if I listen to it right now, I'd hear something that I didn't hear before.

Shannon Hoon: It's very hard for me to think of any song on this record on its own. To me, they all belong together. We put a lot of thought into the sequencing. It's like the chapters in a book. That's how they were written and that's how they sound best—when they're all played together like that. Really, at no point did we even consider making a single. We were there to make this one long record that wasn't just about one song or whatever, but was about a state of mind or a state of place that was whole.

Lisa Sinha: 'Soup' is an album I just *love*. That, to me, is Shannon's best work.

Nel Hoon: I had to put a lot of things together later, because every time Shannon would do something new, he would send me whatever it was he had done. I had his itinerary of where he was, his phone number—everything. He always sent me a first version of this and a first version of that. And on 'Soup,' he did not do that. After I heard 'Soup' for the first time, I thought it was very dark. I don't know if Shannon thought, "Wow, my mom is going to see through this"—with that funeral march [that opens the album] and all that stuff. There were some great songs on there. But I thought that it was dark.

Kim Smith: It was a dark time. But they were making good music.

Heather Thorn: New Orleans was the beginning of the end of everything. It just took a nasty turn down there—as that town does, it seems.

Shannon Hoon: The end result, regardless of how anyone else embraces this record, I see a lot of accomplishment in how we're coping and growing together. I feel like we're proceeding forward, progressing. Our enthusiasm has been reinstated.

'Soup'

Shannon's lyrics were always autobiographical—especially the fourteen tracks that comprise 'Soup.'

Rogers Stevens: The intro part [titled "Hello Goodbye"] was basically the song "Lemonade"—I had that music, and we brought in horn guys. It was the Kermit Ruffins and the Little Rascals Brass Band. They were just a bunch of kids—a New Orleans second line brass band. It was Super Bowl Sunday—we were having a big party. Andy arranged the horns based around the melodies, and those guys just went with it—they were done in 20 minutes. We all felt like terrible musicians—we were spending three months to make an album, and they just did it. The whole intent of that—which ended up being ironic later—was to set up like a New Orleans jazz funeral, where there's a dirge and a march to the funeral. And then the outro of the record is the celebration of leaving the funeral. That's how they do those things—you see them all the time.

Brad Smith: There's not a 'single with a bullet' on the record at all—but there were so many songs that were close. "Galaxie" was really close. I had different lyrics, different melody lines, and Shannon basically didn't even acknowledge them and re-wrote stuff. Which was fine—I couldn't argue with it because he was the singer. But it's a shame that all the relationships in the band had come to that, where things weren't even challenged. At the end of the day, we should have tweaked the songs, and made it more of a concerted effort as a record.

Glen Graham: Brad used to live on Magazine Street in New Orleans. He and Kim had the front apartment. He had a console that was supposedly Creedence Clearwater Revival's board at some point—it was installed in some studio that they used frequently. That may have been some bullshit. But he wrote ["Galaxie"] there—the whole thing. He was playing all the instruments. Then we came in, and gave it 'the Melon treatment.'

Shannon Hoon: [The car] was just my escape, my comfort zone from a lot of places that I found myself during my stay down there. I think a lot of people probably think that [in the song] I'm talking about the galaxies, as in the universe. And I've always liked the idea of wordplay and ambiguously writing about something so simple and making it sound so far out.

Brad Smith: After the first record was done, for some reason, we went back and [rehearsed] in Mississippi again. We needed a place to rehearse, and somebody's parents had keys to this warehouse. We worked up "2x4," "Wilt," and pieces of other songs that never came to be. ["2x4"] was one of the songs that was done in-between records, and two years later, we got to record it. It sat around in the closet forever.

Rogers Stevens: "2x4" was just some riffs that I had and brought into the band. I think I had made a demo of it, and then Shannon wrote those words—I think they're pretty obvious. The verse that I remember is about heroin—"Pouring warm gravy all over me." I love the words, I hate what they're about—but they're so well done.

Glen Graham: From the 'Soup' record, that was one of the more collaborative efforts musically. And I think it sounds like it—it's a little more all over the place than "Galaxie," for instance.

Rogers Stevens: "Vernie" was another one I brought in, and I was really happy with what Shannon did with that. That was a piece of music that I wrote pretty much as you hear it, and the band filled in around it. Shannon wrote those words about his grandmother, who he was quite attached to—a very endearing kind of relationship he had with her. It was really beautiful what he wrote.

Brad Smith: I can't even remember the song—I just remember not liking the song. It reminds me of a Flaming Lips-ish song. I guess it had its place on the record. My general comments about that record is it could have been so much better if it was focused. It was still a great record—some people would contest that it's the best record we've ever done—and that's fine. It is pretty fucking good—we were all mature musicians, we could all play a lot better as musicians. But I still think the songs could have been better.

Shannon Hoon: 'Skinned' though is a happy, skippy kinda song which my mom loves. This guy, Ed Gein, used to make full-bodied suits from women's skin, which he'd dance around in. He'd also make lampshades and coffee tables from their remains.

Christopher Thorn: That was totally done. That was one of those songs that was on a tape—I probably gave [Shannon] like eight things, and "Skinned" was one of the songs. It was a goof—I never thought he would pick that one to sing over. I never would have imagined *anyone* could sing over that one. I remember recording the demo for it in a hotel room, because I had a portable recording thing. One night, he was like, "I wrote lyrics for that, let me sing it." And he sung it in a hotel room, somewhere in the States.

Shannon Hoon: Well, obviously I don't condone this sort of behavior. It's disgusting, but the world creates these subjects and I'm just reporting on them. It's just stuff that fascinates me, even though it horrifies me at the same time. How do you explain the core of evil that makes people, or even a race of people, wish to perpetrate such acts or barbarism? It's just tongue in cheek. There are two sides to the same coin, and you can't take "Skinned" too seriously. After all, it even features a kazoo solo.

Rogers Stevens: "Toes Across the Floor" was a song that Brad had demoed and had done the music for. That was a piece that was brought in with that bass riff. I remember going over to Brad's house and coming up with a guitar riff to go over that—that thing that happens in the verses. He played that a lot—I remember him playing that at soundchecks—and the song was based on that picking bass thing that happens at the beginning of the song. We always really liked that and finally figured out something to do with it. I don't really know what the song is about. I know the thing about God and the dog at the end, that has to do with Robert Hunter's dog—Robert Hunter, the Grateful Dead lyricist guy. He had a dog named God, I think—Shannon thought that was amusing. The stuff was getting really introspective at that time—Shannon was withdrawing into some dark shit for a lot of the songs.

Brad Smith: That was a bass riff I had since Mississippi—when I was going through a Jaco Pastorius phase. He would always do that harmonic thing—he had that song "Portrait of Tracy," which has a lot of harmonics in it, and he made music out of it. So I took his technique, and wrote my own little watered down 'rock version' of what he would do. He was a serious jazz bass player—I'm still fucking nobody as a musician. Everybody always liked that riff, when I would play it in the rehearsal hall. So in between the first and second record, I sat down with an A-DAT, and I laid out a proper bass line, played guitar, and finished the song.

Rogers Stevens: "Walk" was one that Shannon had pretty much written top to bottom. We just figured out how to fill in around it. He had been playing that song for a long time. Going back and listening to it, I think we could have made it better [laughs]. We let Shannon down on that song—what the band did.

Brad Smith: That song is a page right out of Shannon's journal. He was so good at getting drunk, apologizing the next day, and then everything was O.K. And the song is a little bit about that—him being tired of being himself. I think the reason why it stands the test of time is because of the lyrics, and the story about Shannon's soul and personality. And what was going on inside his head—it's a direct look. "Mouthful of Cavities" was the same thing—Shannon was one of the most talented people I've ever known. He was definitely one of the more special people I've known—just with his personality. And he

214 A Devil on One Shoulder and an Angel on the Other

was still, in odd ways, always disappointed in himself. He was always really down on himself. I don't know if it's because of his upbringing—it's just a shame that the guy couldn't stay happy.

Rogers Stevens: I was never a big fan of "Dumptruck"—that song is a mess. There's parts of it that are cool, but it just wasn't my favorite. "Dumptruck" was a song that Brad had this main piece of music for, and the end, where it goes into the half-time, slowed down thing, was a piece that I had—we just stuck that on there. There's a thing during that slow part at the end, I think it's about one of Shannon's high school friends—I know he had cancer, I'm not sure if he survived or not. I'm pretty sure that's what it was about. To me, that song, out of all the songs we did, was probably the one that I have the most issues with. It sounds weird sitting in the middle of the record.

Brad Smith: It's kind of a shitty song. I wrote it—I didn't expect it to make the record. Believe it or not, that song is my attempt at writing a Rage Against the Machine-sounding riff. Which, it sounds nothing like Rage, once Blind Melon gets a hold of it. No matter what you bring into this band, it will never turn out the way you thought it was going to turn out.

Glen Graham: ["Car Seat (God's Presents)"] was in that time when me and Rogers were living side-by-side. I never really seriously considered writing music—I put this idea down. It was piano, drums, percussion, and that was it. The bass line was in the piano thing. I gave it to them, and they were like, "Holy shit, we've got to do this!" I thought they were joking. It's just a straight-up, stock bossa nova—straight out of 'bossa nova 101.' I recorded that on an A-DAT in a bedroom, and the actual recording ended up on the 'Soup' record. I couldn't play it again—I'm not really a piano player, and there are three or four different piano parts. I play them one-handed at times. I had no idea what I did. I also played the drums one part at a time—kick, overdub snare, overdub high hat, overdub toms and ride together. I never actually played a bossa nova beat. So when it came time to do it live on Much-Music, it was pretty rough.

Rogers Stevens: The song is about that Susan Smith story—the woman who strapped her kids into the backseat [of a car] and drove them off into a lake. I think the lyrics are really beautiful that [Shannon] wrote—it was one of his better-written lyrical things.

Shannon Hoon: There was a big story in the news here about a lady in South Carolina who drove a car into a lake and drowned her children. She told the police that someone had carjacked her and made off with the kids. Then it came out that she had been having an affair with a guy who basically didn't want the kids. So she decided to get rid of 'em. She brutally murdered her own children. One of them was eight months old, and the other one was two years old. But she rolled the car into a lake with the children still alive and it wasn't discovered for five or six days. The lady was charged with murder. Anyway, that's what the song is about. I know it's kind of grisly subject matter, but at the end of the song, I try to resolve it, or give it some kind of deeper meaning, I guess. By reading this poem I discovered by my great, great grandmother.

Rogers Stevens: We were in Marlon's apartment, having an all-nighter. We took ecstasy and it was like 4:00 in the morning.

Marlon Stoltzman: On that "Car Seat" song, if you listen at the end, [Shannon] is going at a hundred miles an hour—it's been speeded up. Basically, that's a poem that his great, great grandmother had written—she was very religious—around 1890. I have a copy of it somewhere. Shannon said, "It's [111] years to the day, I've got to record this *now*."

Shannon Hoon: It was February 11, 1995, and the poem was dated February 11, 1884. So it was exactly 111 years from the day she wrote it.

Marlon Stoltzman: It was snowing—it was really bad in New York. He's said, "Let's go to the studio." I hang out and I have fun but I'm always like 'the minder' in a way—I look after people. So I said, "This is ridiculous." He had no shoes on, so he started walking—I was on 12th Street and 4th Avenue—he starts walking to the studio on 33rd Street with no shoes in the middle of winter and snow. He makes it a block, and says, "We can't do this" [laughs]. So we went to the call box down from my flat, he called my answering machine upstairs, and read the poem. And then he took the tape to the studio, and that's on the record—him reading this poem really quickly. When he tried to walk in the snow in the socks, he came back in my house, took them off, and nailed them up on the wall. I still have his old dirty Hurley socks.

Shannon Hoon: I believe that anybody who kills children should die. I don't mean this, obviously, to sound like I don't care, but there's a part of me that can kind of laugh at everything. I can find the horror and the humor. But when people kill children, I cannot find anything but sheer horror. I believe that anybody who kills children should die. I believe that. Because children are too pure, too vulnerable, and not in any way at fault. I just can't comprehend it.

Brad Smith: "Wilt" is one of those songs we wrote in Mississippi between records in that warehouse. We were all jonesing to write new music at that time. We were supposed to be rehearsing for a show that we were going to play in Mississippi, but we ended up writing new material. We didn't practice that hard—we only rehearsed maybe three or four hours a time. But we did that over a period of three days, and we had five or six songs worked up. That's what I remember most about "Wilt"—how easy and effortless it was starting to become for us to finish songs.

Rogers Stevens: That was one that I demoed the music for, brought in, and the band worked it out. The 'elephant ears' thing was a guy [Shannon] knew who was trying to bum money off him. 'Elephant ears' is when someone pulls their pockets out to show they don't have anything in their pockets.

Christopher Thorn: "The Duke" was about this great experience—we played in Hawaii with Porno for Pyros. We spent a week there surfing and snorkeling. "The Duke" was the first 'surfer guy.' He was the guy that brought surfing over to the States, as well.

Brad Smith: I think "The Duke' is an O.K. song, it's kind of a b-side. We should have made an eleven-song record. There are a bunch of songs on there that shouldn't have been on the record.

Rogers Stevens: That was a demo that Christopher had made the music for. I always loved playing that song, because I played lots of solos on it—it was kind of a fun tempo and I could play well on that. When we were in Hawaii, we were surfing on the beach in Honolulu—right of off our hotel. There's a statue out there called the Duke, it's some kind of surf legend. That's what it's about—the statue, being out there, and surfing. A sort of 'escapist' song. Christopher is really good at coming up with riffs that are off-kilter like that— it takes me a while to figure out how to approach it. But once you do, it's complex. I was always happy with it—a lot of times looking back, I'm like, "Oh, that's a crap guitar solo." But on that one, I look back and I thought, "Oh, that's pretty cool."

Brad Smith: I remember Shannon coming up with most of ["St. Andrew's Fall"] while we were on the road—on our first record.

Shannon Hoon: One night we were playing in Detroit at this old church that had been converted into a music hall, called St. Andrew's Hall. And after the show, we were standing up in our dressing room, and it had these windows so you could look down and see all the people leaving the club. And I was standing there looking out when I noticed all these people starting to congregate over on the corner. We were arguing about a monitor mix or something stupid from the gig, I don't know. But my attention was caught by all these people on the corner. I thought man...is there a fight going on or something? Then I see someone point up and I look and there's this girl on the edge of the building, 20 floors up. It wasn't someone from the show; it was a hotel next door to the club. I was like, "Holy shit, you guys, there's a girl up there." We had the most horrific view.

There's about two hundred people, all watching by now, and of course you get all the heartless ones that start heckling and screaming when you should really understand that someone for whatever reason is deliberating life or death here. It was unbelievable. There were people yelling "Jump!" I thought, "My God, what's going on here?" All of a sudden there was this dead calm, and this girl stood up and she jumped, and we were all standing there. And I mean it seemed like it took forever for her to fall. It was one of those situations where you don't want to look but something in your mind makes you watch and will not let you take your eyes away from it, because you're going to learn something from it. I mean, not only did I learn that monitor mixes were irrelevant to life, it just...phoosh! Nobody was able to say a thing for the next three hours. We just got in the van and drove. Rogers had actually left the hall and was down on the street when it happened. It was something that really scarred us all. She was just 26, and no one knew why she jumped. She took her secret with her. They thought she might have tested positive for AIDS, but she wasn't. She wasn't pregnant, she had a job...she just suffered from depression. It could have been anybody. It was really sad. And that's what "St. Andrew's Fall" is all about.

Rogers Stevens: "New Life" hit me flat. I liked what he was saying lyrically—I thought it was really sweet. But the song itself, I never really loved that one. That was Brad's music that he wrote—it was about Shannon becoming a father. It was poignantly written about what that's like. After becoming one myself recently, I went back to the song and really appreciated it.

Brad Smith: I was honored that he wanted to put such a milestone marker into words to my music. I think those lyrics are particularly chilling.

Rogers Stevens: I didn't think "Mouthful of Cavities" was going to make the record. And it ended up being one of the ones people really latch onto.

Glen Graham: Shannon and I cut that together, and everybody else overdubbed. We were upstairs in Kingsway in the big room. Shannon was on an enclosed porch—with French doors in between he and I. He had all the windows open, and I'm sitting there on the drums. We did it a couple of times. That one has one of the best feels than any of them, because he had a really nice rhythmic style on the guitar—when he wasn't burdened by having to

think about other instruments other than just the drums. It wasn't edited—
what you hear on the tape is real. We're sitting in there, he's smoking dope,
sitting in his little chair, and there are cats basically raping each other outside
in the courtyard. They were very loud and they kept going. That was one of
the few times I remember playing with him in a studio setting. We finished,
got up, and it was like, "*Hell yes.* That was great." We both knew.

Jena Kraus: The way I ended up down there—I went up to Seattle, did this
demo with other musicians, and ended up getting a publishing deal from it.
After I did that demo, then they invited me to come sing on the record. I went
there—I had no voice. I had lost my voice for two months—it was nerve-
wracking. I had to go to this doctor that stuck a camera up my nose and down
my throat. And I was on steroids when I went there—my vocal cords were
really swollen and I had [to take] an anti-inflammatory. I get off the plane,
get there—I'm not even there an hour—and [Shannon] shows me this song
that I was going to sing on. I was actually going to sing on "God's Presents"
too, but I didn't. I had my own room at that house, it was amazing. We were
in my room and I had my journal sitting there. He picked up my journal and
started writing in it. He wrote down the words for "Mouthful of Cavities"
for me. They had that film crew there for three days. That might have been
the last day they were there, so they really wanted to get me with them doing
"Mouthful of Cavities." I didn't even know the song yet—I had just heard the
song like five minutes before. If you look at that thing, I have the book on my
lap. I'm reading the words. That was the thing—Shannon didn't want me to
hear the song beforehand. They were going to send me a tape of the song, and
he was like, "No—I want her to learn it on the spot." He didn't want me to
think about it too much.

Brad Smith: Some songs I can really stand behind that I write, and then
sometimes, I don't like anything that I write. I think some songs are the biggest dogs on the planet [laughs]. "Mouthful of Cavities" was one of those
songs that I was oddly detached from until the end. I didn't have a bass line
for it—it was the only song that we didn't work up as a band. That song
was pretty much written by Shannon. They had a late night session where

Shannon played acoustic guitar, Jena Kraus was there, they set up mics, Glen played tambourine or something. And we did a bunch of overdubs to finish the song at Kingsway. I played bass last, which is a pretty odd way to do it-because most of the times, the drums and bass go first on most songs in terms of recording. That song is really an amazing lyric. Shannon knew that he was in trouble with drug addiction, and he knew how he swindled people on an emotional level. Like, he would tell people that he was fine and in control with his addiction—he didn't call it 'an addiction.' He would say funny, charming things and make us laugh, like, "You've just got to know how to do drugs in the right order." That was one of his famous lines.

That particular song, using a metaphor like a cavity, something that is physically the hardest part of your anatomy has got holes in it and starting to decay—to use that as a metaphor for his whole being, his whole personality. Shannon had a way for speaking in really deep terms like that in lyrics, but he rarely did it out loud—at least on that level. He was really good at apologizing—he was really charming. And usually in a good mood—he was always down for a party. But he never got serious and wanted to talk about serious things with people right to your face. So lyrics for him was a way to do that. "Mouthful of Cavities" is like one of those amazing moments, where he just put it all together—in music, lyrics, and melody lines. Jena Kraus sang great harmonies on that. My favorite songs off the record from Shannon were the two songs where he spoke like that—"Walk" and "Mouthful of Cavities." He was talking about his soul, completely. It was a very valid point, and it was crafty enough, it wasn't a "poor me" type song, it's something that everybody could apply to themselves. That is the earmark of a great song.

Jena Kraus: Before we recorded "Mouthful of Cavities," there was an incident in New Orleans. Acoustically we were playing it—and they recorded that and put it up in sync with the track. That was on a Wednesday. On Friday was the day I was going to record it. I was supposed to practice it in between there, but I got 'caught up'—being in New Orleans with them and that crazy house and everything. I don't know why I forgot, but I totally forgot to concentrate on the music. We were about to record "Mouthful of Cavities," and I'm like, "Oh shit—we're recording now?!" I needed five minutes to go and listen to the song—to get it back in my mind. Someone is like, "There's a boom box up in Christopher's room—here's a tape of it." So I went to Christopher's room—Shannon and Christopher were in there. [Shannon] knows I'm about to sing in five minutes, and I'm all excited. He walks by me and he had his hand up. He opened up his fingers, and he had a syringe in his hand. I flipped out. "You're going to go do that *now?*" I freaked out because my father had been a heroin addict my whole life—he actually passed away in the last few years. I found my dad dead from heroin. I don't know how I would have felt if heroin hadn't destroyed my life as a child. But I'd never known [Shannon] to do that. And if he did do heroin, it was really like [he] snorted it or did it a few times. It wasn't like something he normally did.

But he walks past me with this syringe in his hand—and nobody said anything. I think he thought I was just going to be like, "Oh Shannon, you're crazy." But I did not react like that at all—it was really personal to me. I flipped out—to the point where him and I started to fight so bad, screaming at each other. We ended up downstairs in the vocal room, just fucking screaming. I forgot that the mic was on, and we're going back and forth, and everybody can hear us. Then we ended up in the main area where the mixing board was—in the living room. At one point, everybody was getting mad at me—I set the recording back because I was freaking out on Shannon. And you don't tell Shannon what to do—if you tell him not to do something, he's going to do it. We're face-to-face, fighting with each other—for literally three hours. It got to the point where Andy was in between me and Shannon—it seemed like he was 'the dad' and we were 'the kids.'

Shannon's like, "You know what? We're just going to call it quits." And I'm like, "Just because I don't want you to do heroin, now you're going to take me off the album?" Nobody else was saying a word. I think it was like, "Don't upset Shannon. You've got to keep him singing—you've got to do whatever he wants." And I wasn't like that, I was like, "Fuck that shit—you are not going to do heroin right now. You're crazy." I didn't think it was my fault, but I was like, "Fine, I'll back down." My face was so swollen from crying. Then he goes, "*Now* you can really sing the song to me, Jena." He made that whole big scene, but he didn't actually do it—the reason I know that is because I know when people are on heroin. I grew up with my dad doing it, so it's very obvious when someone's nodding. He acted like he was going to do it—he never ended up actually doing it. Then everything was fine. He was really good while I was singing—he was helping produce it in a certain way. At one point, he was in the room singing it with me. He was videotaping it, so I'm sure that videotape exists. He had that videotape on the whole time I was in there.

Brad Smith: That song "Lemonade" is really terrible. I don't understand what a 'Bulgarian national anthem' is doing on our record. And when songs like "Soup" are not on the record and something like that is—it just doesn't make any sense. It made a great intro to "Galaxie"—that's what it was, it was "Lemonade" re-worked up. It made more sense there than it did a 'rock band song.'

Rogers Stevens: The song is about being in New Orleans and fucking up. There was this one night when Shannon got arrested down there [the 'Le Bon Temps Roulette' incident]. There's that line, "Hello Mr. Uppercut"—I think that's what happened to him.

Brad Smith: The standout songs on the record for me are "Toes Across the Floor," "Walk," and "Mouthful of Cavities." If I had to point people in the direction for that 'Soup' record, it would be those three songs.

Shannon '94-'95

Despite being pleased with how 'Soup' turned out, Shannon's personal life is full of upheaval from 1994-1995. Blind Melon almost splits due to royalty disputes, Shannon learns that he and Lisa will become first-time parents (their daughter, Nico Blue Hoon, is born on July 11, 1995), and he moves back home to Indiana—while his drug addiction worsens, resulting in another rehab stint.

Glen Graham: We had some strange, unfortunate business situations happen. When we sat down with our first lawyer to put together a partnership agreement—we hadn't really talked about it. We came to the decision that after much bickering, we would just split everything equally. We shortly thereafter fired that attorney. That piece of paper went away when he went away. So when "No Rain" came out and the money started to come in, Chris Jones sat us down in someplace like Lake Tahoe, and said, "O.K., so how are we going to split the money?" And everybody looked around the room—it was a very strange moment. Like, "What do you mean? I thought we dealt with this?" And he's like, "No, no, no. You guys don't have any sort of agreement at all."

So that almost ended the group—there's no question about that. But we worked it out and I think everybody was happy with it. It's just one of those funny things—I think we started off thinking that we were going to be like R.E.M. or U2. And when given the opportunity to do that, we opted not to do that [laughs]. Speaking as the drummer, who's the low man on the pay scale, I certainly have no complaints whatsoever. But it was a funny thing to watch. "You mean I can get paid *16 times* more than I was going to? Hmmm, that sounds pretty good! It'll all work out in the end." That was one of my favorite Shannon Hoon quotes about money—"It'll all even out in the end." I was like, "I don't know how you're doing the math on that!"

Jena Kraus: I know there were problems with publishing. I think [Shannon] wanted to keep his publishing. There was one week that Blind Melon broke up. Christopher called me and was like, "Well, we're breaking up." It was during [1995]—it was like a week that went by, but then they got back together. But, Blind Melon was broken up for a week, not too many people know. Shannon was really wanting to change the way they had dealt with their publishing. Instead of distributing it equally, he wanted to have whoever wrote what should get the most of the publishing. He wanted to keep his publishing separate.

Brad Smith: Songwriting issues came up, which was a bummer. It's really hard to talk about, because you're so young at the time, and some of the arguments are valid and some are not. It came down to writer splits. It was really fueled by Shannon and I duking it out, because he wanted to split up the songwriting, and I at heart did not want to split up the songwriting. But Shannon had written a pretty hefty portion of the songs at that point, and so had I. So I got dragged into a situation where I had to fight for my own splits. And one of the songs I had written all of was "No Rain." That was the song that became successful, and I think that bred some resentment. Like, I knew 'No Rain' was going to be a hit and I was going to make a lot more money than everybody else, and that was what I was fighting for. When in reality, I was just having to go along with defending what I did write. Which is a bummer. It's a real shame, because there's bands that do it the way we should have—everything gets split evenly. There's none of that unspoken for resentment and grievances towards each other that I think we had. Whether people want to admit it or not, I think that's just what happens in any situation where someone makes out better than the others—but everybody had the same amount of effort. I got really lucky. In my mind, "Change" should have been the hit, or "Holy Man." There are several songs on the record, where you're like, "God, why wasn't that a hit?" And it just blows my mind that "No Rain" was the hit, and I own more of the songwriting. But you know what? Everybody had the same amount of effort in that band—everybody put the same soul into that record. Everybody put the same amount of time on the road—behind the microphones and the writing process. We did it all together, and it's a real shame that it didn't end up that way. I wish it would have.

Rogers Stevens: It was sorta a brutal battle, but we got it sorted out in a way that everybody was happy with it. We all compromised, and I was really proud of that—that in the end it worked out.

Lisa Sinha: I got pregnant, and [Shannon] was just so excited about this baby. I really thought it was going to be what would straighten him up—I really did. He was absolutely wonderful with children. Desired to have kids, and wrote the song ["New Life"]. He wrote the song as a psychological thing, like, "I'm writing this song and I'm making a promise to myself to behave myself." I had a million conversations with him about whatever I could do to help him get through it. And the conversations we had, he'd be very sincere—"I need to get sober, I want to get sober." Nico was a planned pregnancy—it wasn't an accident. I used that too, to enlighten him that he had to get sober. I couldn't go on like that—especially with having a baby.

Shannon Hoon: I have a girlfriend and we're getting ready to have our first child in July. I'm so happy. I haven't prepared myself to be a father. And my girlfriend, Lisa, we've been together for like ten years. We went to our senior prom together. All that sweet, Midwest bullshit. Hmmm, it's weird, because when I'm holding the baby, then I'm going to be a father. But up until then, anything that I've ever prepared myself for never turned out right.

Chris Smith: He was actually at my apartment—we were doing cocaine in New Orleans—when he got that phone call. He was kind of stunned and left. He was excited though.

Shelley Shaw: I think she got pregnant in New Orleans. She went down there during the recording. I'm pretty sure that it was November [of 1994]. But I don't remember his behavior changing.

Marlon Stoltzman: One night, he's like, "Dude, I'm having a baby." He must have made a hundred people the Godfather of Nico, but said to me, "I want you to be the Godfather of my child." I said, "I appreciate that, but don't cop out here—this is a huge responsibility. Don't go dying on me now."

He said to me, "Marlon, I'm a professional drug addict." And I answered, "Shannon, that is so lame. You can't hide behind that. You have a child coming. It's so much more important than your obsession with drugs." He's like, "I know, I know. I'm really going to try." Of course you're going to want to give up drugs for your child—and for yourself. But it's not that easy.

Brian Whitus: He wanted to have ten kids. That's all he talked about, and I always said, "Man, you're nuts."

Melissa Whitus: When we were a little older, we liked hanging out, cooking out, going golfing. We just did a lot of the 'regular things' with him. He did take us to a concert when he was in Blind Melon. Lisa was pregnant with Nico at the time, and they were going to have their ultrasound the next day, to find out if it was a boy or a girl. He said, "Whitey, if it's a girl, we're celebrating with water. If it's a boy, we're having a six-pack."

Domenique Johansson: When she got pregnant, again, that child-like fascination of a new experience. I remember him wanting to document everything with Lisa, and her big belly—there are some beautiful pictures. That was when he was wearing that funny flat hat. He had these different periods—whether he wanted his hair dyed really dark, or wearing his hair back in side ponytails. He had his moments when he played with a look. They had that house—it was like a typical house with a white picket fence out front. I was blown away when I saw that [laughs]. It almost seemed too normal. Shannon was really excited about it—he was expressing more interest, excitement, and love for the idea of being a father than he was for the fear of it. Shannon always thought that things would take care of themselves in a certain way.

Brooks Byrd Graham: I think he was happy and scared—just like anybody that is going to become a parent. He'd known Lisa for a *long* time. She was a grounding force for him. When he got a cell phone, he'd call her four, five, six times a day—all the time. She knew him and could be truthful right to him. And they talked about having a kid forever. I think in a way, he was ready for it and not ready for it. He was glad it was Lisa—"She's good and she's going to take care of everything. I hope that I can live up to what I'm supposed to be." He was excited about the possibility of having a kid to show things—I think that's part of why he was glad he'd done so much videotaping.

Heather Thorn: We honestly all thought that that was 'it.' That was the turning point in his life, because he and Lisa were so stoked. It was in New Orleans that she got pregnant, and as soon as they found out, they ran out and went to an antique store, and bought a little baby spoon or something. They were super-stoked about it. He would even mention it in interviews, and he showed the sonogram picture on TV. He was so excited about this little girl. Honestly, that was where everybody thought, "O.K., he's done now—he gets it. He's going to have a kid, it's all going to make sense to him, why he needs to get his act together." It just never happened. It got worse and worse basically, as time progressed.

Shannon Hoon: No matter how much I could try to prepare myself for it, there's no way you can. How do you prepare to be overwhelmed in every part of your body? It gives meaning to the big picture now. I'm gonna be a father longer than I'm gonna be a singer. I don't know which will be the most exhausting, actually.

Jena Kraus: In February [1995] they came to New York. They might have been mixing the album, but I remember they were mastering the album in March. I remember hanging out with Shannon and Shannon wanting to go get crack. He had this guy he called 'Felix the Crack.' He's like, "Jena, you can hang out as long as you want, but if I come back and I get it, then you have to leave. I don't want you see me turn into a werewolf." He came back and he didn't get it. Sometimes with Shannon, as much as he did party and do drugs, I think sometimes he acted like he did more than he really did. So it was sort of weird—you never really knew. Like, "Is he just exaggerating, or is he really that fucked up?" But I remember he got the phone call to sing "Three is a Magic Number," and that was at River Sound. He recorded that at literally 3:00 or 4:00 in the morning—after he had tried to get crack, couldn't get crack, came back, went to sleep, and then got the call. He was up and out of there.

Danny Clinch: One time he said to me, "Danny, you're a photographer. You've got to come down with me to the Westside—you've got to see this guy that I buy crack from. You've got to come and take pictures—it's just ridiculous." I'm like, "Shannon, *dude.*" That was at a point where I said, "You're really making me nervous—you've got a child on the way." I remember that, and I remember him saying to me one time, "Now I've got my little girl—I'm totally going to try and be a good dad. I'm going to not be so selfish." He was a good talker—he was a guy that one minute you'd be so pissed at him, because he'd do something so rude, and then ten minutes later, he'd sweet-talk you into loving him again. You'd be so pissed at him, and the next thing you know, you're like, "Oh that Shannon, man, he's great." He'd manipulate the heck out of you. And not just gullible people like myself, *seasoned bullshitters.* At a certain point in his life, his fingers were all burnt and shit—from smoking crack. It was really scary.

Jena Kraus: One night we did mushrooms or something. I don't know what came over me, but I started freaking out, and was like, "What happens if you die?" And he's like, "Jena, if I die, I die. I look at my life as a mission for other people to learn from and not to follow." He also told me to keep everybody at arm's length. Christopher and I had talked about it. I remember saying, "God, what if Shannon died?" And I remember Christopher saying, "If Shannon died, that would truly be a tragedy." I guess after that, he went back to Indiana.

Rogers Stevens: When we finished 'Soup,' Shannon went back to Indiana and bought a house.

Nel Hoon: I know that he wanted to live in Lafayette. [Shannon's house] was just a few blocks from my house. Nothing really prompted him—he always wanted to live here in Lafayette.

Glen Graham: The lowest was the time we went to L.A. to do the "Galaxie" video. He was nuts then—he was off the deep end. He was leaving the hotel at 2:00 in the morning, on foot, heading towards parts unknown, looking to buy crack. You're like, "Why are you doing that? Look, you are kind of a little rock star—if you want crack, call the crack guy. Why would you put yourself in this precarious situation?"

Lisa Sinha: When they were doing the "Galaxie" video, he walked off the set. Shannon wanted [Timothy Leary] on the video. I remember Shannon calling me and saying, "I just smoked crack with Timothy Leary in the bathroom!" He was all psyched about it, like, this is the coolest thing. And of course, I'm just sitting there going, "*Oh my God.*" That's not O.K. That was right before he was scheduled to go into rehab, I think. As I matter of fact—I was pregnant with Nico. Chris Jones called me at like 1:00 at night. He's like, "Have you talked to Shannon?" I said, "Well, I talked to him earlier." "No, have you talked to him in the last five hours? We can't find him—we're really worried about him." And then of course, I'm sick to my stomach. I would get so upset when they would call me—I didn't know what to expect out of him, he was a big worry for me all the time. I can remember Nico getting an adrenaline rush, freaking out—I just had a bad feeling about that night. I could feel her moving in my stomach, real violently. He just did that to a person—you didn't know if he was going to wind up dead. And then he called me at like 5:00 in the morning. That same weekend, Shannon called me, and he said, "I'm on the balcony and there's cops in my room." I called Chris Jones after I talked to him, and I'm like, "What's going on? He's on the balcony?" Chris is like, "*There is no balcony.*" There was a lot of stuff at that time, he would call and you would not know what he's doing.

Heather Thorn: The "Galaxie" video, he was just super out of his mind. We couldn't even get him to come out of the hotel room to lobby call—he swore there were cops out on his balcony. He was so paranoid—he couldn't be talked out of his room, because he was sure that he was surrounded. But finally, they coaxed him down. We got to the "Galaxie" video…he was so ugly when he did drugs. But he always had that underlying charm, so he would be walking around the video shoot totally gaked out of his mind, being really charming and sweet to the seamstress or the caterer people. He just got this look in his eye, where you're like, "*Ugh.* Dude, you're evil right now." And then he was back there doing drugs with Timothy Leary and thinking he's all cool. I remember him coming up to me and going, "Heather, are you mad at me?" I'm like, "Shannon, just get away. Come back when you're done with what you're doing."

Everybody in the band knew him well enough to know that he was an asshole at that point, but then you have the people on the outskirts who will always indulge somebody because they are who they are. I remember him smashing the car window [in the video]—smashing it with his head, smashing it with his feet. I mean, it was great—he was going crazy [laughs]. But in the same breath, he was really *gone*—just that look in his eye of like, he's beyond sanity at that point. He's completely out of his mind. It made for a great video, but he was a pain in the ass to be around. He got really ugly—I wish I could explain it better. Just not a good person. Still sweet, but evil. It was a stressful day—trying to get him there and getting him to realize there weren't people trying to sabotage his every move, and he was there to do a video. It's funny—I'm actually looking at [Shannon's] Galaxie right now. We own the Galaxie—I took it out of the garage.

Rogers Stevens: That was just bad all around. I remember him showing up underweight—hadn't seen him in a few weeks. He had been in Indiana—running with his old crowd there. It was out of control. We had this video shoot set up, with a soundstage rented—which is huge and expensive—[and] an expensive director. We thought, "O.K., we're going to get this done today." But it ended up the first day we were there, I think Shannon punched one of the production assistants, and then split. So that day got cancelled. He was definitely fucked up. Then the next day, we go back to do it again, and Timothy Leary is in the video. I remember being back in the dressing room—doing blow, basically. I think we were putting it in joints and smoking it. Timothy Leary said, "Is somebody smoking coke? Give me some!" So he proceeded to jump in.

We go out, and we're filming this thing. The scenes in the car...I can't even watch it, because that day was fucking horrible. They were sort of egging Shannon on to do crazy stuff. He's barefoot, and he's jumping up and down on the windshield of this car, and he puts his head through the windshield at one point. Just stupid. It's like, at that point, a straight jacket was required. It was totally disgusting. There was a dark mood over the whole thing. People in the band were really upset, but there was a feeling of, "There's so much money being spent, we've got to get it done." And rather than just pull the plug on it, we did it. I don't think it looks that great, and I can't watch it. It's a bad memory. I think Shannon skipped out and they found him somewhere later. The whole thing was just fucked. That was a point where we had surrendered our ability to control that day or what was happening. Rather than just saying, "No," we were so fucking spun out, that we didn't have the ability or the wherewithal to do that.

Glen Graham: There was no talking to him. Any talking to him in that state to him was a threat. It's like, "No man, get annihilated if you want to—just show up and do your thing." I remember calling him from New Orleans—I guess right before the ['Soup'] tour. I would call him often and he would call me often in the middle of the night. You'd talk a while—I was stoned usually, I'd smoke pot. That was my thing every day. I don't know what he was doing—I think he was coked to the gills and just wanted to talk. I was probably the last person he would call. After about ten minutes, I would start breaking through the bullshit, and start talking to him about, "Hey man, I think you're manic depressive—I think that's why you use drugs. That's why I use drugs. And I think you've been doing it so long and using such heavy drugs that you can't see outside of the whole box. You go up, you get depressed, you start doing heavier stuff, you swing back up, you feel good, so you feel good about doing drugs, then you feel good enough to stop for a little while, because you have your reason to stop, because you're in a band that's supposed to be doing stuff. You're very pleasant to be around for a while, and then you get super-manic, and you start drinking." And then that would lead to depression again. I would talk about that with him. I got through, but getting through to Shannon at 3:00 in the morning doesn't count, because as soon as he hangs up the phone, it's like, *"Whatever."* He made an art out of dismissing things. It was almost a 'performance part' of his personality. You could talk to him about anything—he would always have the last word, and that word would be to dismiss whatever you had just been talking about, so he wouldn't have to think about it anymore.

Lisa Sinha: That's when he went into rehab [Exodus Recovery Center, in California]. He was emotional about it too—I felt sorry for him. I felt really bad for him and the situation he had gotten himself into. He had so many people that wanted to help him, but it was really hard—he wasn't very help-able. You get treated special all your life—you don't have to account for your behavior. You feel invincible.

Marlon Stoltzman: He wrote me a letter. It says, "Marlon, a little boy goes to his dad and says, 'Dad, I want to play.' And the dad (who is working at the time) says, 'O.K. son,' and walks over and pulls out a map of the world, and tears it all up and throws it all over the ground. He then walks back to his son and then says, 'Son, when you put this map of the world back together, we'll play,' thinking this will enable him to have the time to finish his work. Then in a quick minute, his son returns with a map of the world all taped up and back together, in all the correct places. The father, obviously surprised by this, asks his son, 'Son, how did you do this so fast?' His son replied, 'Dad, there was a man on the other side. And when I put the man together, the whole world came together.' So this is what I'm out here trying to do, Marlon. I hope your [sic] well, tell all the friends hello from me. I miss the old me a lot and I miss all of you guys as well, give my love to Mary Cullen and tell John hello for me." He wanted to send another few tapes of the new album—"But I only had a few copies, and I had to trade some for meds. Gotta kill some pain, you know. The body will come around through some of it. Kiss the forehead of Carolyn for me, kiss your fingers and smack yourself on the cheek as well. Paradise in Exodus, your friend, Shannon."

Heather Thorn: Whenever I talked to him, he'd be really into it. He never made it far enough to realize, "O.K., your parents are screwy but you are now the adult, and you've got to clean up your baggage." He was gung-ho about it. "Savor the raisin"—they used to make them put a raisin in their mouth, really keep it there, acknowledge it's there. They took something like that and made them focus on it. But like I said, he never really got it. He never got out of the point of saying, "I'm like this because of this, because of that."

Brooks Byrd Graham: I don't remember thinking anything, except, "Well, it's a nice try, but it's not really going to help anything." He wasn't ready for it. If you have a chemical imbalance in your brain, you can't control what you're thinking, you can't control your actions, your emotions. So rehab was nothing, really.

Jena Kraus: There was something that happened when he was in rehab too—I only heard this through Christopher—that he left rehab with a girl, I don't know who it was. I guess they went and did heroin or something, and his heart stopped—I don't know if she called the paramedics, but something like that. I never heard it from him, but I totally remember Christopher telling me something weird like that. I never asked about it again.

Lisa Sinha: He went into rehab and came out about a month before I had Nico. He ended up leaving rehab in a huff. He used the excuse of, "I just want to be home. You're getting ready to have the baby." He got sick of being there I believe. There was a lot of drama—he was very dramatic. And I'm not saying that it was fake or anything like that, but he would create this drama—he was very high maintenance as far as his life and the way that everyone tiptoed around him. "Whatever you want." You couldn't tell him no. He would agree and then in two seconds disagree. He 'escaped' or whatever from rehab. He did have a sponsor—they were looking for him at the airport and he was dodging them. I really don't think it helped—*at all*. I didn't see much of a change in lifestyle. The second time was more like, "I'm going to get sober for Nico." It turned into this attention thing. When he came home, I don't even think that he was rehabilitated at all.

Duff McKagan: I talked to him. He was trying to get sober, and I had gotten sober—much to mine and everybody else's surprise. And I started doing martial arts—I got so into it. I was doing it every day, and it really got me sober. Especially that first couple of years, where it's touch and go. So Shannon called—this is probably '95—he was like, "Man, I can't fucking get it dude. You got sober—what did you do?" And I told him I was doing martial arts. I said, "You should come down man, to my dojo." And he told me—I never fucking knew this, out of all the years I'd known him—that he was a Junior Olympic Tae Kwon Do champion! He was in the Junior Olympics—at least that's what he told me. And I'm like, "Dude, well you've got the fucking basics of martial arts—can you pull some of that back up?" I think because he'd grown up with it, it wasn't like a new sort of thing to kicks his ass. The guy was searching to figure it out.

Shelley Shaw: He left rehab, bought a car, and drove to L.A. I was walking to a show at the Roxy—he was driving on Sunset, saw me, and sort of cut me off. I was like, "What are you doing here man?" He said, "I left and I went out and bought this car—it's amazing!" I think it was an Impala or a weird old white station wagon. I go, "Do you want to go this show?" I can't remember who it was—it was a Mudhoney kind of band. We went to that and then we went over to the Viper and we were talking. He didn't order drinks or anything like that—he was full of news. He was talking about how hard it was for him. He really unloaded about what he had been doing. He was like, "I used to have eight balls in my guitar case and needles." I had no clue. No idea. He was like, "I'm going to go home, pull a baby out of my woman, and get on the road for this record." He had done some therapy around his family situation at the rehab. He was really full of questions actually, about his mom—there were deeper things there that he was alluding to. He wanted to distance himself for a bit and just focus on the work. He actually stayed on my couch that night. He was really tired, because they had put him on so much medication.

Kim Smith: I remember picking the phone up one night—[Shannon] sounded really out of it, and he said he was on a bunch of meds. After he got out of rehab that time, he came up to Seattle, and he was just kind of quiet. He was more quiet than I had seen him—*ever*. He was only in Seattle for a few days, and then he was on his way back to Indiana, for the birth of Nico. It was in May, and then she was born in July.

Marlon Stoltzman: Shortly after he came out of this one, he's like, "Dude, it's not working." The one thing with me, like, a lot of people from a celebrity point of view, they just want to be friends with a celebrity. So they're not prepared to contradict, they're not prepared to say, "This is not a good idea." They'll be the first to buy a drink for a guy that shouldn't be drinking, because they want to party with the guy. Whereas I try to go, "Well, there's nothing really going on tonight—why don't we have tea and go home?" If you're really somebody's friend, then you're going to look out for their best interests. I would talk to him about it and try to encourage him, and go, "Come on. You were just in rehab." And he's like, "Well, obviously it didn't work." And then definitely, it started getting *extremely* frustrating for the band. Christopher and Brad are pretty serious guys, and you can image, "Fuck, we're a good band, we've got something going here, we're trying to move ahead, and you're just fucked up all the time." It's your second album, you're not *there* yet. And imagine trying to want to work or do things, and you've got this irresponsible 'child' around all the time. It became very frustrating.

Jena Kraus: Both times out of rehab, I think he started smoking pot not too long afterwards. And that was O.K. in his mind. And then it seems like pretty soon, other things started to happen.

Heather Thorn: He was smoking crack right up until the day she was born, basically. I remember Lisa freaking out because he was still doing drugs.

Lisa Sinha: 7/11/95—we said [Nico] was our 'convenience store baby.' We just kind of waited for her to be born—worked on the house. He was very excited, very involved. And then when we had Nico, he was just so excited—it was very touching. The birth of her, he was very emotional, and a really good dad. Stayed around, called and checked on her all the time if he was gone. Very in love with his daughter. He named her. He came up with Nico from the member of the Velvet Underground. At one point, we're like, "When I get pregnant, we're going to name the baby Blue. The 'Blue' just came strictly from [a] Zippo lighter that somebody had given him. We're like, "That would be a cool name!" We were going to name her Blue, and then we decided we didn't want it to be too terribly trendy. Where, who knows what she would be when she's older—Blue might not be...'Dr. Blue' [laughs]. He came up with

Nico Blue, and then everybody tried to say it was the flower Nikko Blue—we had no idea that even existed. We were at this flower shop—we were looking for bushes to put around our house, and I ran across Nikko Blue.

Marlon Stoltzman: When the child was born, he phoned me. He had a lot of love that guy—tons and tons of love. He was absolutely thrilled. Those moments were very precious for him. But as you know with drug addicts, like he said to me, you put the drugs there and a picture of your child, and you say, "I'm going to stay clean for my child." But again, no drug addict thinks they're going to die. I guess there are some—I think the guy from Alice in Chains locked himself in a room until he died. But Shannon wasn't like that—he liked to get out, have fun, party, talk to people. He was a 'positive' drug addict. But I believe it got quite negative.

Glen Graham: I remember that freaked him out badly, but it was just a momentary jarring of the senses. He knew he was going to have to get it together and also knew he couldn't do it alone. In addition, many people around him thought about his 'getting it together' in terms of ceasing to break promises to himself, his child, and others regarding drug use, rather than realizing the depths of his addiction and what would be required to overcome it.

Shannon Hoon: Lisa and I are trying to build a very good home for her, and I don't think that me being in jail somewhere is the appropriate way to go about it.

Kim Smith: He was so excited after Nico was born. He said now he had something to live for, because of the birth of Nico.

Rogers Stevens: He was such a kid in his own way that. This girl is beautiful to this day, and she looks just like him.

Shannon Hoon: And I think with having a child really made me look at a lot of things that I used to find enjoyable, and then when you really step back and look at them they really aren't enjoyable. They seem like they're enjoyable at that time, but you know what? The time you spend getting high there's twice as much time spent recuperating from it, and I'm sorry, recuperating from anything is not an enjoyable thing. And I don't know, I think it really paves a bumpy road for what you could possibly have as a happy life.

Melissa Whitus: Shannon and I both liked candy—he was a 'candy kid.' He loved Sprees and Sweet Tarts. We would eat candy the whole time we'd be golfing. We had a pretty good heart-to-heart at times. I'm very steadfast—set your mind to do something, you just do it. And he liked that about me. I was cutting his hair—I said, "I don't understand how if you know something is going to kill you, you can't stop it. You have this beautiful child now, but you're going to go on the road, and you're going to be tempted. You need to look at her picture every day and know what you have to live for."

He said, "Melissa, I don't know how to make you understand it. What do we do when we go golfing? We go get candy. Let's say you can never have another Twizzler for as long as you live. Would that be kind of hard to do? It's because you've *done it*—you've tasted it, you know what it's like, and it would be hard to give up those Twizzlers. If I brought a pound of Twizzlers to you, you'd probably have a hard time saying 'No' to one of them." It was the first time I kind of got it. I said, "But you know what Shannon? I honestly think if I knew Twizzlers were going to kill me, I could give them up. As a matter of fact, I'll never eat another Twizzler if you never do another drug—I can promise you that." He goes, "I wish I could have been like you. I wish I could have never touched the stuff. The first thing they teach you in rehab is you never meet a drug addict that hadn't tried drugs—because that's how you become one. I've never met another you." That was kind of his line for me- "I've never met another you when it comes to that."

He was a freakin' horrible golfer. The summer [of '95], he probably golfed four times a week. He swung like he swung a baseball bat. He pulled out this club that was the size of a shoe, and I'm not kidding you—he tees off, and the ball did something I've never seen a ball do before. It goes straight up, straight to the right, hooks around, and it goes two fairways over, two holes ago. We went to find the ball, to see how ridiculously far it went. I said, "Shannon, you better stick to singing, *because you really suck at golf.*"

Shannon Hoon: Obviously now being a father, there's a lot of things I need to take into consideration. Staying alive is one of them.

Lisa Sinha: Our whole take on marriage—we had been together for so long, and we were so young. At that point, I said, "If we have more kids, we're going to have to get married." We just never really felt the need—our relationship was good the way it was. We had Nico, which we always said was more of a commitment than marriage. That was the biggest commitment of all—having a child together. I wasn't that girl that "I needed to get married." So at that point in time, it just didn't matter to me—I really didn't harass him about it. I think when we were younger we talked about it a lot more. He was always trying to be trendy, hip, and cool, and I think he thought it was cool to not be married.

Shelley Shaw: He, Lisa, and Nico were a tight little unit—I didn't have any communication after he left my house in L.A.

Lisa Sinha: Shannon was a huge antique buff. Our dream was to one day have an antique store, and we would 'antique' all over the place. I remember being in Tennessee, they did the Rolling Stones tour—it was the first day—and I had taken some friends. I ended up coming back with a U-Haul attached to the back of the Blazer, because he wanted to go out antiquing, and then I could drive it back. This garage was just packed with antiques. We refinished furniture together all the time—it was our little thing to do together. Half the furniture I have now is furniture that he and I refinished. Really into it. Fixing up old fans was one of his hobbies. And along with that went vintage clothing. I did a lot of vintage clothing shopping for him. That's why he liked the cords, Levi's, the old shirts. I have just tons of that stuff—I actually had to part with some, because it was too much. That was kind of just the style that he took on. He had his favorite stuff—army pants. I guess before it was even popular— we'd get shirts for like a buck at St. Vincent de Paul. He probably had like 50 fans that he had bought and started working on. The fans was something that he was really into. And then the furniture—he refinished tables, our dinner table. He and I refinished a Hoosier cabinet, a pie safe. We were always doing one piece and then going on to the next. That was something he did when he was home—we were hardcore [laughs]. It was funny, because we'd sit out on his mom's porch and refinish stuff, and all these Blind Melon fans would go by, and he's out scraping on an old piece of furniture.

Brian Whitus: When he'd come back, most everything he would talk about other than the band would be opening up an antique store. He was in town and I'd come home, and my garage was full of antique stuff that he'd bought. I had no clue that he was even in town at that point—he had loaded my garage! He liked driving down the road, and wanting to pull over and sift through some trash, because he thought he'd seen something. He did that quite often—whether it be an old sink, an old stove. I actually just got rid of an old couch a year ago. I had that couch for twelve years, and got rid of it because I was getting other furniture. That one probably was an antique—all the other crap was just crap. We'd stop at a store from time to time, and he'd spend hours in there. I'm like, "C'mon, *let's get out of here!*"

Melissa Whitus: One time, we were cooking out at Shannon and Lisa's, and Nico was little. He thought I was a pretty good cook, so we would cook together. We were outside, and Lisa was in the house, and Brian's kind of in and out. Shannon didn't have his shirt on. Shannon is really into landscaping—he takes this piping, and puts miracle grow…like, every shrub that he put in his house, he had that piping, so he could fertilize his freakin' plants. He's watering as I'm checking on the chicken, and we hear this buzz sound—it's semi-dusk. It was at the time that people were hearing about Japanese Beetles, so we didn't really know what they were yet. I was like, "I wonder if those were those Japanese Beetles?" Just as I said that…it was like a cartoon—they swarm and sting him! He's running and screaming like a girl into the garage. The hose flies up, sprays the windows in the house, Lisa flies out the porch, she's like, "What the hell are you doing?!" Later, he's got welts all over him. We're laughing about it, he's like, "It's like Melissa completely offended them—that's why they attacked me!" My husband said it was some kind of mud hornet.

Lisa Sinha: He loved tattoos, obviously. A lot of them, I don't think there was a major meaning to it. A lot of the things he just liked. The one that's in cursive on his forearm, that was something that his great grandmother had written [the lyrics to "God's Presents"]. So as far as family went, that had a lot of meaning to him. The one on the back of his neck, I can't remember exactly what the meaning of that one was, but it had something to do with giving, peace, love, and all that. The one around his hand, he really liked that. The roaches I deterred greatly—*"Don't do the roaches around your neck!"* He thought that one was hysterical. It was something to do with he hated roaches—it was his way so he wouldn't fear them anymore. I was like, "Picture yourself at 90 years old with that around your neck." But he was hell-bent on getting that tattoo, so he did. A lot of it was just art that he liked. He had the big fish on his back. It was more to cover up this 'chick on a snake.' The first time he went to L.A., he got this tattoo of a girl on a snake. At the time, it was all 'heavy metal era.' It was a horrible tattoo—whoever did it, did a terrible job. He's like, *"I've got to get rid of this."* And then the fish covered that—it was more to cover up that tattoo then to cover up the scar [from getting stabbed].

Melissa Whitus: We were at the Seattle Beanery—a little place on the west side, a deli-type place. Lisa and I liked to go there for lunch, and Lisa has this hair phobia—even if it's her own hair, if she sees a hair on the plate, on the table, she's done. She won't eat a thing. We're eating there one time, and of course, she finds a hair, and that was it. So we go there with Shannon, Nico, and Lisa—I think it was after we golfed. And these guys are like, *"Is that the guy from Blind Melon?"* All whispering behind the counter. I go up to get a coffee later, and they're like, "If we gave you a shirt, do you think you can get his autograph for us?" I said, "He's a cool guy—if you want his autograph, just ask him." They were too shy, and I finally said, "Shannon, those guys want you to sign a t-shirt, just go up there and do it." He had known the story about the hair, so he writes on the t-shirt, "No hair in my food please. Shannon Hoon." They hung it up on the wall—I think it's still there.

Shannon Hoon: I'm an old car fanatic. It was a Matchbox fetish that turned real. But I don't smash my new cars the way I did with Hot Wheels. I have seven [cars] now. I just love them; they're like old pieces of time. The gadgets and the dashboards, and everything is so inefficient. They're so gaudy and big and you can get your whole block in your car. I have an old farmer who lets me store them in his barn, and I just bring them in town, fuel them up, lube them up, bring them right back out there, and enjoy the little life I have in the drive from the farm into town.

Lisa Sinha: His first car was the LTD, which we still have—that was an LTD 1973, I think. Pea green, but he suped it up—stereo, tinted windows. It was our car for years. We bought a Blazer, it was a huge deal—he paid *cash* for it [laughs]. All the other cars were like a thousand bucks or something. He got really into the whole car thing. And the Galaxie he bought in New Orleans. Then he got another Galaxie—I think it was a 1968 or a '67. Because then, it was an excuse to buy a car—"Oh, it was the year I was born." He bought the second Galaxie on the day Jerry Garcia died—"I'm going to get his car, it will represent the day Jerry Garcia died." And then he bought a 1938 DeSoto. He came driving up in it and honked the horn. Nico and I came out, I didn't know he was going to buy this car. And of course, that one signified Nico being born. I remember him giving us a ride around the block in it—she was three weeks old. And then he bought a truck, I want to say it was Chevy, it was like a 1970, and he bought a Cadillac. These cars, a lot of them were junk. We kept the DeSoto and the LTD, but Christopher wanted the Galaxie— that was the true Galaxie, that's what the song was written off.

Melissa Whitus: He called me [and] said, "Melissa, I need your help. Lisa has a doctor's appointment, and the Blazer's battery is dead. Can you take me up to get a new battery for the truck?" I come to get him, we go to the Auto Zone to pick up the battery. We went by his Galaxie—it was in the process of being redone. He wanted to stop by the body shop and show it to me. We checked that out, then we went back. We're standing there, and I'm looking at the battery in the Blazer—it's a 1994 Chevy Blazer—I said, "Shannon, did you tell them what kind of make/model you had?" "Yeah." "O.K.—this is a top post battery, and they gave you a side post battery. They're not interchangeable." It was just funny, I thought, "What an idiot"—this guy's got all these cars and all this money, and he's completely clueless. I'm a chick and knew that!

Lisa Sinha: He liked Pink Floyd—especially when I first met him. Pink Floyd was plastered all over his room. He liked Van Halen too [laughs]. But not a huge fan. A huge fan of the Rolling Stones, Neil Young, Soundgarden. 'Dark Side of the Moon,' 'Sticky Fingers,' and Jane's Addiction—especially 'Ritual de lo Habitual.' He loved Tom Waits, the Velvet Underground. He liked the whole concept of the Grateful Dead. He loved Janis Joplin. He liked a lot of different stuff, like Liz Phair. He loved Zeppelin. He had very good taste in music—a lot of old stuff. Tom Petty, Social Distortion, Reverend Horton Heat, the Meat Puppets. He *loved* Alice Donut.

Melissa Whitus: We went to this Tom Petty concert—we had third or fourth row seats and backstage passes. Probably one of the neatest things I saw Shannon do, Brian and Lisa left a little bit early to use the restrooms, and we had watched these kids in the second row—they knew every single word to every song. They were true Tom Petty fans. We walked over there, and Shannon says, "Hey, we noticed you guys, and we thought you may like these more than we do," and hands them four backstage passes. They were like, "Oh my God! Dude, are you the guy from Blind Melon?" I said, "Shannon, those kids are going to school the next day, and they're going to tell everybody that they met Tom Petty, but the dude that gave them the backstage passes was the guy from Blind Melon. And no one's going to believe them—because you didn't sign the backstage passes" [laughs]!

Release of 'Soup'

Despite both the band and many of their longtime fans feeling that 'Soup' is a more than worthy follow-up to 'Blind Melon,' the group's newfound pop audience and critics feel otherwise, as the album is panned upon its release on August 15, 1995. As a result, album sales and chart placings ('Soup' peaks at only #28 on the Billboard 200) fall well below what was hoped for.

Shannon Hoon: I'm happy with this record. I'm not going to equate the success of it by the amount of copies it sells.

Danny Clinch: I remember them getting Rolling Stone Magazine, and that they had given them two stars for the 'Soup' record, and had given them an average review. I remember specifically Christopher being really bummed about it—he had the Rolling Stone in his hands, and was like, *"Bummer."* I think I remember Shannon being bummed about it too. I have a picture that reflects that.

Brooks Byrd Graham: It effected [Shannon]—it definitely effected him. He was one of those people that should not read those things [laughs]. He always felt a lot of pressure—I'm sure any frontman feels a lot of pressure. They had worked hard—they were very good, hard workers—and they'd been let down by the record company. When Gary Gersh came in, he had no interest in them. *At all.* They could have had a couple more charting singles from the first record, but Gary Gersh didn't want to do anything with them—and that made Shannon real mad. With 'Soup,' it's such an amalgam of things. Everybody's attitude was, "We're going to go out there—we're going to work this record as long as it takes."

Domenique Johansson: I think that Shannon's mood—general outlook— changed on the way to 'Soup.' Shannon's approach with the press on the second record was more defensive. People might not have immediately taken to a record [when] they didn't hear another 'bee girl song and video' up front. There were some criticisms or observations, that might have been hard for him to overcome—it was a very personal thing for them. There was a certain 'loss of control' he might have felt, that played into his drug use. It's a loss of control the band felt, but Shannon handled it differently. It was with the label—again, a new president. They had their same marketing and publicity people, a few of the radio people, but I think a lot of the people that they really liked...they just felt things unraveling, and not quite the [same] control. It all gave a general overall uneasy picture.

Tim Devine: I think the debut album was so strong in terms of material, that it was hard to follow up. And the band started to become a little scattered and a little frayed around the edges. I mean, we had difficulty deciding on the first single—not because there were too many choices like we had before, this time, there weren't *enough* choices. I think the album proved to be very difficult when it came to singles to promote to radio. And that was probably the ultimate demise of that record.

Christopher Thorn: It's great to blame other people when your record doesn't do that well, and that's what I'll do right now [laughs]. But it goes both ways. We made a crazy record—a really dark record, and a lot of the lyrics are about drugs—Shannon going through a lot of intense deep shit, and struggling with drugs. In the record company's defense, they came back to us and said, "Hey, we're not so sure you have a single." Gary Gersh in particular said, "I think the song 'Pull' has potential, but the arrangement is kind of whacked." When I wrote the song musically, I never intended for it to be a single. I wasn't even thinking about a single—I wanted it to be this epic song with this long outro. And that was the problem he had with it—he just said, "If you guys could re-work this song, possibly, this would be the first single we would go with." And sure enough, at that time, we were still in 'we've sold lots of records, no one can tell us what to do mode.' We said, "No—*that's* the record." And we learned a lesson—you can't really do that with a record company. In the end, either they say, "We're going to spend money to sell this record, to make sure people hear this record" or "We'll move on to something else." And I think Gary had a really different agenda. He came in; he had signed the Foo Fighters. We were in trouble when we had a certain release date, and our release date got bumped—Dave Grohl wanted the July 4th release date. We had it, Dave wanted it, and then suddenly, "Oh, now Dave has the July 4th release and you guys are getting bumped." At that point I remember thinking, "Uh oh, shit. We *used to be* the priority." Everything changed when Gary came in. And we gave them a crazy record. So I don't know—it goes both ways. I think we have to take some responsibility for that. I don't want to call it failure—I think we made a great record. But the fact that it didn't take off and we didn't deliver a song that would get on the radio easy, that is partially our fault.

Shelley Shaw: That first single ["Galaxie"] was not the greatest song on the record—but they always wanted to come out with 'the rocker,' because ["No Rain"] was sort of 'pussy-esque.' It's a really well written song, but they felt like, "We don't want that to be us." So they come out of the box with a fucking blasting rocker.

Hale Milgrim: I do know that if you do everything you possibly can—you do all the right set-up that you have to do for a record before it comes out, and you have the right songs that you feel have a good opportunity to go into certain different areas/segments of the community—you should be able to get X amount [of sales]. If you don't, then there's a tendency—and I think there's been more and more a tendency the last ten or twelve years—to pull the plug. To say, "Well, we didn't get what we expected in the first week or two." It's almost like a film—if a film doesn't show that good the first weekend, they go, "We better cut back our expenditures—we already spent X amount of hundreds of thousands of dollars. We're not going to take it to the next level to see how deeper in the hole we're going to get." I don't know what the discussions were [at Capitol].

When you sell that much of your first record, you may have a lot of resistance on your second record. There have been very few artists that have had that phenomenal type of success on the first album, that have come back with their sophomore record and had an equal success. Yes, it has been done, but it's so few. I worked with Dire Straits at Warner Brothers. We had that first album ['Dire Straits'] that took a good thirteen/fourteen months to succeed, with "Sultans of Swing." Then it took off, and we started selling a million eight of that. The next album was 'Communiqué,' and I believe in its first twelve months sold roughly 300,000 copies. We were all shocked or dismayed that we didn't have the follow-up that we were hoping to have. But, in Europe and other places around the world, 'Communiqué' was as big as the first album. Every subsequent record they had was a huge record. And I can think of numerous artists that had a similar situation.

Tim Devine: Hale was certainly a big supporter of the band, but I don't think that Gary was any less interested. It was just a matter of it being a more difficult record that a lot of people had trouble getting their head around. We kind of reluctantly went with the first single, "Galaxie," shot a video, and we put a lot behind the launch of the record—a lot of promotion and advertising for it. But it just wasn't taking off from where the last record had ended. The reviews on it were mixed at best and there were a lot of people that just did not like the record.

Denise Skinner: If you sit in a marketing meeting, and the head of the company goes, "I don't hear a single on this record," it sets the tone. That pretty much dictated the way upper management was going to handle it. "We don't hear a track—we'll put a sampler together and see what radio picks." It was handled really poorly. They just didn't want to spend the time on it. And Tim—if he signed you, he's probably one of the hardest working A&R guys I've ever met. He could not get Gary's ear, because he was not one of 'Gary's boys.' Whatever corner we tried to head towards, we got pretty much bashed. And again, it stems from the top—when the president says he doesn't hear it, what are you going to do?

George Nunes: I don't think you can really blame Gary. I don't care what label you are—you have success with something and the label wants exactly the same thing. I remember hearing ['Soup'] early on, and going, "Wow, this is really different." It was much more ethereal—a much more open record.

"Galaxie" was an awesome track, but it was not "No Rain." I think 'Soup' was a great record—the bad part was I think it was sadly ahead of its time and nobody embraced that record. And I think it went away pretty quick from what I remember. And we did everything for it—Gary had created a special packaging for it, there was a hidden track on there. The marketing of the record I don't think was lacking. What was really lacking was the acceptance both critically and [from] the public. Sadly, the early reviews and feedback were not great—I think that's what hurt the record more than anything.

Rogers Stevens: We were surprised and hurt by the response it got in a lot ways. But that's fine—it's *still* selling. Publicity-wise, I don't know if some-body didn't have their eye on the ball or whatever, but we got *hammered* in the press. It really effected us. That was when I realized, "Hey, maybe people *do* pay attention to critics and reviews." Sort of get this general bad vibe about a record, that permeates through, and people are less inclined to check it out. On our second album, [it] seemed to not be what people thought they were going to hear. We didn't get a chance after that. Maybe we would have turned it around, had we been able to tour longer, because it was one of those albums I don't think people liked when they first heard it.

Tim Devine: I think at the end of the day, a lot of people felt that the songs were not as strong on the second record as they were on the first. In fact, I was pushing for them to add a few songs that go back to the original E.P, that I thought could add some depth to the album. We always wanted "Soul One" and "Mother" to get their day in the sun.

Hale Milgrim: I really liked the second album. I don't think it had the one song that I'd heard with "No Rain," but I thought it was a very, very strong second album. It was a perfect—in a strange sense—sophomore record. I can understand why it didn't do the numbers of the first record. I think the first record just captured a moment, and I think the video was the climactic moment in a strange sense. When you get that visual experience everywhere for as much and as long as it got played—unless you have a follow-up that could do something to the same level—you've already lost X amount of the people.

My favorite artists are the artists that I've been able to watch go through the whole cycle—the up's and down's. Neil Young being one of the kings.

Owen Orzack: I stayed in touch, and got the heads up when the 'Soup' tour was going to go into pre-production. You heard all kinds of issues and stories. We were like, *"It's going to be an interesting tour."* We were concerned about the last tour was pretty big, this tour we were starting kind of small. We were worried about ticket sales and things like that. "Is the record going to sell? Is it going to go over?"

Rogers Stevens: It must have been a weird time for [Shannon]. He had a baby, a new record that was getting panned. So yeah, it was a real stressful time—a lot of pressure. I wouldn't say that he was blissed out or in a great frame of mind, as he should have been with a baby.

'Soup' Tour

Although Shannon voices mixed feelings about going back on the road so soon after rehab and the birth of his daughter, Blind Melon move forward. Apparently sober at first, it doesn't take long before Shannon falls back into old habits.

Shannon Hoon: I would be lying if I said I was 100 percent enthusiastic about being out on tour right now. It's hard to be away.

Nel Hoon: Shannon did not want to go. He had said to Dick, "Dad, I don't really want to go on this tour—I just don't feel right about going on this tour." And Dick said to him, "Son, you have to, because there's so many people counting on you. You have to fulfill your obligation." Also, he said to me that he didn't want to go. I think he was looking for somebody to talk him out of it. And God, how many times I wish that I had, because I told him the same thing that Dick did. I said, "The guys are all counting on you—the fans want to hear you. You have an obligation, you have to go." For so long, that really bothered me. I hardly could stand it when I heard, when one day his dad and I were talking—this was probably two years afterwards—that he had gone to both of us, and we had both told him the same thing. I think, "God, what if I had just said, 'Shannon, don't go if you don't want to go'"? I truly believe in my heart that he was afraid to go—maybe he knew he was going to get back to doing the same old thing.

Lisa Sinha: He did not want to go out. He wanted to stay home—he wanted to be with Nico. He didn't feel like he was ready for it. Just the pressures of feeling that he had to do it for other people. It's a job, y'know? He felt like he had to go. I told him straight up, "I don't care if you make another penny. You don't feel like going out? I've got a college education, I can support us." I gave him lots of options, because I didn't want him to go—I knew he wasn't ready. But he did anyway. So, I supported him. He had to make the decision. But no, he didn't want to go. I don't know how much he voiced that to the guys in the band. But to friends and family, I know he did not want to go.

Shannon Hoon: It was just the fact that I'm not really, really ready to jump back into this with both feet. I'm not a business; I just want to be home with Lisa during this pregnancy. That's my pride and joy. That's more important to me than this band is. I'm going to be a father longer than I'm going to be the mother...motherfucker [laughs]! The baby had the hiccups the other day.

Brian Whitus: He knew what he was going to do when he went on tour. He didn't have any self-control. He wasn't ready to go on tour. He was just tired. He didn't necessarily tell me he didn't want to go because he was afraid he was going to do drugs, because I'm sure deep down in his head, he thought he *wasn't* going to do drugs. He would never show that side to me, because he was 'the tough guy.'

Rogers Stevens: But he had a lot of connections [in Lafayette]. We caught a lot of flack later on, but that's what I always told people, "Look, this guy is showing up twenty pounds underweight"—and we hadn't even been around him.

Lisa Sinha: I have to agree with Rogers. Anywhere he went, there were the drug dealers—especially in Lafayette. There was a whole group of people that he knew that had drugs. He could easily get them in Lafayette—and did. I sometimes thought he was worse in Lafayette than he was on tour. Yes, there was a big supplier there. It was *bad*. I can remember at that time, all the spoons in our house were destroyed, because he was doing crack. I can remember coming home from shopping, and I could smell it in my house. Ugh—terrible.

Heather Thorn: The bottom line is it doesn't matter with Shannon—you can go anywhere and get yourself in trouble. You can get drugs everywhere. But yeah, he tended to get in more trouble because it was his hometown and he was a little rock star there. He had all the connections before he left to go do what he did—so they were all still there when he came back.

Brad Smith: It was hard for us to make those calls back then. Do we leave him on the road? Do we leave him at his house? Do we keep him busy? Y'know what? That guy was just an addict and he was always going to find a way to get into trouble. That was our thinking at the time, Rogers is right—"Let's get him on the road and away from Indiana, because he has a lot of dope dealing buddies in Indiana." And they would supply him with everything from crack to crystal. It was ridiculous in the worst way. We were desperate to get him away from that environment at any cost. I don't know if the road was a better environment for him, especially after he'd gotten out of rehab.

Shannon Hoon: We can prepare for it a little bit better now. We'll know the cities better this time. I think I'll be doing a little more sleeping, too. This time we'll be pacing ourselves. Trying not to live at 90 miles an hour. I think the band and crew are probably a bit relieved when they call my room and I happen to be sleeping. Usually I'd be calling their rooms at 6am, going, "Hey man, what's going on? I got nothing to do."

Jena Kraus: I think it was August of '95—they had played at the Troubadour [as a warm-up for a European tour]. Later, at the Mondrian Hotel, I went to his room with my friend. We knew he was in his room, and he was not answering the door. We could hear the T.V. The next day, he says to me, "I was looking through my bag, and I found heroin in my bag." He normally didn't do heroin, but he'd done it here and there. He said he did some—I felt like maybe it was coke, I don't know. And he was like, "The cops were knocking at my door!" And I was like, "That wasn't the cops...that was us!" That's why I think maybe it was coke—he seemed awfully paranoid.

Rogers Stevens: Then when we got out on tour—he was clean for a while, in the beginning. We went to Europe and that was pretty fun—with Soundgarden, and Kyuss was on the bill. The band had a bunch of new songs to play and it sounded better.

Shannon Hoon: I like outdoor festivals. You can feel the grass underneath you.

Susan Silver: It was a big show outdoors. Shannon was all giggly, and came and told me the dirtiest joke [laughs]. A happy, giggly, child-like face, telling this really nasty story.

Paul Cummings: A couple of times, he would do the thing where he would throw the mic up into the lighting rig, and try to spin around on the cord, as it was dangling from that. He did that a few times—once at the Reading Festival. It was funny, because it took him three or four throws to get it over the light truss because he kept missing. Then he spun around on it, and they'd have to cut it off him, because he was all tangled up. It seemed like that was going to be a big deal at the Festival. Then Pennywise came on after them, invited the crowd on stage, and people kinda forgot about them.

Shannon Hoon: I was just sitting in my room, and the concierge came in and took all the alcohol out of my mini bar. He was from Zaire or something, and he was saying, "Ha, ha—I take away your lager now. You can't have none." It's pretty weird when someone from Zaire knows who you are, and knows about your alcohol problem.

Glen Graham: Cocaine was the big problem. But he knew a lot of heroin dealers. I have a strange chemistry as far as drugs go. I used to smoke pot like crazy, I don't like cocaine, and the times I've done heroin, it's purely been optional. Fortunately for me, it's that way. During the 'Soup' era, Shannon couldn't say "No." It was as if he didn't want to offend the dealers, so he would take whatever they gave him and hoard it rather than toss it. Eventually, he would start to feel guilty and give it to me and others.

Rogers Stevens: When we got back over here, a week into it, it was definitely the best the band had ever sounded. We had gotten good at playing together. We were playing theaters—that sized venues—and most of them were selling pretty well. There were times it was spotty in the Midwest. Otherwise, it was good.

Lyle Eaves: We didn't take production out. It was a 'cut back tour,' doing clubs. I just never felt like they really had it together from the start of that tour on. I mean, I *think* they were fired up to back on the road.

Paul Cummings: It didn't seem to me like they ever recovered from that first 18 months of touring. They were just like, "Ugh…we're doing this again?" They just weren't into it.

Owen Orzack: The band and the crew were together [on the bus] on that tour.

George Nunes: I think the plan was to keep them touring, touring, touring. The hope would be that this record would catch enough fire with people hearing it while they were out on the road.

Danny Clinch: They played at the Tradewinds in New Jersey—I think I sat in with them that night, I played harmonica. After the show, they had been asked to go play [Neil Young's] Bridge School Benefit, and everybody was super-psyched to go. Shannon said to me, "Hey Danny, we're going to Uncle Neil's—*you better bring your harmonica!*" I was like, "Fantastic dude—I'll see you there."

Brian Whitus: They had a concert in Indianapolis. Got us some tickets, talked to him just a couple of minutes prior to him going on stage. We didn't go backstage, and I remember Lisa saying the next day, "Shannon said, 'That Brian and Melissa, aren't they funny? I don't understand why they never want to come backstage.'" That just wasn't us—didn't want to be back there with all the hoopla and autographs. Because people knew that Melissa and I knew him, and they would call us, "Shannon's in town, do you think you can get us an autograph?" He gets that enough from everybody else, he's certainly not going to get that from us.

Nel Hoon: I saw the show in Indianapolis, and the next day I had to work. I was working at an antique store and I was going to get off a little early. Something told me, "Go see the show in Chicago." So I called my sister immediately, and I said, "Caroline, come on—we're going to see Shannon's show in Chicago." I had just seen him the night before—I don't know why I did it or what got into my head. It was just a spur of the moment decision. So my sister and I got there a little late, and Shannon was coming out of this little restaurant that was right beside it—all the guys were coming out of it. Shannon said, "Hi mom, hi Aunt Caroline—I've got to go, I've got five minutes!" He headed straight in. Well, that show, honestly—speaking as a mom—was one of the best shows that I had ever seen Shannon do. I went to many of his shows—if they were within 300 miles I drove. But that to me was the best show I had ever seen him do.

Rogers Stevens: I remember being [at Chicago's the Metro] and thinking that our sound was really together. Like, "Wow, this is really better than the first record-tour cycle."

Paul Cummings: Before we did Vancouver on that tour, we drove up through the border and stopped at immigration. We were standing at the immigration desk with Shannon, and they run his name through the computer. The immigration guy, when Shannon's stuff came up on the screen, went, "*Whoa!*" and stepped back. [Shannon] was very charming when he wanted to be—they got in. I've seen people turned back for less stuff than that. After we got back on the bus, they start pulling stuff out that they smuggled in. I was pissed that they would even *attempt* this.

Kim Smith: I went to a couple of shows, and Lisa came out with Nico. It was when they were playing with Page & Plant. And he seemed *great*. He was sober, the best spirits ever. He really seemed like he was going to make it. He loved having Nico out there and he was all excited about that.

Lisa Sinha: Nico and I flew to San Jose, shortly after they went on tour, and did a week/week and a half with him.

Marlon Stoltzman: They did the Page/Plant tour on the west coast. Shannon called me, and said, "I've never been happier. The baby's here and Lisa's here."

Rogers Stevens: It was cool—Robert Plant liked our band. He would talk about us in interviews. Obviously, we were knocked out by that—all of us being big Led Zeppelin fans. And so, we did those shows, and they sounded great. I'd seen Jimmy Page play really badly before on television, but man, he was amazing. Amazing on those shows. And they had a cool band—it sounded really good. I remember walking backstage at that show the first day, and Robert Plant being there—bronze and bare-chested! They were really nice people. [Jimmy Page] showed me some of his guitars—that was the only time I really talked to him. But he was really nice.

Glen Graham: The biggest memory of that was, for us, we played, it was great, people liked us—we were known at that point. There was a connection between…*we are playing with half of Led Zeppelin!* It never really dawned on any of us. Those were shows where the audience [was] as rabid as they would be in Europe, at a festival, watching Rage Against the Machine. The most energy I've ever seen in a crowd.

Bill Armstrong: We were up in San Francisco—they were opening for Page/Plant. We were hanging out, and I remember being in Golden Gate Park. Shannon was smoking weed at that point. Me and Rogers were sitting there, and I remember Shannon walking with Nico in a backpack. Shannon came over and hung out, and we were looking at Nico—she was really beautiful. Shannon went walking off, as he did. Rogers looked at me—we started laughing, and he's like, "Can you imagine if Shannon was your authority figure? That's that little girl's *authority figure!*"

Brooks Byrd Graham: Lisa and the baby were out—all the girlfriends were out and we were all together. They went to do a radio station thing, and I remember because we were all standing outside playing with the baby. I loved Led Zeppelin, and so did Shannon. I have a couple of pictures from that show, and he looks bad. He did look pasty and kind of sickly. He didn't eat right—he avoided milk for his singing. He used to get sick a lot—from not taking care of himself and doing drugs too much. But it was obvious at Shoreline.

Bill Armstrong: I really feel that as a live band, when they were on the 'Soup' tour is when they were really kicking into their own. I remember seeing them at Slim's in San Francisco, and it was like, "Wow, these guys have really come into their own." They had their fans that loved them, they really had their defined sound. At that point, they had become *Blind Melon*. They'd had a lot of time on the road, they were great live, they had their sound—all the kinks it takes in a band to work out. They were really pro. It didn't feel like 'my buddies' band' so much anymore, as it felt like, here's this real professional, world-class rock band.

Christopher Thorn: Things were great—Shannon was sober. I remember going from Seattle down the coast, and Lisa and the baby were there on the bus. It was great—it felt like, "Cool, this is the next phase of Blind Melon." I remember playing really well, kinda loving it.

Mike Osterfeld: Shannon was the cleanest I'd ever seen him up to that moment. He was so pure and his body had purged everything. It cleaned out his system and he was totally away from it—he didn't need it anymore. Then we hit L.A., and for some fucking reason, they let us stay after the show.

Jena Kraus: I was supposed to do "Mouthful of Cavities" live with them that night [at the Palace in Los Angeles]. And soundcheck...I lived in Venice, got stuck in traffic, and didn't get there on time. They were trying to teach me a lesson about being late, and they didn't let me sing. They were like my big brothers—very parental roles they ended up taking on with me. Lisa was there at the show with the baby—actually, she was on the bus. She went back to the hotel, and Shannon, me, and Christopher drove to the Hollywood Athletic Club and met everyone else. I remember Brad beating George Clooney at pool—and winning a lot of money from him. Everyone left, and me, Rogers, and Shannon got a cab back to the Mondrian Hotel. I had to go back to pick up my guitar, it was in Rogers' room.

We were all in Rogers' room and Shannon was talking about going to get drugs. Shannon's like, "Hey, aren't those guys from Alice in Chains here?" He called and found out that they were in room 911. Now that's really weird, because that's the same room that I recorded in [earlier], with Christopher, and I was getting all weird vibes in that room. So we went to that room, and I felt bad—I didn't want him to go do drugs, but I didn't stop him. Rogers was in the bathroom—I had my guitar and I wanted to sing this song. [Shannon] had my guitar in his hand, and he was holding it up by the neck looking at the back of it, where the note was still on the back of it. He's like, "Jena, you kept the note! I really meant this. I am really sorry—I haven't been myself the past year." He starts apologizing for the things that happened in New Orleans, and I cut him off. I'm like, "You don't have to explain to me—I already understand."

Then Rogers came out of the bathroom and they were ready to leave. Now I'm holding the guitar, and Shannon is standing across from me—he's got his hand on the doorknob, and he's like, "Wasn't there something else you wanted to do?" What I wanted to do was play this song that I had written ["No Obligation"]—it was a little different than the other songs I had written in the sense that my songs are always honest, but this one, I really was like, "I'm just going to say whatever I think." And the song was about Shannon—it was about his drug use, and it was correlating it with my dad's drug use, and how I felt about that. And just how I wanted him to live. I felt like he couldn't even feel anything anymore in a certain way. So I was going to play this song—and I know this sounds weird—I just know that if I were to play that song, he wouldn't have gone up to that room. Because that song was all about drugs. Hindsight is 20/20. I mean, I know Shannon—he wouldn't have gone up there if I'd just played the song. We probably would have ended up hanging out or whatever. I could have hung out with him anyway, but I felt weird because Lisa and Nico were there. And he was like, "Wasn't there something you wanted to do?" And then all of a sudden, this stupid voice in my head—I felt this feeling like, "Let him go—it'll be better next time."

Mike Inez: It wasn't really a party more so than we were using the Mondrian as 'Gypsy Camp Central' [laughs]. We were doing press—I can't remember what it was—but our management team was there. We were doing press and those guys happened to be staying at the same hotel. There were certain 'camps' that were pretty close to Alice in Chains. I don't want to speak out of school—we were *all* doing a ton of partying back then.

Jena Kraus: I thought I was going to see him in two weeks, because Halloween, they were supposed to play Philly and I was going to fly back for that. Because I didn't get to sing at that show at the Palace, I was going to sing at the Trocadero in Philly. Then we went upstairs to room 911. We got there and Layne Staley was sitting there, and they were all doing coke. It was Layne, their bass player, and the drummer too. There were two girls there. I had the weirdest freaking vibes in that room. So I go in there—the way the room was, it was like a living room, a little kitchenette, and then there was a door behind that. So there was a bedroom and then a bathroom. Shannon never actually did the coke in front of me that night—it was sort of weird, because I'd seen him do it other times. But he went into he backroom—in the bedroom—with Layne and a couple of other people, and I guess they were doing it. I waited a few minutes, and then I went in that room, because I didn't want to see them. And once I came in there, he took everybody to the bathroom. He kept it away from me. And then they went out into the front room again to go get more. Him and Layne left—he never said goodbye.

Jerry Cantrell: [Shannon] was always a great guy, man. We hung with him in L.A. I remember he was there with his girlfriend and their baby. I was in pretty bad shape at that time. He was really excited—he took me down to his room to sneak me in to see his baby. He was really proud—he showed me some pictures. We got down to the door, and he's like, "I don't think this is a good idea," and I'm like, "Yeah, I don't think it is either" [laughs]. "We don't need to wake up your girlfriend and baby—I come stumbling in the room. That's cool man—I'm really happy for you." We spent the night together. I think he had been sober for a while, and I think he also was wanting to *not* be sober that night. Whatever memory of that night was that we had enough of our own struggles going on that we realized a little bit at least [of] what the gravity of that situation was. So nobody wanted to party with him—nobody wanted to set that train rolling again. But it ended up happening anyway—I think by his own accord.

Rogers Stevens: I don't remember anything specifically about [Alice in Chains]. I remember there was a party in one of their rooms. We just went to it and got drugs, basically. Don't blame them—blame us.

Lisa Sinha: He ended up partying all night, and really upset me. A lot of times I dealt with Shannon—he's not the type of person you tell what to do. You tell him to do one thing and he'll do the opposite. That night, I was horrified. I know he was scared that I was going to be mad. But I didn't want to come down on him too hard. He was really bummed to leave Nico, and I truly believe it—Nico was his one proud…he was psyched about her. They kept calling downstairs wanting to come see the baby. I was like, "*No way.* I don't want this around my child."

Kim Smith: They were all really, really pissed off. I got a phone call from Lisa, too. She left from L.A.—she said that her and Nico were up in the hotel room and he didn't get back to the hotel room until 6:30 in the morning. She was furious. He took her to the airport, and she said when she left, she was so disappointed, because she knew he had been partying, obviously. She was really disappointed in how things turned out. Because honestly, those first couple of weeks, everything was good—everything was great—until they got to L.A. If it was put in front of him, he was going to do it. There was nothing in particular that set him off; I just think he couldn't resist doing it.

Rogers Stevens: And then the next day, we bought more drugs. Fucking stupid.

Glen Graham: Other than [the "Toes Across the Floor" video—which was shot during this time in L.A.] being one of the most ridiculous things I've ever been involved in, I remember Shannon was in bad shape. He was at the beginning of his sort of 'Alice Cooper eye make-up' and 'Let's not bathe for many days' [phase]—no telling what exactly was going on there. But it was not good. This was at the point when things seemed to be way out of control in every way possible. You show up at this building, there's trailers with assistants, and there's this huge crew. It was just like the "Galaxie" video shoot—this big production. We don't need to spend $100,000 on an advertisement for a song that's not going to get played on the radio. I was having none of it. Shannon wasn't being abusive or anything, but it was obvious that he was ready to get back to the hotel room to get on with more 'important things.' By the time we got to L.A., the heroin people came out, and we had a 'minder guy' come out. The dumbest idea ever—like Shannon didn't realize what was going on. Didn't trust him, and the guy wasn't very good at it—let's put it that way.

Rogers Stevens: That's where the guy came on tour with us. This big, huge guy, and his job was to keep drug people away from Shannon. The guy flips on the headlights of the bus, as we were in the parking lot of the hotel to drive out of L.A., and Shannon walks into the headlights and buys drugs right in front of him! That was the big 'fuck you.'

Lyle Eaves: We were all on one bus, and it started getting real uncomfortable when [Shannon] started getting high again. ['The minder']—pretty nice guy, but he didn't really do a lot. Shannon would be in the back lounge getting high, and the guy's sitting in the front lounge watching a movie. Shannon needed somebody like that, but I just don't think that guy was right for whatever reason—he didn't click with Shannon. Being in the band's space and being back on their bus, they're used to having their own private bus, and then the whole crew gets stuffed in there with them. So we kind of hide out in our bunks and stay away most of the time. Because hell, most of the time we were getting up early in the morning to do load-ins. They're in the back doing drugs.

Paul Cummings: One of the problems was ['the minder'] was the thirteenth person on a twelve-bunk bus. There was just no place to put him. Shannon's heart wasn't in it—didn't think he needed to be there, didn't like being watched. That's unfortunate, because he really needed someone to keep an eye on him. So he was gone because there wasn't much room for him and Shannon just didn't think he needed to be there. For some reason, instead of warming to it, Shannon took it as a challenge to get away from the guy.

Christopher Thorn: Shannon's in the back of the bus doing drugs, and the guy's up front, taking up room in the bus. We were like, "Why is this guy here? If he's not actually doing his job, this is stupid." At a certain point, either Shannon's going to do drugs because he wants to, or he's not because he doesn't want to. And having a guy on the tour bus didn't change a thing. So we said, "Send this guy home, he's not doing his job." I don't know, I go back at this point—whether I regret that decision. We sent the guy home in Colorado, or something.

Owen Orzack: Paul got robbed at the hotel [in Boulder, Colorado]—the band lost all their money and passports.

Rogers Stevens: It was a hectic little run there. We got ripped off for a bunch of money in Boulder, in the hotel. And that pissed everybody off. Because somebody at that hotel...they had our number, and stole a briefcase with a couple of night's money. I don't really specifically remember to be honest with you. I was kinda 'spinning' a little bit at that point myself.

Nel Hoon: He called me. He said, "Mom, there's a friend of mine that's really bad on drugs—I think he's going to die. I don't know what to do for him." I said, "Well honey, try to concentrate on yourself." He said [the friend] was Layne Staley. I said, "Just be happy that you've been through rehab and that maybe you can talk to him and help him out." We didn't talk very long that day, and I realized later that he wasn't talking about Layne Staley—he was talking about himself. He was trying to tell me that he was back doing the drugs. And he said, "I think he's going to die." I know in my heart that Shannon was talking about himself.

Brad Smith: I remember things becoming more unhinged as the cocaine use got out of control—on everybody's part. Cocaine was basically destroying the band in a live capacity—I felt that standing on stage, I don't know how the audience perceived all this. We were rushing songs—it was just mayhem on stage. We sounded like a metal band playing Blind Melon songs. No one's a saint in this band—I'm not going to point any fingers. But you can make a blanket statement that there was some cocaine abuse going on, and some marijuana abuse, heroin, and whatever else. It was a secret I had between me and my now-wife—I might just slip off in the middle of the night, get a plane ticket, and go home. Because this is fucking stupid. I was really frustrated. And I think part of that was because I didn't use cocaine at all. I never have—I've never touched the stuff. So when you see your friends start crumbling around you from that kind of substance abuse, you're out on the road and you're trying to make the best of this 'people waiting on you to fail'—you're giving them a lot of reasons to follow through with that emotion. Y'know, "Wow, this band's failing." And sure enough, we did because of the cocaine use. It was really hard on me, personally. We could do better than that.

Rogers Stevens: I was the last guy to get the severity of the situation. I was living in a bit of a bubble, and not necessarily the most 'together guy' myself at that point. I don't think I saw it as clearly as they did. But my impression was that once we got started, things were O.K. But no, I didn't think that stuff—I didn't think I was going to cancel the tour. But it might have been hidden from me—I don't know. I wasn't on that level, but I was definitely doing the drugs here and there. That clouds your judgment. It just didn't seem so bad to me—everyone was there and together. We were playing shows every night, we're touring, crazy stuff happens. You're a rock n' roll band—people do drugs.

Lisa Sinha: [Shannon was] very upset that the album wasn't doing well. And Shannon was one of these people, things had to be going really good for him to be happy. And that meant all the cards in place. If one little thing wasn't going right—such as the album wasn't selling quite the way he wanted it to—he would be bumming out and depressed over it. If you recount the last six months, a lot of that was the end of the 'Soup' [recording], the release of the album, Nico being born. It was very much like a rollercoaster—lots of highs and lows. I think that when the album wasn't doing well, that just stressed him out terrible. And it wasn't even that the album was doing poorly, because really, it hadn't been out long enough to do bad. He needed instant gratification and wasn't getting it, so he was worried, and I think it was a pride issue, too. That really bothered him—he got really worked up over it.

He and I had many a conversation. Of course, me being an optimist, I was like, "You have to give it time. You have to not beat yourself up over it—a lot of people's second album doesn't do as well as the first. It takes longer to break." He just couldn't stand that it wasn't doing as well as he thought it would. And I think a lot of that stemmed from this was *true Shannon stuff.* I don't know if it was like, "My art is not being appreciated." And I think that was depressing for him. Having Nico was really exciting for him, but having a new baby is also very stressful, too. Having this little person that's relying on you—for normal, everyday people having a baby is stressful. I don't know that he was that stressed out about Nico. I just think being in show business and any kind of music, where you're selling your heart and soul, he was a very passionate person—as far as his lyrics, the things he wrote had meaning. He didn't really do a lot of love songs—his songs were personal experience. I just think that it was hard for him not to sell as many albums as the first album did.

Tim Devine: He had called me and was noticeably depressed. He was depressed about the fact that the album had fallen off the chart, and what were they going to do about it? What could they do, what were we going to do, etc. At that point, it seemed like he wanted to come home and come off the road. I tried to tell him that these things take time—going back to the path we followed on the first album. America was a big country and the world is even a bigger place. I tried as best I could to encourage him to keep his head down, stay out there and work through it. Get out there and do what had worked for them in the past, which was steady touring—bring these songs to the people and let these songs come alive in the concert setting. But I think it was a frustrating experience. Here was a band that had just come off a very successful run of magazine covers, TV shows, big concerts, and a lot of attention, to being in a place where the reception was not as warm and friendly as it had been. He was definitely in a funk. We talked for about 20 minutes and I think he didn't necessarily want to hear what I was telling him. But he also probably understood parts of it. My goal at that point—my mission—was to try and lift his spirits and keep the ball rolling. It was too early in my mind to be giving up on an album after all the work that had been put in—both in making that record and all the work associated with the prior album.

Brad Smith: By the time we made it to Fort Worth, he had done an eight ball of coke.

Mike Osterfeld: The band broke up three times. They broke up in Dallas [on October 19th]. They couldn't stand each other anymore—they were just so fed up. A lot of this had to do with Shannon's substance abuse. They came walking off the bus saying, "We broke up." I think it was Christopher that told me that. "We're going to play the show, but we broke up." It was just like, *"What?!"* We had been through a frickin' washing machine. We had been to the highest of highs—"No Rain" being the hit, we had the semi's, and whatever we needed we got—to being, "Here we are all living on the same bus trying to do a club tour." Starting all over. Then the next day we hit Houston, and somebody showed up with Bolivian flake—the purest of pure. Gave it to him, and it was bad news. It was the worst fucking show they ever did. We were playing *a discothèque*—it was the lowest point ever. He was choking on his microphone. He was so high that when he was singing into his mic, he shoved it all the way into his mouth. He had no breath—he couldn't produce the lyrics. The kazoo, he couldn't play it. That's how bad that Houston show was.

Paul Cummings: I remember Mike Osterfeld saying, "Man, it looks like [Shannon] is going to have a heart attack out there." He was out of breath and just didn't look good. He wasn't sleeping and he wasn't taking very good care of himself. I could tell he shouldn't be out there, and looking back, maybe would have done things differently. I was thinking we should have just gone home. And I remember thinking on the day of [the Houston performance, on October 20th], "We shouldn't be here, we should be going home—he's not up for it. It's not working. It's not worth it."

Christopher Thorn: Other than just the normal sorta crazy mayhem of drugs and stuff like that, it wasn't always all bad. That's sorta misleading in a way—to just think about the drugs and it was terrible. I mean, we laughed a lot, we had a lot of fucking fun. I remember the [October 20th] show specifically, feeling really awful—I just wanted to get off stage. Feeling like, "Fuck man, *we're sucking.*" It was just really sloppy. None of us made a habit of doing drugs before we played, too often. I mean, there were times that we went through a little pot smoking phase before we played. But for the most part, there wasn't heavy drug use going on before we played, it was sorta the 'after' that was the party. And I felt that Shannon was high before he went on, and it felt like a terrible show—I remember feeling kinda bummed out. But it wasn't like we were fighting, it wasn't like that.

Lyle Eaves: The shows were definitely suffering. It was obvious I think to everybody. And along that point is where I called Chris [Jones] and said, "I don't know how much you know about what's going on, but you need to do something. I know Shannon's getting way back into drugs, and the shows are not very good—this isn't doing anybody any good." That may have even been [October 20th]. If I remember right, [Chris] started getting the idea of that, but I don't think he knew it was to the severity that it was.

Glen Graham: The place we played, Numbers, right next door to it was a nice restaurant—I remember eating there, coming back, playing the gig, and then waiting to get on the bus, because Shannon was signing an autograph for a kid, who had a poster and record. Maybe like a ten year old—a little blonde haired kid—his parents were there with him. Hippie kind of parents. I remember this distinctly—he was talking to the kid, and the kid was saying all this stuff to him. Praising him. And he was in this real sort of like, "I hope I see you next time, I hope to make it back." A lot of really depressing, down sort of stuff. And then, his coke guy showed up. And I saw—and Rogers can confirm this—the largest ball of cocaine I have seen in my entire life, except in television or in the movies. The size of a golf ball. I mean, *it was a big fucking bag of coke.* And he sat in the back lounge—and he had help—but basically snorted most of it by himself.

Lyle Eaves: Shannon was sitting in the back lounge. When I got done, I walked on the bus, and he's sitting back there not looking very happy. He said, "What did you think about that show?" And I said, "It definitely wasn't one of your better shows." He just kind of sighed, and I was like, "Truth hurts."

Christopher Thorn: He gave me a Warhol book, just like, "Hey, check out this book." And I could tell he was in 'party mode' and was going to be up all night. For me, I'd had a bad night. The show fucking sucked and I was really pissed off about it, so I was like, "I'm going to go in my bunk and kick it." He stayed up all night doing drugs.

Brad Smith: I can't remember exactly what he was talking about or what he said. You know when someone's really drunk, high on coke, or really out of it, and they're rambling about stuff? You're kinda like, "We'll talk about it in the morning." I disregarded everything he said—he was telling me what he wanted to do. I was like, "O.K. Shannon, let's talk in the morning—I'm tired, I'm going to go to bed." I got in my bunk. The last meaningful conversation I had with him, I think it was after he got out of rehab. We were talking about how things are going to be better and different, and how he was sorry.

October 21, 1995

On the morning of Saturday, October 21, 1995, the band's tour bus pulls into New Orleans, Louisiana for a scheduled show at Tipitina's.

Christopher Thorn: Unfortunately, we were accustomed to drugs being around. People ask me, "Was that a weird day?" It's like, "Yeah, but that happened all the time." It wasn't that out of the ordinary—Shannon would do drugs, get sober and clean for a little bit, then do some more drugs. A lot of us in the band were doing drugs too, so it wasn't like, "Oh God, he's fallen off the deep end!" It was like, "Oh O.K., he's having some fun tonight."

Glen Graham: I had stayed up all night. Like I said, I was not a 'coke person'— I'd done a little coke here and there, but I'm not into it. Rogers and Shannon were doing coke in the back lounge—I was in the front lounge. Rogers went to bed at some point, and I remember Shannon was on the phone—cell phones were new, and cell phones that you could talk to anybody in the country on were very expensive. He was pacing back in forth in the front lounge, coked to the gills, and he is screaming at our accountant's voice mail—it's like 4:00 in the morning there—over some little piece of nothing. At some point, he disappeared in the back. I always stayed up and talked to the bus driver—we had this guy, I can't remember his name, but he was a younger guy. The television is right behind his head, and I put in 'The Out-of-Towners'—that Jack Lemmon thing. It was just obnoxious—it's got Sandy Dennis [mimics a nasally/whining voice] *talking like this.* It's an hour and forty minutes of that, and I've watched this movie probably 15 times in the last few weeks. I remember him going, "Oh my God, no! Not again, please don't! Anything—get Shannon back up here screaming, I can't take it!" So we drive into New Orleans, I'm sitting there on the little steps by [the driver]. We're talking about his family problems. His father committed suicide—some very unfortunate story.

Mike Osterfeld: We got onto the Ponchatrain, and I woke up at the truck stop at 5:00 in the morning. And here's Brad, Glen, and Shannon—I think maybe even Christopher—hanging out in the front lounge, having a *deep* conversation. And Shannon was making complete sense. Up to that point, from L.A., he was so far gone, that the band had 'broken up' and couldn't deal with him. And here they are, Shannon making complete sense. I'm thinking, "What the hell are they doing up at 5:00 in the morning?" I went back to bed.

Glen Graham: We pull into the hotel, which was a block off of St. Charles. It was the first time I had come home from a tour to a house I owned. I walk off the bus, got my bag, walked around the corner, got on the streetcar, rode down St. Charles Avenue to Napoleon, where I lived. This is probably 7:00 in the morning—cool, very light, breezy. New Orleans in the fall. I remember getting off the streetcar, and walking four blocks to my house. And thinking about how great this was. I told Brooks that—I woke her up—"It's finally coming together. I like it." And went to sleep.

Christopher Thorn: I saw [Shannon] in the morning. We got to New Orleans, we all checked into our hotel rooms. He seemed fine, he didn't seem fucked up by the morning. It was a long trip, and by whatever time it was—6-:00/7:00/8:00—it seemed as normal as it ever was in the Blind Melon world.

Rogers Stevens: As I remember it, us being in the elevator, and we were talking on the way up. I told him to go to bed—"You look tired, go to bed."

Lisa Sinha: About that day, I did speak to him. He called me—not a day went by that I didn't speak to him three or four times. The night before, it was weird—he talked to my dad, and my dad said he was acting a little strange, because he was looking for me. I think he thought I was at my parents' house. When he called, I was home—I may have been busy with Nico. The next morning he called—they had went to New Orleans. I was pretty good at telling when he was doing drugs, and he really sounded normal to me that morning. He sounded tired, but he didn't sound screwed up. I got the story later that he'd been doing drugs the night before. He called and said, "I'm really tired—do you think you can get me a flight to Florida?" They were going to Florida next. And so all morning, I was on the phone getting flights booked for him. I talked to him I would say 9:00—I was getting everything figured out. And then I went to a friend's house, and I came back. [Shannon] was going to go get something to eat, and he was going to call me in a little bit.

Glen Graham: He got in his hotel room, called Lisa, went downstairs, walked around the corner, got something to eat, went back on the bus.

Owen Orzack: Because the band and crew were on the same bus—they parked at a hotel. The band would go to their rooms and then our load-ins were usually at 11:00 or 12:00. So we stayed on the bus. That one was different. Lyle, his girlfriend came down from Mississippi, and Randall—the other guitar tech—his girlfriend drove down, and those guys had hotel rooms. So they weren't on the bus. The guitar tech at the time, Vince, had left. He had gotten married, so he had off, and we had another guy come out—to fill in. A guy named Pinsky—a guy I knew from Minneapolis. Him and I were on the bus, but everybody else was in the hotel. I was in the top driver side front bunk, and I remember at some point, hearing something that didn't sound right—some sounds, some grunts. I actually thought it was Pinsky—I thought he was talking in his sleep or had sleep apnea. It was weird—there was banging. I was like, "What's going on?" It woke me up. Didn't think about it. Then later on in the morning, I got up. I noticed right across—on the passenger side middle bunk, which was Christopher's bunk—there was a foot sticking out of the curtain. I had to move the foot to open the door—I didn't want to wake him up.

So I went up to the front lounge, and saw Shannon's clothes strewn all over—his pants, his bag, his room key was lying on the floor. I was like, *"This is great."* I looked in the bunk, and saw it was Shannon. I was like, "What's he doing in Christopher's bunk?" His foot was sticking out and he was facing the wall—with his back to the curtain. I actually got dressed, went into the hotel, and called Paul. I said, "Hey Paul, just F.I.Y.—we're due to leave here in about 45 minutes, Shannon's on the bus, he's in Christopher's bunk, his clothes are all over the lounge. What do you want us to do? Do you want us to wake him? Have him go to the room?" He's like, "No. Just wake him when you're fixing to leave, and he can stay in the bunk, or he can come in the hotel. But let him know before you go to [Tipitina's]." So I went back to the bus, and a few minutes later, Lyle and Randall came on board, and I told Lyle what was going on. He goes in, opens the curtain, and he's like, "Shannon... Shannon." He shakes Shannon and nothing happens. When he rolls him over, he takes one look at him, and he's like, *"Holy shit!"* We knew something was wrong—we thought he might still be alive. He was still warm. There was no pulse—I took his pulse.

Paul Cummings: It never occurred to me that he was dead at this point. I don't think it occurred to any of us—I thought it was some kind of stunt.

Mike Osterfeld: Half his body was blue, half his body was red. We put him down on the floor, started giving him C.P.R. I was holding his head, and the last bit of breath of air came out of him—*it was smelling death.* We wrapped him in a blanket, put him on the front bunk, called 911. It took them *forever* to get there. The E.M.T. walked on the bus and said, "He's dead," and walked off. I wanted to kill her. All's I could think was the drug enforcement showed up before the frickin' ambulance. They wanted to bust us. After we wrapped him up and called the E.M.T., I went through the bus and started cleaning it out. Because the last thing I wanted was for someone to get arrested. So I found his stash and got it off the bus. I knew it was going to be a drug over-dose and it was going to be all over MTV. The last thing I wanted was the band going to jail for it.

Paul Cummings: [Shannon] went back out to the bus and had a heart attack. Too much and just couldn't take it—he wasn't eating, wasn't taking care of himself. I'm still mad at him for that. The first thing I said was, "This is so typical of him."

Owen Orzack: Paul came down and the rest of the crew. We all just stood outside the bus. A lot of people were crying. I don't know when the band members came down. I remember at one point, we weren't let back on the bus, because it was a crime scene. We ended up getting rooms in the hotel for the rest of the folks. We were all stunned. Then the cops started asking all kinds of questions. I was like, "He's 28 years old and he's got a history of drug abuse."

Paul Cummings: The manager had already been called at that point, so he knew what was going on—he flew out. I guess they just left [Shannon's body] in the front of the bus until the coroners came and took him away.

Shannon Hoon: It touches me when someone young dies. [Their life] is just cut short. It just seems like there's a lot of people who tend to make the drugs part and parcel with the music, and I don't know why. You think, "If this person would have worked at Thrifty, would they be doing heroin?" It's just a shame.

Aftermath

While some expected Shannon to die at an early age, the news still proved to be a shock to those close to him and the band.

Glen Graham: At 10:00, the phone rings, and my wife answers the phone. I saw her walk to the other room and [say], "It's Chris Jones." He said, "Are you awake?" "Yeah." "Shannon's dead." Just like that. I said, "Are you kidding?" "No, I'm not kidding—I would not kid about something like that." I said, "Well, tell everybody they can come here." And they did. All the crew, Rogers' parents, my parents, Brad's family—they were all down there because it was 'New Orleans.' So we had this wake in my house—it was the most grim kind of thing. And my house was a dark place to begin with—it was a lovely place, but it had very dark colors on the walls, dark woodwork. There's 25 of us in there, fielding phone calls all day and sitting there in disbelief.

Lisa Sinha: And then I got the phone call from Chris Jones. *Thank God my mother was there.* Chris said, "I have bad news." "What?" "Shannon's dead." Which was horrifying for me. It was just lots of things going through my head—my daughter no longer has a father. My grief for her was overwhelming, along with my own for myself. I ached for her—I was horrified. Things have turned out a lot better than what I've ever thought they would—the way she's handled it. She's handled it like a complete trooper, as far as that goes.

Nel Hoon: It was mostly shock. Lisa's mother and her sister-in-law came to the store where I was working. They wanted me to know before I heard it on the radio. When they came there and told me that, there were costumers. I was getting sick and I went into the bathroom. I don't remember this, but when the manager came, I had crawled underneath the sink of the bathroom—I must have been in shock. I don't know how long that went on—I'm sure every mother on this earth that has lost their child goes through the same shocking experience. They don't know what they did until somebody tells them.

Heather Thorn: We lived in Seattle, and I was looking for trees for our front yard. I pulled over to the side of a pay phone on Aurora Avenue. I called Christopher, and I was like, "Listen, do you want maples in the front yard?" He said, "You haven't gotten any of my messages? *Shannon's dead.*" I remember collapsing in the phone booth, sitting there, just going, "Oh my God, what do you mean he's dead?" He proceeded to tell me that they found him on the bus. He died in Christopher's bunk, which Christopher to this day, is still haunted by that, because he doesn't know why he was in that bunk. Everybody's space in the tour bus was their own, and it was taboo to go into anybody else's space. But I don't know, that's just as far as he made it before he died. Nobody knows what happened. I remember focusing really hard to get myself home alive, and trying to get in touch with Brad's wife. You're just in shock. You expect it, but when it happens, it's like, *"Fuck."*

Kim Smith: It was a shock. I was going to school at the time—I got home, and there were all these messages from Brad, saying, "Kim, you have to call me, you have to call me. I'm at this hotel in New Orleans. *Shannon's gone.*" Honestly, it did not click that Shannon had died. I'm like, "Shannon's gone? What happened?" I thought he left the tour—like he did when we were in London that time. I thought maybe he left to go home—like he couldn't handle it again. I was trying to call the hotel, and finally, I called Heather. I was like, "What's happening?" She's like, "Have you talked to Brad? *Shannon died.*" I was in complete shock. I was blown away—I could not get over it. I did not think that was coming.

Brooks Byrd Graham: It was so stunning—it took so long to sink in. And it did for everybody—I remember Christopher saying he didn't unpack. He went home and he lived out of his suitcase for a while. He just couldn't face reality, that this whole thing that they'd been working so hard on for so long had just suddenly ended. There was nothing. But God, it was so hard, because Lisa wasn't there. I was glad that we had a house and everybody could come to our house. Everybody could talk on the phone there—it wasn't like hanging out in a hotel lobby or something. It was our house, we could all be there together. But talking to Lisa was just crushing.

Glen Graham: The crew—they were all mortified. Absolutely blown away. Not only is this thing that they had affection for gone, but the realization that so is there livelihoods. You can't say anything. You can't talk. It was grim. I remember us going into my office, which is right next to the room where everybody was, and I remember saying—with Chris Jones and the four of us—"I don't want this to end." I remember Christopher saying specifically, "Well, now's not really the time to think about that." And I said, "No—what I mean is I don't want this to stop. And I don't think it should stop. I don't mean that I want to find another singer, I mean I think that we should continue to make music." Then it got very, very morose.

Mike Osterfeld: Losing Shannon was huge—I thought it killed me. I thought I was done in the business.

Owen Orzack: As my career went, it pretty much changed my whole career. At the time, I was working for bands—I was hired by bands and working with musicians very closely. And after that, I ended up working for sound companies and at arm's length sometimes from musicians. I was very upset and I was very angry at the whole thing—the whole loss of somebody that was very cool. But being angry as well because I had a one-year-old kid and I was out of work. How was I going to feed my family—because somebody couldn't stop doing drugs? I remember being very pissed off about that—a lot of us were. The crew certainly was and the band members were, too. Angry, as well as sad—for many years. Lyle completely got out of the music business not too long after that. He went back to Mississippi. I actually hired him to go on tour with a few other bands. He did a Tracy Chapman tour with me, and him and I did the Dave Matthews Band on the 'Crash' tour—we worked together for a sound company that did their tour. He was very interested in motorcycles, and wanted to open a motorcycle shop. Music was something he just did in the meantime. After a few years, he just gave up, and now owns a bike shop in Mississippi.

Brian Whitus: Was it a shock? Yes. Did I think it was going to happen? Yes. His mother had called—me and a buddy had just got done doing some deer hunting here. I walked in the house, and my wife was bawling—hysterically. *I instantly knew*—for some reason, I just knew it was about Shannon. And it was. Nel had called Melissa and gave me the phone. That was it. I remember dropping to my knees on the kitchen floor, hanging the phone up, and then going down to the basement and sitting in a chair, thinking, *"Oh my God."* Hoping it wasn't true, [that] it was just some nasty dream. But it wasn't.

Jena Kraus: Shannon had left his pot pipe with me. I was like, "When I see him on Halloween I'll give it to him." I had no pot and I was dying for pot—I scraped the bowl and remember taking the very last hit of resin. As I blew the smoke out of my mouth, I watched the smoke go up, and thought, "You're going to remember this moment for some reason." The [same] night, I said to myself, "What if he died?" I swear to God I thought that. The next morning, I had to get up early for work. The woman I worked for, I normally wasn't supposed to work that day—I was going to work a double shift because she had to go to a wedding. And she circled in red Sharpie twice, October 21st—like a few days before. I remember her saying, "I have a bad feeling about this day, you're not going to be here on this day." That morning, October 21st, I was like, "Something is weird about this day." I remember sitting at the bus stop waiting for the bus to go to Santa Monica where I worked. I'm sitting there and dreaming about two weeks from now, I'm going to go to that show, I'm going to sing with them, it's going to be great. I'm like, "God, what would I do without them? What would I do without Shannon?" I went to work, everything's fine. I'm there by myself, and I decide I'm going to check my messages. I call, and it's one new message—it's Christopher. He's like, "Oh my God Jena—pick up the phone, pick up the phone." He's going on, and he's like, "Jena, I don't want you to hear this on the news—Shannon died this morning." I heard that and slammed the phone down. I was in shock. I left and stayed in my apartment by myself—couldn't even go out for three days. It really fucked me up—for years. I feel like only in the past few years I just started to get over it.

Shelley Shaw: I remember that I woke up—my answering machine was blasting and it was Axl. It was like 10:00 in the morning on a Saturday. I was sleeping, and he was like, "Shelley, it's Axl—I've got to tell you something. Call me back, it's really important. *I've got to tell you this.* Before you talk to anyone else—please call me." I was scared to death. I was like, "What the fuck is going on?" And Axl always had 'things,' so I thought, "Oh, it's Saturday. I don't want to hear whatever it is—whatever's going on now." So I got in my car a little bit later, around 2:00—I was doing my Starbucks run and checking my machine at work on my car phone, and he was on there too, saying the same thing. He goes, "I think this is your office, I don't know." And I was like, "What is going on with this guy?!" I'm just going to have my day, and I'll call him when I've had some of my day. And this agent from our New York office…my car phone rang, and he goes, "Shelley, it's Phil. Are you driving? Pull over." I'm like, "What's going on?!" And he goes, "Shannon's dead." I remember it was like I wrecked my car. I called Axl back, and I don't remember anything about that conversation. I remember I went to the Cinerama Dome, and there was a movie playing. I sat there for like two and a half runs of it—just sat in there in a coma. And then I talked to Chris Jones, and they didn't really want anybody to talk about it. I had some sort of event that night—I drove myself to it, put my 'showbiz face' on. I went home and slept, and then the next day, my phone was ringing off the hook. I never knew anybody that lost the battle. And it's funny, because this past year, my mom lost the same battle. It was the same Goddamn thing—every time, she went back to drinking. I couldn't believe it! But I think in the end, looking back and going through all or her stuff when I cleaned out her house—they don't really ever leave it. They're hiding it.

Danny Clinch: At my life at that point, I don't think I had ever known anybody that young that had died—where *everything* was going for him. But I wasn't surprised, to be honest. Chris Jones called me. I remember him saying, "Danny, I never wanted to make this phone call, but Shannon died." I was like, "Ugh, God." I told my wife, because we had all become friends. At this point, when they came to town, they were coming to my apartment, and we would hang out and have jam sessions. My wife got to know them and their girlfriends—who are now their wives. We all became good friends. We were all sharing in the excitement of what these guys had going for them.

Mike Napolitano: We were supposed to have a session in the early part of that day—they were supposed to come by and O.K. some final mixes for "John Sinclair" or "Three is a Magic Number." It was a shock, but not surprise—you knew it was coming. Still, it was, "*Holy shit.*"

Bill Armstrong: I'll tell you—I wouldn't put him on my list of 'friends to die.' I would have maybe put him on my list of 'friends to get sober at some point.' It was a surprise, that's for sure. I have some friends who I do consider drug addicts, and it hasn't been a surprise when I heard they died. It was like, "It was a matter of time." Sad, but not surprising. Shannon was a real surprise. Because he's also the guy who would throw on sweats at some point and go jogging or something. He was a guy of extremes.

Domenique Johansson: His death and the way he died was a complete surprise, as far as I was concerned. It was just so totally unexpected. You see other people that have been so far gone—you just knew it was going to happen. Like that guy from Alice in Chains. It was just no way thought he'd be long for this world. It was not what I think you felt around Shannon. You did wonder if he was going to take it too far one day, but I didn't think it was something that would end in death. He was responsive to people when the concern came, he seemed to have some level of control. Alcohol I always felt was his biggest demon—he didn't control it well. His biggest problems and fights seemed to be more with alcohol.

Susan Silver: That was the 'shock call.' To get that call, and know the horror that the guys had to have gone through. We had a similar situation with Layne. I didn't even know [Shannon] had a drug problem, so it just shocked me. Chris [Cornell, who Silver was married to] was never one to have phone chat relationships with people—he and Jeff Buckley were as close as it got. They didn't talk often, but when they did, it was definitely a deep connection. But Chris adored Shannon. When I got the call, Chris was over at our cabin at the time, writing. I was trying to get him to come home, so I could tell him in person, but he could tell that something was wrong and wanted to know what it was. It was another incident where to me it felt like he buried the grief—Chris buried the grief. He didn't react, he didn't respond—he went dead silent. I think it had to do with his continuing depression—unresolved grief. And Shannon's death was another significant blow.

Curt Kirkwood: He didn't seem too fucking 'far out' to me. Even when he died, it was probably an accident. I don't think he was that eroded, he had a brand new kid and was doing pretty good. It was an accident, y'know? He was a pretty tough guy. He was strong-minded too—in an almost bulldog mind-set, really a passive sort of thing going on. But there was a lot of that weirdo, 'Guns N' Roses' sort of thing in there too. That's how I always looked at it-Midwestern rock/barroom sort of thing, too. He didn't seem self-destructive to me though.

Tomas Antona: I was gutted. We were in France on tour. We found out in the afternoon—we were playing that night—it was just like the wind taken out of us. The rest of this drive was completely silent. It was sad, and then after we got back and read more—the press made Shannon out to be this freak. And it wasn't the case.

Sissi Schulmeister: I was really depressed about it. He was so young, and it's such a tragedy that he just had a baby. It just made me really sad. Even today, thinking about it makes me sad, because he was such a great guy. He died way too young.

Craig Ross: He was extreme. A lot of guys I grew up with had that kind of vibe that Shannon had—they could get really out of control. I was used to that kind of person. I remember keeping in touch with him and his girlfriend, and thinking that they were turning a corner—things were going to get pretty stable for him. So in that respect, it was a shock.

Buz Zoller: It didn't really surprise us, because we had 'been there.' Whenever things would come up in the news or the magazines, we would be interested—

so we heard the bizarre stories that would start to come out. It was like, *"Here we go."* Because we knew how dynamic of a person he was—and obviously, the whole band had kind of a 'tie to the history of rock n' roll.' They had a respect for the past and classic rock thing—obviously, he idolized the way that the stereotypical '60s rocker' would go, and things he would do. Dying young is probably something that he thought about, as great rock n' rollers do. It was obviously a shock because [it was] somebody that you know, and at such a young age. And unnecessary.

Jon Plum: In some ways, it didn't surprise me that much, but it was really disappointing. Some of the people I've met, they just have that energy—that crazy, over-the-top energy. I know some people like that right now, and you question what's going to happen to them. I definitely had that feeling about Shannon—"What's going to happen to this guy when he gets out there?"

Nicholas Bechtel: He was not this 'death person.' I partied and grew up with a lot of guys like him—but he had so much energy in him. That to me was a shock. Was it a shock that he put himself in that situation that he could have died? We all do when we party like that. I wasn't seeing it firsthand, so to me it was a shock.

Kim Smith: I think we had all seen Shannon much worse than that. The days in L.A. when we were partying—before he hit it big. That was when he was really bad. You would have thought he would have died then—not at that point. I didn't see it coming.

Heather Thorn: There were always general discussions of, "He's going to end up dead." But I don't think there was that sense of, "Here it is, it's coming right now." No more, no less than we always had of, "Jesus Christ, are you kidding me? He's doing it again—he's going to end up dead one of these times, he's not going to wake up." Hindsight is 20/20—it got worse and worse. When we first moved to L.A., he was more of a drinker, although he would do a little bit of everything. But once you go to crack and crystal meth and that kind of stuff—that was the point of no return for him. Knowing more now, it's like, "Dude, are you crazy? You're going to kill yourself."

Brooks Byrd Graham: I definitely thought that he was going to kill himself with drugs—at some point—if he continued the way he was. There was just no way his body could continue that way.

Marlon Stoltzman: Jena called to tell me. Jena's father had been quite sick, so when she called and was hysterical, I thought that her father had died. And she told me Shannon had died. I couldn't believe it. But no one was surprised. All the people he met with me, everyone that this guy touched, was devastated. And I really believe that it was secondary to the music. He really made impressions on people. He gave you something and left you with something. The whole group was just very somber for a while—"I can't believe it" type stuff.

Denise Skinner: It devastated me. Chris Jones and I were talking on the phone, and we both started crying—it was so sad. It was a waste of a very precious life. Shannon is the same age as my youngest brother, so a lot of this hit home for me—as far as this could be my son, this could be my brother. Here he has this beautiful baby. At the end of the day, I think that Shannon would have done this to himself one way or another. And that's the unfortunate thing. There was a lot of hope, especially when his daughter was born. But I think he wanted to be liked so much that he let people near him, and unfortunately, the bad people got to him. He had a hard time saying no, and God bless the other guys—they saw that and they could only do so much. That's where Chris Jones was so important. I don't think Shannon would have ever gone to rehab if it weren't for Chris Jones. So at least there was a lot of heartfelt concern for Shannon. Unfortunately, he just didn't make it.

Lisa Sinha: Chris Jones was always really good to me. Shannon loved Chris Jones—they were very tight. He got them great tours, and he was really responsible for that. Even after Shannon died, when I had my interview with VH-1 'Behind the Music,' he came and hung out with me during that, so I didn't have to do it by myself. Shannon had a great relationship with him— he really did. I did a lot of communicating with Chris—especially during the hard times when [Shannon] got in trouble. Chris and I had to get him out of jail, like in New Orleans. Shannon looked up to Chris as a father figure in a way.

Eva Pfaff: When the baby was born, I was like, "Here's something that will keep a little part of his day ordinary every day." I felt like they were both robbed—he was robbed of that opportunity, she was robbed of her father. It was so sad.

Hale Milgrim: I was so saddened obviously with Shannon. I like to think I would have had more strength in myself to be able to sit down and talk with him, or try to help in whatever way—just like the band members tried to help, just like management tried to help—with his substance abuse. I spent time with him, I never saw that side of Shannon. It's so sad when anybody so young and so full of life as he was—and had so much of a kid in him—that we couldn't have reached him some way.

Glen Graham: And the next day or two days later, you're on a plane to Lafayette, Indiana, where we'd all been once or twice. It's just surreal, but what do you do? We're at a funeral for our friend. And then everything is over—your life as you know it is over.

Shelley Shaw: I flew to the funeral, and I had to connect in Denver. I get to my connection, and the whole band is at my terminal. It was just like what you would expect. We were just all 'hound dog.' And I didn't ask anybody about it, nobody talked about it. The funeral is a blur. We were in a hotel and got driven places together in a van. I remember going to the house that he and Lisa remodeled, and how beautiful it was—he was so talented at fixing it up. She took me out to the garage—you opened the door, and it was this towering, almost sculpture, of junk furniture. *Teetering*, it's so high. She goes, "Look at this mess, what am I going to do?!" She was really strong—she really took care of all of us in the house. God...I don't know how she did it. I really fucking don't know.

Axl was supposed to come to the funeral, and then he put his own drama ahead of the whole situation. Doug Goldstein was still the manager, and he strung out Doug—like, at the airport, missing his plane, calling from the limo, screaming and yelling. Doug arrived to the funeral a frazzled mess from what he said he put him through. And Axl didn't make it. I don't think that Axl and Shannon were talking on a regular basis after Shannon moved back to Lafayette. That was a time when Axl was out in Malibu. He always had a Halloween party for the people that worked for him—and [their] kids. And he had Christmas parties. I was always invited to them, but I only went to maybe two out of the five years I was there. I don't know if Shannon was invited or around. I think they kind of went their own ways.

Heather Thorn: I remember going to the funeral and sitting in the limousine. I kept feeling that somebody was missing, like, "Wait, wait, hold on—we forgot somebody." You're always doing a headcount to make sure that people were there. Looking around at everybody sitting in the car and just going, "One, two, three, four…oh, that's right. This is how we are now." And seeing Lisa and Nico—Nico was so little. Lisa was such a trooper, boy. I swear to God, she looked like Jackie O.—she had on big black sunglasses and had Nico on her knee, bouncing her up and down on her knee, trying to keep her calm. Saying goodbye is crazy—not fun.

Glen Graham: You got Lisa, who is absolutely…she's wearing his clothes, she's got a child, she's known him since they were in high school. It's the most devastating thing. It's the most devastating thing that I've ever been through in my life. Without question.

Denise Skinner: When Shannon passed away, I went back to Indiana, along with Domenique and Tim Devine, for the services. The assistant I had at the time, she loved the band. She was great—she'd bend over backwards for them. Well, when Shannon passed, Gary called the whole label together, and started to pontificate on how much of a loss this was. And then he went off into how he tried to help Shannon—my assistant knew better. She was so mad at his blatantly standing up in front of the company and pontificating on things that he hadn't done. She called me and said, "I'm going to quit." I went, "No, no, no. You don't work for Gary Gersh, you work for Capitol. Think in terms of what's going to happen to the rest of our artists if you leave and I don't have you here to help me—then he wins." As far as I was concerned, Gary was very good at taking credit for what happened with Blind Melon, but when it came down to getting in the trenches and helping out, he was too busy with whatever things he thought were his priorities. It was interesting—when I went back for the services…I'm a homegrown California kid, so I'm used to tolerance and a large mix of people. When I went back for the services, I started to understand that 'small town thing' that Shannon was talking about. The narrow mindedness of people. I found it very uncomfortable. If nothing else, I was glad that Shannon got to experience something different than the upbringing that seemed to have tortured him so much. And then to be there and have my assistant call me to tell me Gersh was doing what he was doing—it just put more fuel on the fire.

Danny Clinch: It was just terrible. I remember taking a lot of photographs of everybody hanging out together and being sad. I went to L.A. right after that, and somebody stole my camera with all my pictures in it. But it was sad, it was a drag. There was all this friction because Shannon's mom didn't trust everybody—she thought that everybody was out to get her, and that Lisa slept with someone else and Nico wasn't Shannon's kid. If you ever see pictures of Nico—it's 'Shannon II.'

Shelley Shaw: There was a really rough thing there. I think it was a bit of struggle over the estate. Then I heard the family had dug up a woman that they thought had born Shannon's child as well. So they were sort of siding with her and trying to get some of the estate, or have her recognize…I don't know what happened with that. I thought that was very strange—money does funny things to people. Not that I would think that there would be that much there—just maybe enough to be smartly invested and hopefully last. But certainly not a fortune. So that's a shame.

Nel Hoon: If a person could die just from wanting to, then I would have. He was such a big part of our lives—his dad, mine, his sister, his brother, his aunts, his uncles. We all just loved him so much and we admired the fact that he had come from this little farm area and come so far and such a short time. It's hard to describe—six weeks after Shannon died, I tried to go to a bereavement group here in Lafayette. And oh my God, people were standing up, and their child had been gone for like ten or twelve years, and they were making these speeches with tears rolling down their face. I thought, "If these people are still going through this pain like this, how on earth am I going to be able to live with this for all these years?" Because the pain was just so unbearable. I remember Dick was there, and we would go out at like 3:00 in the morning, sit on the back steps, and try to figure out how we were going to go on. It was that devastating.

I mean, it gets easier—it really does. I think of him every day, probably every hour—something comes into my head about Shannon. I'll pick up something in my house and I'll say, "Shannon used to like this or that." I've become such a packrat—I always was a packrat, but I'm even more so now, because I can't let go of anything that I had at that time. Two years later, I was able to go to bereavement group meetings. And when I first signed in to go, I said, "My son was Shannon Hoon, he died from a heart attack." I could not make myself say that he had died of drugs. Middle of the meeting, I thought, "If I'm going to get help here, and everyone in here probably totally told the truth about how their child died—because the bereavement group was all people that had lost their children—and I lied. So I got up, went to the back, and wrote in the book that he died from an accidental overdose. At the time, I felt I was still hurting over the fact that he had died from drugs. But at least what I feel about that, he died comfortably numb. The way I felt the other night when they gave me morphine [for Nel's cancer treatment]. He just went to sleep, he felt no pain, nobody shot him, nobody slit his throat—he didn't have to die of cancer like a friend of his did. Shannon had always hurt so badly over that. So he just died comfortably numb.

Domenique Johansson: It took them months to release [the cause of Shannon's death]. I understand that it was definitely a cocaine overdose. Inevitably, you do end up having a heart attack, but frequently with those kinds of overdoses, if he had emergency care right away, he might have lived.

Brian Whitus: I feel sorry for the band members. I feel sorry for Nico and Lisa as well.

Heather Thorn: He never got it, is what it comes down to. Obviously—he's dead. But he never got what it took. I've seen other people, where you're like, "You don't get it—*it's about you.*"

Post-Melon

The four surviving Melon members keep busy by completing and releasing the odds and ends collection, 'Nico,' as well as a Grammy-nominated home video, 'Letters from a Porcupine,' on November 12, 1996—almost exactly a year after Shannon' death. An attempt to find a new singer and carry on fails to pan out, however.

Mike Napolitano: They called me. At first, I think [they were] still sort of spinning a little bit. They didn't know what they were doing—they didn't say, "Hey, come produce a record." They said, "We've got all this outtake stuff. Will you help us figure out what we can do with it?" So we went into the studio. It was an exploratory mission—what's here and what can be done with it? I think instinctually for all of us, once the reels got up, we just started recording on them. It immediately started going somewhere cool. That's just how it happened. Radically different [comparing the 'Soup' and 'Nico' sessions]. It wasn't anywhere near as structured—it was almost completely 'fly by the seat of the pants.' Also, it was sort of the reverse way most records get recorded, by the fact that they started with an acoustic guitar and a vocal, and a band wasn't around half of it.

Glen Graham: That was great. Actually, that was the easiest thing we ever did. It felt weird going in, we were all apprehensive. But as soon as we got in there and put the DAT's up and started listening to them, it was like, "O.K., this is alright." It was basically, "Let's use some leftover stuff from the 'Soup' record"—I think one of them was Christopher's and two of them were Rogers'. "Pull" is Christopher's, "Swallowed" is Rogers'. I remember Christopher being furious that "Pull" was not on 'Soup.' We had some pre-recorded shit already, and these DAT's. I guess it's one of those lucky things—I'm one of those drummers that can overdub on stuff that's already recorded, even if there's no click-track. You can tell it's loose, but it sounds pretty cool. It was those guys sitting in the control room, watching me overdub on these things— "Hell," "The Pusher," "Glitch," and the other "No Rain" thing. Usually, we do our shit, we finish, Shannon comes in and does his thing, and then, surprise! And this was like, "The Shannon parts are already done—all we have to do is finish it." It didn't feel cheesy, it didn't feel wrong—it felt great. I would have never imagined on the flight there that I would be saying this.

Rogers Stevens: Looking back on it, "Soup" is one of the best songs from the ['Soup'] sessions. In a way, I'm glad it happened like that, because a) we had it for the 'Nico' record, and it's such a strong tune it really helps that album. And b) it's weird to have a song named 'Soup,' and the song isn't on the album. It's a little twist. That was not intentional at the time—I just thought it was going to be a b-side. Christopher had written that whole acoustic guitar intro thing. It was just the two guitars basically and the vocals. So we did that, and I had that whole other outro part, where it's all big and rock. That's a part that I had written and stuck on there, basically. Actually, that part that's on the end of the song, was one of the things that I had been working around when I was doing "Vernie," but I ended up chopping it out, and it got stuck on that one. And Shannon, I thought one of our best moments on any of our records was where the lyric builds up at the end of the kind of mellow part of the song. There's a real tension there, and then it gets held over into the other part—the way he holds off on the last word.

Christopher Thorn: I thought the song was complete, personally. I was like, "Here's the song." And Rogers was like, "What about this as an outro?" Which turned out to be the climax of the song. That's one of my favorite songs we did. I think those lyrics are about a bunch of things—it's not always easy to follow. But I do know that the outro was about Kurt [Cobain]. I remember the first time he sang that, I got goose bumps. I was like, "Holy shit—*you're going there.*"

Brad Smith: I really like that song ["Soup"]. That should have been on the 'Soup' record, instead of the 'Nico' record. It was also one of those songs where I wish that the band would have spent more time on, in terms of getting the arrangement a little more solid. That groove—which is a James Brown groove—Glen can play that old school funk style really well. You hear that opening guitar line and that super-funky ass drum beat, and you just wish that it would have stayed locked into that a little while longer than it does. And you wish that it could have been a little more developed. But as Blind Melon often does, we'll write a hook or two, and then go into 'left turnville,' where all of a sudden it breaks down into double time or half time, changes keys, and a whole new song happens at the end [laughs]. It's like, "What happened to where we started?" Part of me thinks that that song is unfinished, but it's full of credibility, so it's hard to go back and change what actually worked, because that happens to be a lot of people's favorite song. I wish that the band could have been communicating a little more, and got that song to the next level. That song was a 'world beater song'—that song could have gone out and made a real mark on everybody. That song should have been a 'ten,' and it ended up being a 'seven.'

Mike Napolitano: I do remember being shocked when they took the song "Soup" off of 'Soup,' which I thought was a great song. And a perfect liaison between what the world perceived Blind Melon as a band, and what they really were.

Rogers Stevens: "Soul One" was written by Brad and I. There's a couple parts that were finished off by Shannon. But it was a little bit sentimental—it didn't strike us as being all that cool. A lot of people love the song, but it's not my favorite. It's one of those ones we wrote early on in the process of starting to write songs. I felt we were doing better stuff. But looking back on it, it's often those simple, first ideas that people end up gravitating towards. I understand that it's a first-listen-type-song, and it's a very sweet song. But I felt like we wanted to be more of 'a rock band,' than 'a band with a ballad.'

Christopher Thorn: That song is funny—people say that they love that song, and we just thought that it was the cheesiest song. There was a fight between us and the record company. They really thought it should have been on the record. In hindsight, it's a beautiful song. I don't know why we really turned against that song at some point. And then it became a struggle between who's got the most power between the record company and the band. Back then; they did want to please us, so we had the upper hand. As much as they wanted the song on the record, we said "No"—it was this back and forth fight. And then we got our way. In the end, the record probably would have sold more if that song was on the record. That could have been a single.

Brad Smith: I wrote ["Soul One"] before Shannon was even in the band. It should have been on the first record—it turned out to be a great song. I don't know why we didn't re-cut it. Once the band got together, they probably thought the song was like a 'ballad pussy song.' I really wish "Soul One" would have been on the first record—it's too bad it wasn't. I was really on the fence about the whole thing, because I had written the song myself, and it's hard to go in there and fight for your song when the rest of the band didn't want to hear it. It's kind of a bummer. It reminds me of living with this girl at the time. I was going through a severe hippie phase—dreamcatchers, tie-dyed shirts. The whole nine yards. That song became more about the 'anti-Soul One' song. Because if someone is your soul mate, than you should be with them forever, right? Well, that wasn't the case. I was like 19/20 years old; we were calling each other our 'soul mates' and all this crap. And in the bridge, it says, "I never got a chance to say goodbye"—like, "Well, I guess she wasn't my soul mate—all this is just a load of crap." So for me, that was kind of what I was saying for the song—but almost in a 'love ballad' type of way.

Rogers Stevens: I remember we tried to do a take of "John Sinclair" in this guy's apartment in New York. Some guy that worked on some other records, and he was going to try and record us. It was a disaster—sounded horrible. I know there was a failed attempt to do that. People like the way the "John Sinclair" thing came out. To me, it's not as good as "Three is a Magic Number" [which would be released on 1996's 'Schoolhouse Rock! Rocks' compilation], but they both came from the same session. I remember John Sinclair himself was contemplating suing us for using his name or recording the song. And of course, you can't do that—it was a John Lennon song and you can sing about a public figure. Anyway, he was upset about it. Glen ran into him at a bar in New Orleans, and he saddled up to the bar stool next to Glen, and threatened him with lawyers or something.

Glen Graham: The little riff thing that I do with Brad is good—that's the funkiest we ever got.

Christopher Thorn: There's a song called "Glitch"—never heard [Shannon] play it or sing it. After he died, his friend who had recorded it, said, "Hey, I got this song." It's one of my favorite songs. So it makes me go, "Man, we would have been doing some really good stuff."

Glen Graham: I remember "Glitch," I said, "Let's do Mellotron and percussion." Blank stares. That's the first time that we did anything like that. Laid down tons and tons of percussion. We pulled the Mellotron down the hallway—they were laughing at us in the studio. "Why are you using that thing? It's a Mellotron!" This is Heart's studio [Bad Animals, in Seattle]. Three of us are playing the Mellotron at once—one guy's working the foot bank, one guy's working the weird control knob, the tapes are all off, and one of us is playing the little line or whatever. It was cool.

Brad Smith: I thought "Pull" was a great song that possibly could have made the 'Soup' record. Another really great riff. But it took that 'left turn thing' that Blind Melon often does, and that particular left turn did not work out as well. That's probably why it didn't make the record. That last part of "Pull" is this droning thing—it doesn't really go anywhere. There's no hook in it. But the beginning was good. If we would have been communicating better back in the day, that song would have easily made the record.

Christopher Thorn: That's another song that was on that same tape [as "Skinned"] that I'd written in Seattle, given to Shannon, and he wrote lyrics for. My memory of that is being somewhere in Europe and him explaining the lyrics to me. [The lyrics] were a little bit about a fishing trip that we had and a little bit about drugs.

Mike Napolitano: I am a producer instead of a musician mostly because of Blind Melon. That experience let me see how creative and cool this job could be. And it turned out to be more creative for me than actually being a musician. Those guys giving me a chance to do it on a level…it's just unheard of, for somebody of their stature at the time to just use me because they thought I'd be good. Regardless of what my track record was—which was nonexistent basically at the time.

Jena Kraus: I ended up getting a record deal just a couple of months later, and I'm like, "Oh great, *record deal.*" I didn't want to feel like that, and I was very grateful for opportunities that I had, but I couldn't focus on making a record. I did end up making a record with Christopher and Brad—nobody knows about it. It was after they did 'Nico.' I got dropped, because I couldn't concentrate on making a record. I handled [Shannon's] death worse than I ever handled anything. My own father just died, and Shannon's death was harder. I was really close to my dad, but [Shannon's] death really took a toll on my soul.

Brad Smith: People around us wanted to keep us secure because we'd been through so much after Shannon died. It was like we had the world at our feet, and now we're scratching for a career—what the fuck do we do now? Blind Melon had a really tight knit family, people that were authentically close to the music and the band, and they wanted to take care of us. They said, "You guys just need to find somebody and move on."

Glen Graham: Everybody had their pick [for a new singer], and nobody was very good for us. They were great at what they did, but they weren't for us. And then there was talk of Brad, and it wouldn't have worked. I don't think we ever actually did anything with Brad, except talk about the fact that he might sing. I don't think any of us were really into it. Now, since that time, Brad's gotten a lot better, but I still don't think that Brad would have filled in for Shannon. We would have needed somebody with a much more powerful voice—as distinctive as Shannon's was. Brad can sing, write, and come up with good melodies, but he doesn't have that 'frontman uniqueness thing.'

Marlon Stoltzman: They actually found a guy—who was in a band with his friends, and he turned them down. He said, "I want to play with you guys, but I can't abandon my friends. We've been in high school, we're trying to do this thing together." I would be interested to see if this guy got anywhere.

Glen Graham: As far as the whole 'getting a new singer' deal goes, we tried to do it, but what's the point?

How Does Blind Melon's Music Stand Up?

Years after their initial release, how do the songs on 'Blind Melon,'
'Soup,' and 'Nico' sound today?

Glen Graham: I talked to a guy from Spain yesterday [from Popular 1 Magazine], and he was saying, "'Soup' is the top album of the '90s according to our readers." It was like, "*What?*"

Shelley Shaw: I was looking on Myspace, and I put 'Blind Melon' in their search engine. I must have gotten like 5,132 hits or something. I was clicking through—they were all these kids, all different ages. I'm surprised that it's still so much out there on these kids' minds, because it seemed at the time, they were left behind.

Domenique Johansson: I think Blind Melon's music has shown a lot of resiliency, which has made me happy. I've seen a lot of things in retrospect—people that have grown to like something they weren't too sure of, like 'Soup,' when they first heard it. I see huge fan sites, I meet people still that really love the band. There are people in their late 20's now, that Blind Melon defined their whole high school experience. And these people just love them. Blind Melon has held up. I think they didn't have enough of a catalog and stuff out for them to have the thing that could be mined forever. When you go to YouTube, people are posting their videos, [they're] all over Myspace. So I think they are being remembered, and I'm happy about that—that it's alive.

Heather Thorn: Blind Melon's music today is bigger than it ever was, and it completely holds the test of time. They would have gone on to do great things and been one of those bands that never really ended. Their career would have gone on and on. The musicianship was obviously there, and I think they were doing something that nobody else was doing. They pulled from everything classic—and had that flavor—but made it their own. I honestly do think to this day that they would still be touring.

Hale Milgrim: I miss that freshness. There was something very fresh about that band. Fresh, but at the same time, borrowing from their roots, and making it something special. There's very few brand new things out there, but if you can take something from your past, and meld it into something that's different, you can make something very special. And they did.

Tim Devine: Any time I hear one of their songs on the radio, it comes through like a breath of fresh air. I think their music holds up pretty well, insofar as it's real, and although it's a little rough-hewn, it's still comes out of a classic sound that falls within the lineage of the Crosby, Stills, & Nash's, the Neil Young's, the Blind Faith's, and the Traffic's. I'm very proud of the work we did together and I think it holds up to this day.

Owen Orzack: I went through a long time where I never listened to it. I'd hear it on the radio and I'd turn it off. But I started putting CD's on my iPod, putting all the Melon stuff on there, and listening to it again. And y'know, I really like it. It does hold up. It's hard to distract it from all the emotional B.S.

Marlon Stoltzman: The documentary that's on the band ['Letters from a Porcupine'], I show it to a lot of new bands, and people are extremely inspired by it. Also, there's a lot of lessons in that. As fans go and speaking to people, it's just incredible—for the little they did that years later, [the fans] are still there. Plus, one wonders where they would be today, because there was so much music there. I don't think it's aged a day. The interesting thing is that they're still selling albums. If you're not selling albums any more—that's the proof. And who are they selling it to? It must be new converts.

Lyle Eaves: I think Blind Melon was highly underrated as a band. They were much better than the one hit video wonder they are remembered for.

Danny Clinch: I'm always the one saying, "Oh man, Blind Melon is a completely underrated band—you've got to get that 'Soup' record." I was trying to push it on Ryan Adams, because I think Ryan would get something out of it. Y'know, Ryan is very similar to Shannon [laughs]. I'll have to stick it in his hand or play something for him particularly. Think about this jam band scene that goes on right now—can you imagine if they never lost any steam, and kept making music? They could have taken over that whole scene. For a while there, they had such a bad rep because of "No Rain." I always tried to flip that on people—"Man, you've got to give that another chance, because this stuff is fantastic." It *totally* holds up.

George Nunes: They were so far ahead of their time—you hear their influence in music in what's going on today. You've got to remember, back in that day, Triple A, Americana, all that stuff, wasn't around. They'd still be current today. They could come out today and still have a current record. Easily. Any jam band has taken stuff from Blind Melon.

Bill Armstrong: They didn't sound like 'a band of the moment.' They were really their own band. I can't lump them in with a genre—they weren't a grunge band, they weren't a metal band, they weren't a punk band. They were genre-less in a way that they were their own music. I think ultimately, over time, they are their own thing—so they're timeless. They aren't like anything else—there's not another band that you can really compare them to. I think that's given their music a timeless quality.

Lisa Sinha: I can hardly listen to his music—I have a hard time. I haven't listened to those things for years.

Nel Hoon: I really don't listen to his music—I've made New Year's resolutions every year to start listening to Shannon's music again, but the only time I ever listen to his music is at the vigil every year [an annual vigil is held at Shannon's gravesite, to commemorate his birthday].

Brooks Byrd Graham: I like the live stuff—I think they were good live, and they got better and better. There was a lot of energy, and you could really see/ hear that they were all such good musicians. And Shannon was such a great frontman. He was such a performer—even if he was having trouble with his voice, he still was that energetic guy up there. Really passionate about what he was doing. For me, it's too emotional—it brings back so much that it's really hard to listen to.

Jena Kraus: I remember all these details and stuff—I knew the music really well. But I cannot listen to it—hardly. I know it sounds crazy—as much as I love it, I have to really be in the right mood to listen to it. It's painful. I don't listen to it as much as I should. I think also that he's gone, that when I listen to it, I don't want to listen to it too much, because it's all I have now.

Marc Pollack: To this day, it brings back such memories to me that are almost uncomfortable. I mean, I love the first two records—they're almost like 'classic rock classics.' A song comes on the radio, they're instantly recognizable—you know exactly who it is. They stand out, they stand the test of time—which is very important for a band's legacy. I think that they belong alongside other classic rock songs—and they will stay there for years to come. But on the other hand, when I hear "No Rain" on the radio, it takes me back there and it's sad. I get sad—for what was, would could have been, and for Shannon.

Melissa Whitus: The hardest thing isn't hearing his music—I think that's the neatest thing about the fact he was what he was. When you can pop in a DVD and see him move around, hear him talk, and hear him laugh—it's a gift. And to hear his music's a gift, because that will always live. Those memories are always there, but it's sad, because we miss 'Shannon the friend,' not 'Shannon the rock star.'

Nicholas Bechtel: Still makes me choke up. I think it's timeless. I don't think 'Soup' got a chance, and I think 'Soup' was ahead of its time—it was such a switch of what the first record was in a lot of ways. There was something that was more 'grown up' about it—more polished. I don't think it was getting its chance to shine. If that record came out today with a proper push, I think it would be huge. I'm 42 now, and I started going to college working towards a bachelor's. I was at this coffee place in San Diego on campus. This guy who plays music, we were talking, and I turned him onto 'Soup.' The next day I saw him, he said, "Man, you don't know how many people came up to me and asked me who this band was." The music and energy still transcends into that age group.

Christopher Thorn: Sometimes somebody will say [Blind Melon was an influence], and the band will sound so drastically different from us—I'm always shocked by that. But yeah, we hear that. [Brad and Christopher] have been working with some people—this girl Cheyenne Kimball, she was thirteen when we met her, and the reason why we got to work with her is one of her favorite bands is Blind Melon. She knows *everything*. She knows all the stuff I forgot—guitar parts, lyrics. It's so completely flattering and it's really fun to be around somebody who you influenced. I feel so silly saying that. There's a friend of ours who was producing the Used, and they called and wanted to borrow a lyric. We were flattered and said, "No problem." Something in "Mouthful of Cavities"—"Haven't seen him smile in a little while."

Brad Smith: I think that period of time in music was really passionate. It was before ProTools, before all these consolidations of the companies, and I think you hear the emotion of the music back then. It wasn't tidily packaged, there were off notes here and there. It sounded really genuine and authentic. It was the last period before it got really tight. Contrived is a bad word—*controlled*. It was the last period of music where things were really honest sounding and emotional. There's something about Shannon's voice, lyrics, and the way that he delivered it. It connected with people on such an emotional level that it's survived.

Christopher Thorn: I think the records sound real. Shannon had something to say. The songs are 'real songs,' I think that stuff lasts longer than a pop song just written to get on the radio. We never had those expectations. We were writing songs from the heart, and people related to Shannon as a frontman for sure, and the band in general.

Brad Smith: Music has an uncanny ability to mark periods of your life—like a milestone or a photo album. You hear three notes of your favorite album from ten years ago and you're right there in your 1980 Honda Civic Wagon. It takes you back immediately. That's the beautiful thing about music.

Rogers Stevens: What I do like about the first album is that there's an energy to it, that comes from really going for live takes. And there's bad chords and fucked up shit on there—I like that. We didn't leave that stuff on the 'Soup' record—we fixed everything.

Glen Graham: The truth is that we were a band that was very lucky. I think we were pretty damn good, considering the lack of effort we put into it.

Rogers Stevens: I think we would've made, easily, another two really good records. We would have made our best records—that's the way it was going with 'Soup.' If we would have sorted out our less-then-desirable activities, we would have been able to do something better. Because musically, it was getting better. ['Soup'] was a stepping-stone to something else. It didn't always work on that record, but on the next one, it would have really sorted itself out.

Christopher Thorn: We were going over to the Capitol vaults and trying to pull together some 'Classic Masters' stuff—songs that everybody knows. Going through all this stuff, I got turned onto stuff that I completely forgot about. When you're in a band and you're selling records, every time you got to a radio station they ask you to record. Acoustic versions—you're just constantly recording, and some are live and off the cuff. But I came across some really great stuff—Shannon by himself playing acoustic versions of "Galaxie" and "Vernie," really cool songs that I'd never heard before acoustic. And I was telling the guys, "I'd really love to just get this stuff out. If anybody cares about the band and they want some stuff that has never been heard before, these are great things." It's all eras of the band.

For awhile, I had a portable recording studio that I took on the road, and there's a few songs from literally, Shannon knocking on my door and going, "Hey, I need to lay this down." He'd lay it down, and then I'd forget about it. There's a song called "Ever Had the Feeling" which never got released, a really dark song. I think maybe it scared people—I don't know, maybe it's something that we still don't release. It's a song about killing yourself. It's sung—which only he could do—in this tongue-in-cheek voice.

There's just nothing like hearing songs stripped down—you really get a sense of the band and the songs, you really hear Shannon's voice. It's going to be raw. For me now, it's kinda charming—I can smell the room [they were recorded in] from hearing the recordings. There's also live recordings—I was given a box of A-DAT's. For a while, we were recording every live show—right around the time that "No Rain" hit, when we were playing bigger places. I'd like to have the stuff get out, I would love people to have it—I don't feel good about it just being in a box somewhere. I can't promise anything other than they're just some really cool things that I think if you're a fan you'll love to hear.

Nel Hoon: If you have a friend that has the music, go and just have them make you a copy. If they don't have the money to buy it, give to them—share his music. That is how I would like him to be remembered. And this is what the vigil does. A couple of years ago, there were people from five different countries that came to the vigil. A girl came all the way from Serbia, a girl came from New Zealand. This year, a girl from Italy has already bought her ticket. And now I'm worried about my condition, about being able to be there and host this event of my life, which is what I live for now—just to be able to have all these people together. And we all have one thing in common—we love Shannon. At the time this year of the vigil, I'm going to be on chemo and radiation combined, and it's going to be really hard for me, because the doctors don't want me to be in any crowds, catch a cold, or anything like that. But I can't let these kids down—they've come from too far and I have to be there. If I have to be in a wheelchair—I'll be there.

Glen Graham: It didn't bother me when Shannon died and everybody started saying unkind things. It was like, "So what?" They said it about Jim Morrison, Keith Moon, Janis Joplin. "What a shame, what a tragedy. Well, he was already on his way out anyway." You know what? Fuck you. Our music will stand the test of time. The revenge we will have will be the children of our most harsh critics blasting our music through their parents' houses and telling you what short-sighted fools you were for not getting it the first time around. We do not claim to be Led Zeppelin or the Who, but for a certain cross-section of the music-listening population, we may as well have been.

Jena Kraus: They really taught me a lot about music and art. Mostly what they taught me was to be myself. I grew up in a small town in Pennsylvania, where people were really narrow-minded. It was kind of scary to be yourself. What Shannon, Christopher, and everybody taught me was, "Don't be afraid. Be yourself, embrace it, and be proud of it. It's O.K. to be different—it's a good thing." They were really good people.

Shannon Remembered

Shannon Hoon certainly left an impression on all those he came in contact with—those closest to him recount memories and how they'd like him to be remembered.

Marlon Stoltzman: I saw Robert Plant in New York, shortly after Shannon died. Robert put his hand on his heart, looked at me, and said what a tragedy it was. I'm sure he's lost enough friends to drugs—maybe not that many recent as Shannon, but in the day. He felt that Blind Melon was arguably the most talented of all the bands coming out of that era. He loved them.

Domenique Johansson: Shannon was a big personality. He was controversial. He could step in shit as much as he could charm you to death. He was just that kind of guy, and he lived for every moment. He's the kind of guy that people would gravitate to. He didn't hold back. It was easy to see that Shannon was going to draw a lot of attention. He had a very generous nature. And he cared for his fans and friends a lot. He showed an extraordinary capacity for care—that you just didn't see in people. A lot of integrity.

Tim Devine: Shannon was predictably unpredictable—always the 'lightning rod' of the band. The guy that stood out—the others seemed much more similar to each other. Shannon was the magical—sometimes whimsical—frontman, that made it as special as it was. Shannon was a very intense being and his mind worked on a lot of different levels, although he always had a pretty good handle on what it was he wanted to be and how he wanted to project himself. And that was always in an organic way.

Owen Orzack: He was great—he really was a super guy. Super sweet, warm hearted, nice, pleasant person—90% of the time. And it was that 10% of the time that he was 'evil Shannon/the drug Shannon.' It wasn't 'Shannon the person.' You just had to separate your perceptions. I never took anything really personally. We were friends, but I tried to keep it on a professional level as well. And that's how I wanted to keep it—*because he was a handful.* But a super nice guy. We hung out actually a lot, considering we didn't drink or do drugs together.

Marlon Stoltzman: He totally lived for the moment. I think he saw himself in a band forever—the music was his life. He'd kiss you, hug you, and tell you that he loved you. A lot of love that guy.

Miles Tackett: The beautiful energy that the guy put off—that exuberance.

Jena Kraus: I remember good memories and happy thoughts—like he would tell me, "Happy thoughts, Jena!" He was such a huge influence on me in so many ways. He helped me so much, in ways that I can't even tell you— spiritually. And he got me to write my own songs. Such a loving person, just amazing spirit. He lifted me up. He helped me in my life.

Lisa Sinha: Shannon was very good to me. I did not work—but part of that was so that I could be at his beck and call when we were living together. And he was very good to people around him—a very generous person. And sincere, that's the other thing. He got into fights and all that wild stuff, but that was under the influence of something. When he was not drinking or just smoking pot, he was cool as a cucumber. And funny—he and I would have so much fun.

Brooks Byrd Graham: He was funny to be around because he talked *constantly*—just stream of conscious. And that's why I think so many people have these fond memories of him, because he was just talking all the time, and whoever would come around, he'd talk to them. Whatever was on his mind was going to come out—he was without inhibition.

Hale Milgrim: He and that band were full of life—full of a positive energy that we need in this world. We maybe need it in this world more today then when we needed it even when I was fortunate to bring them in. There was an experimentation and improvisational side of the band that I just loved. The band was a wonderful 'groove machine,' with this wonderful vocalist that was all over the place. Full of energy and life—the opposite of what drugs do to you over time. I'm sorry that pressures were so extreme for him that he just couldn't cope. I'm very saddened about that. And I'm so saddened for his family—his child. And his other family—the band.

Rogers Stevens: He was a really talented guy who didn't get to do everything he could have done, because he had a fucking stupid substance abuse problem, which is tragic. In some ways, it fueled what he did, and in other ways, it hindered him from being as great as he could have been. He was a bright guy—he had a really active mind, that he enhanced and distorted at times. One thing led to another—I think a lot of the crazy stuff that he did, even before we met him, gave him things to write about. And for that reason, when he sang those songs, they came off as being totally real. Because they were—he lived it.

Brad Smith: He already is being remembered. It's years after his death, and people are remembering him for the right reasons. There's this shock value of pissing on the audience, going to jail, going to rehab, and stuff like that. But what's made his memory last this long is his songwriting, voice, and music. That's why people are hanging around for years. If it was just shock value, they would go on to the next thing. There's some real depth there—to what he had to say and his voice.

Christopher Thorn: Being remembered as a great songwriter would be nice, instead of being remembered for like, pissing on an audience. But that's kind of cool, too [laughs]! It would be nice if at the top of the list was like, "What incredible songs he wrote," and not "He peed on an audience" or "He got in a fight at the American Music Awards." The songs were great—*his* songs are great.

Glen Graham: I'd like Shannon to be remembered as a great frontman, a great singer—somebody who was an individual. He may have sounded like other people, but he certainly wasn't trying to. And at the same time, I think you can hear that he wasn't trying to be different just for the sake of being different. He was himself. People read things and get the idea that he was a casualty. Shannon would be dead anyway—even if he hadn't been in Blind Melon. Probably a lot sooner. Rock music didn't kill him. I would like him *to be* remembered.

Nel Hoon: When I go on those thousands of places on the internet, the way he is remembered is by his beautiful music and how very intelligent he was. Some of the things that he wrote—which I found in some of his personal things that were brought home, things where he started a song. I want him to be remembered by his music.

Heather Thorn: I say to Christopher, "I still cannot believe that Shannon is dead." It still blows my mind—on a personal level, it's such a bummer. Like all the things now we go through our lives and say, "Wow, Christopher and I just had a baby—Shannon will never know my kid, his daughter, Brad and Kim's kids. Rogers just had a baby." All these events that happen, I still look at Christopher and go, "I cannot believe that Shannon is not here for this—it's crazy." It's just unimaginable to me, still, to this day. It's like, wow—*that's it.* We're not going to see you again. He was a great singer. He was so passionate. He was a great lyricist. I'd want him to be remembered as one of the nicest, most charismatic guys, who lived 110% every single day of his life…and that's what burned him out so fast. But he honestly had one of the biggest hearts, and lived life with more gusto than anybody I've ever known. He was a killer singer—nobody else sounds like him. He was amazing. He was the real deal. He was fucked up like every singer, but equally, he was talented as well.

Denise Skinner: A friend of mine—on the day that I heard that Shannon had passed—brought me a new little kitten. I wasn't going to take her—I [wasn't] emotionally equipped. I wound up keeping her—she's my little 'Shannon reminder.' Every time that I see her walking around, I think of him. And I have an office for our little internet label for my husband's music, and I have one of my favorite pictures down there—of me and Shannon. It's funny, because when my husband saw the picture, he looked at him and goes, "Who is that?" I said, "That's Shannon Hoon." And he goes, "Oh my God, he looks exactly like Matt Damon!" I looked and went, "I guess he kind of does—but he had a lot of different hairdos, honey" [laughs]. I hope people remember Shannon as someone who really loved his music and loved to perform. And had a very good heart. Any more than that would be icing on the cake—at the end of the day, this was a good hearted, kind kid, and his creativity unfortunately didn't get to shine as long as it should have.

Marlon Stoltzman: Shannon could write lyrics in 15 minutes sometimes. He was a genius when it came to this stuff. They would be jamming and he would go, "There it is." Shannon was such a free spirit, and naïve in many ways. Like, they'd come to town, they'd be playing a concert, and Shannon would not organize anything for me. I would work my way eventually to the back-stage, and I'm like, "Dude, I didn't hear from you." He said, "No—I knew you'd get here." You know how hard it is to get backstage if you've got nothing? [laughs]

Rogers Stevens: Everything he wrote was true. He didn't make shit up—it was all about stuff that happened to him.

Owen Orzack: I think he should be remembered for the music. I still have mixed feelings. There's plenty of other people to look to, to reference why drugs are bad, and Shannon is just another shining example of somebody who was totally cut short—way before his time. Those guys could have really been a force. He was part of a great band—that's how I think he should be remembered. He was a nice guy, that's the other thing—deep down inside. Everybody's like, "He was angry" or "He had emotional issues." He was a nice guy, he really was. I miss him.

Lyle Eaves: I want Shannon to be remembered for the true artist he was. Not just another cliché rock star who O.D.'d. His music and emotion speaks for itself.

George Nunes: Who knows how successful he would have been—such potential. A truly beautiful person. An unbelievable voice, an original voice. I'm sure he would want to be remembered as a loving father. He was a very special light in the world.

John Fagot: I was looking forward to working with this band for a long time, because I felt that their creativity wasn't just in one song or one album. Shannon was going to be able to come with a lot of great music over a long period of time. Not just missing the person, who was a nice man, but also missing the talent that was wasted talent—that didn't happen. He was a true artist.

Glen Graham: Shannon's deal was plumbing the depths of his psyche. I think he would have gotten to be more of a craftsman at that, as time went on.

Lisa Sinha: He always lived on the edge and would say things. Shannon is a hard person to explain, because he had very highs and lows. Like, high on life—"I can't wait to live to be 100!" And then one day, "I'm not going to live past 30" or 'life's not worth living' kind of attitude. It depended on the day, it really did. It depended on what mood he was in. He never said "I want to die" or anything like that, but sometimes, "If I die, I die. If I live, I live." But I don't believe that Shannon wanted to die in any way, shape, or form. I think he was bummed.

Kim Smith: He always used to say he was going to die young. I'd say, "Shannon, stop saying that—it's morbid." And that time on the bus [during the Page/Plant shows], he was joking, "Now I'll probably live 'til I'm 38!" Two weeks later, he was dead. He always would joke that he was going to die young, but after Nico came, we all really thought he was going to make it.

Mike Napolitano: I think it was understood—Shannon knew as much as anybody else what he was doing. He was killing himself, and he knew that—he was acutely aware of it. The evidence of that is in all of his songs. It was pointless to tell him something he already knew. And I certainly didn't know any magic phrase that would make him act on what he already knew.

Glen Graham: Oh my God—yeah, he knew it. The thing that the Blind Melon camp will always talk about is, "Shannon is one of those guys you think will survive anything." It's like, "No, no, no." I think Shannon knew full well that he was not going to be around forever. He did not know his limits—that's for sure. But as far as lyrics go, yeah, that whole thing was prescience personified. He was writing about himself—'I know I am doomed' was the theme of 'Soup.' That was the 'Shannon Hoon autobiographical record.' New Orleans was the perfect metaphor for Shannon Hoon's personality and mental state. And we should have never gone down there. I really apologize, because I was the one who really wanted to go.

Brooks Byrd Graham: I'd like him to be remembered as that really impassioned person, who went through life without inhibitions, and who tried everything. He was really loving—he loved a lot of people, a lot of things about the world, music. He brought a lot of energy—*a lot of energy*. He had a presence—when he was in the room with you, you knew it.

Danny Clinch: The best songs for me are ones that can be interpreted a million different ways, through everyone's life experience. And Shannon had a way of writing these songs that didn't completely make sense. But when you put them in the context of your own life, they made sense to you. But I bet it didn't mean the same thing to any one person, because his lyrics were so abstract in a way. Everybody could take something different from it. He should be remembered as a guy who did what he wanted to do. He didn't really seem to care what anybody thought—he just put his heart out there and said, "There it is—take it or leave it."

Gilby Clarke: One thing I always remembered about Shannon was he was one of those people that had fun in life. He was just one of those 'happy people.' I never saw him depressed. I always saw him happy—maybe 'cause it was always around shows, traveling, or just living in the moment. He really did live it to the fullest. Every moment was precious, and he just lived it—he went as far and fast as he could.

Duff McKagan: The guy was a really special guy—he was so full of life. A really funny dude. He was a guy I liked hanging out with. He didn't fit that typical 'singer mold.' The typical singer mold in a big band, they're precious, y'know? And he wasn't that at all.

Craig Ross: It seemed like he was going to become a friend, because him and his girl connected with me and my wife. He was going to have a kid, get stable, and I've always been that way myself. He was a really sweet guy. He was emotional, and he was kind. To me, he seemed like a normal, good-hearted guy who's involved in this business, which can be a little crazy and can allow you to be as crazy as you can get. But I considered him a friend, and he seemed normal to me. He was a really cool guy—a bit extreme, but I've got friends like that.

Susan Silver: Someone who instantly made other people feel comfortable and feel good. He had a way of instantly putting people around him at ease— making them smile.

Nicholas Bechtel: Not as this person who was a druggie. Somebody who had the kindest heart in the world. He was just full of life, and he would do any-thing for you—he really would. He had good senses as to who had a good heart and who was good. Just as this loving person who really did care about people and had a lot to give, and for one reason or another, cut himself short. Maybe he didn't see that—I don't think he saw his potential as a lot of us on the outside did. I remember he had such a childlike quality about him, but no matter what it was, nothing could fill whatever hurt was going on with him. If you watch the Woodstock video, you know when he's just going off and he's laying on the stage? People who didn't even know the man looked at that and said, "Jesus Christ, he was hurting." That was evident. I do wish to this day that I had been in the capacity to be out on the road with them. I don't know if that would have ever stopped anything.

Brian Whitus: As a fun, crazy, good friend, and in the three months I'd seen him around his kid, as a father.

Lisa Sinha: He would have been an awesome father—I feel bad because he wanted her so bad.

Melissa Whitus: I miss his laugh—I wish everybody could hear that laugh of his. I can still hear it. He always rubbed his fingers—he had a little patch, I don't know if it was silk, a little thing in his hands. He always rubbed his fingers together. Everybody's flawed—I heard people say things about him when he was first dead, and people judge people. I think my reaction was it wouldn't matter if he got hit by a bus or crashed in a plane—he was still my friend, and he's still somebody that was somebody's brother and somebody's boyfriend. Just because he did bad things and he didn't have that control, didn't make him a bad person.

I want people to know that he was a good person, and that if he loved you—and Shannon loved my husband, Lisa, and that little baby—you knew it. There was no question. He gave my husband his double platinum album for Christmas—the last Christmas he was alive. Shannon loved my husband and loved the way their friendship hadn't changed. He gave that to Brian because he said there's not many things that he's done in his life that he's accomplished or that he's very proud of. And he was very proud of that. And he even said, "Brian, you'll dust it and take care of it—I wouldn't." It's sad, because I think of all the time that's passed since he's been gone. I just want people to know that he was a good person.

Kim Smith: The guy didn't have a mean bone in his body—besides when he was drunk [laughs]. He was just lovely—an amazing guy. He was perfect. He was great.

Marlon Stoltzman: All the girls loved him, but he was a friend—he was never a 'rock star playboy' type.

Heather Thorn: Incredibly cute—every girl of course was oohing and aahing over him wherever he went. Everybody instantly liked him. He was super charismatic—always the loudest voice in the room.

Jena Kraus: I know he wanted to do a solo record—he had talked about that. Christopher I think was going to help him with that. But it was only talked about, it wasn't set in stone. He wrote a lot of songs—maybe some songs that weren't right for Blind Melon.

Shelley Shaw: Shannon at some point—when things were O.K. and he was doing well—was like, "Down the road, I'm going to do country solo records, and me and my mom are going to make these records. Because my mom has got a beautiful voice." He was really excited to do it.

Riki Rachtman: He had a great relationship with his mother.

Tim Devine: Shannon always wore this turquoise necklace [made by] Nel Hoon.

Nel Hoon: Shannon was more intimate with the fans than he was the big label people. He was more on the 'fan level.'

Bill Armstrong: Everything with Shannon was an adventure. He'd come home, and always have some kind of a story of something that happened. He got a lot out of everything. That's really how he lived his life. And he had a really good sense of humor. My memories of Shannon is him laughing a lot. He found humor in everything.

Lisa Sinha: The camera went everywhere where we went. He was into video-taping *everything*. I'm giving these videos to Glen shortly, and he's going to make a DVD out of it—I believe that's the plan. It was a huge deal—if we were on tour, all the other girlfriends got to hang out, while I would have to video the show. And he would critique me—we'd get back to the hotel, "God Lisa, you've got to zoom in here!" It was ridiculous. He was very, very into getting as much on video as possible. He's just the type of person that wanted to document his life. And these videos are precious. There's been so much controversy over these videos—I was under *strict orders*, if anything happened to him, I was to snag the videos and guard them with my life. I mean, *seri-*

ously. And I have, I've guarded them with my life. It's the one thing I did grab and was like, "O.K., until I feel the time is right for Glen to have them." They've never asked for them, and I would have given it to them a long time ago, if the guys in Blind Melon wanted them. But now they're ready for them. He just wanted to video everything—he carried it with him all over the place. *Hundreds* of videotapes. The Rolling Stones and all that. It's all documentary-style stuff, like, "We're going to the show, we're at the show." It's been a long time since I've seen these videos, too. He documented not only on the road, but at home—Nico when she was a baby. When we went to the hospital to have Nico, you would think that there was a camera crew there! He had two video cameras going...three cameras. Video was a big part of his life. I think if he would have lived longer, he would have done some video stuff. He had a knack for it, for sure.

Eva Pfaff: Shannon made no bones about the fact that he was in this—other than love of music and his talent—because he wanted to be famous. He wanted everyone to be a part of him becoming famous. He was all heart and soul. He struck me as a very passionate person—maybe because of what he said to me, of really wanting the fame aspect of it. I think a lot of artists aren't so honest about that—it's sort of like they're almost embarrassed to say it out loud. That made him a very direct, honest, tell-it-like-it-is person.

Jena Kraus: I wish Shannon was remembered more than he is. I feel that the world needs to know more. Sitting in the room with the guy, I mean Mammoth Mountain, him just singing acoustically. Sitting around in the kitchen, he started singing "Wish You Were Here." I heard that song a thousand times in my life...and then I hear this guy sing this song. I heard the lyrics in a totally different way than I've ever heard them. He did that song better than Pink Floyd [laughs]! The world does not know how talented he really was, how much he had to offer, and how much he gave. I've never met anyone like him. This guy had a spirit that shined brighter than anything I've ever seen. And anybody that met him could see it.

The other thing about him—he was a tough guy. He could kick ass if he wanted to—he didn't take no shit from nobody. But at the same, I've met a lot of guys that could kick ass, but most of those people aren't able to be real sensitive. He had this whole other side to him—he was not afraid to express himself. So he had this tough exterior, but was really quite sensitive really. He didn't need to put up any front—he was really real. I wish people could have had the chance to hear more of him—and I hope that in the future, they do hear more of him. He was an amazing person and he would do anything for anybody. He never had an ego—the fame never changed him. They all really remained the same people they always were—that's not an easy thing to do when you've got people kissing your ass all the time once you become famous. He had trouble trusting people because of that.

Glen Graham: We knew he was doomed basically and we knew there was nothing we could do about it. The great tragedy of 'the rock star' is that they are supposedly on top of the world and are supposed to be feeling that way. And the tragedy is you have a guy who is supposed to be feeling great about what he is doing, and can't. So he's getting fucked up all the time to make himself feel better, and it not only makes everything worse—it becomes his demise. It's the archetypal rock experience. The history of rock music is littered with this story.

Nel Hoon: I never, ever knew how bad he was. But I do know that Shannon was like a binger. If he was like a continuous drug user, he may have still been alive today. I'm afraid to say that—I don't want to encourage anybody, but I think what happened to Shannon was because his system was so cleaned up, that he maybe went right back to where he'd been and that his heart couldn't take it. I guess because I never did drugs, I don't really know what…I mean, the closest I have come is this past thing with the cancer where I've been put on morphine. Last week when I went into the hospital, I thought about Shannon because I went there with so much pain—I felt like I was going to die. They gave me morphine and almost instantly, the pain was gone. The first thing I could think of was my Shannon. He was on those drugs, and maybe when it was physical or mental pain, he would get a shot of something or do whatever it was he did, and then he would feel the way I was feeling at that time. That's all I could think of—"This is how Shannon felt when he would do whatever it was he did." Maybe this was the relief he got. And I could totally understand it.

Brad Smith: Blind Melon had a way of sabotaging a song to the nth power, and still have hooks and keep people interested. I attribute most of that to our musicianship and Shannon's voice. His voice is one of those haunting voices—you hear it one time and you know exactly who it is. He's up there with Ozzy Osbourne, Marvin Gaye, and Robert Plant. In my mind, a world without Shannon is like a world without Ozzy. I know that's comparing apples to oranges in a lot of ways. It might be taboo to Black Sabbath and Ozzy fans—but fuck it, that's the way that I feel about it. That's what Shannon meant to me.

Rogers Stevens: He was interested in all kinds of things—serial killers, dead rock stars. And that definitely plays out in the lyrics. I think if you live like he did, you'd better be acquainted with it—because you're definitely playing around with it. And he did lots of things throughout his life that were risky. He was a total risk taker. It's like when I was talking about him snowboarding—he didn't just snowboard down the mountain and take a couple of little two foot jumps. He had to go over the things that you're not supposed to do with his experience level. He had to jump those hills—do crazy shit like that. It's amazing he didn't break anything. That's just the way he did everything. It's one of the things that was so cool about him. But it was also one of the things that's fucking tragic about him.

Mike Osterfeld: I want the guy to be remembered as everyone's best friend. He was as good a guy to everyone that I've ever met. Even when he was bad, he was good. He was a true artist, a true talent, which made him a very upset and confused person, because it's impossible to harness that kind of talent. But the guy was the most talented guy I've probably ever come across. He was stolen from us. Maybe he did it, but at the end of the day, he should have never been gone. We didn't get as much as we should have gotten out of that guy. He had easily 10-20 more years to give us.

Melissa Whitus: When I was pregnant, Lisa had talked to us about using Shannon's name for our child, and I thought that was just really special. She said, "There's nobody else in this whole world that he would want to have their kid named after him. That's what I want and that's what Nico wants—so we would be honored if you would consider using his name for your child." I wasn't having a good pregnancy, and I actually lost that baby. So when I got pregnant again, I didn't know what we were having, and we made a decision that we were going to wait and be surprised. We named our daughter Mylee, which is Hawaiian—we were married in Hawaii—and her middle name is Shannon. We have a picture of him—we tell her who he is, that she was named after him, and that he's in heaven.

Jena Kraus: In a lot of ways, I feel that Shannon's death prepared me for my own dad's death. My dad almost died before he died, and that's why he got sober. When my dad almost died, I felt like Shannon sort of helped me-what I had experienced with him and his death helped me, because I was really aware. The rest of my family was so over my dad's drug use, and they were doing 'tough love.' I'm like, "*No, no.* I can't do tough love—this could be the only chance I had." And I had wished that I tried to stop Shannon that night when he went to [room] 911. The reason why I didn't stop him also was of that time in New Orleans when I did try to stop him and there was this big fight. I said to myself, "If I try to stop him, he's going to do it more." So I didn't. But now, here's my dad, and I knew everything I had learned from this experience with Shannon. I'm like, "I have the time with him now, and I'm not going to make the same mistake. And even if my dad ends up dying, I'm going to know I did everything I could, and at least I'll be able to live with myself. Because I do regret a lot with Shannon—I regret that I didn't stop him. I'm sure everybody feels that way. I just wish I would have followed my gut a little more.

Marc Pollack: It's important to know that in death, he saved lives, including my own. A day didn't go by after he died that I didn't think about what happened. I may not have cleaned up my own act the next day, but he was surely responsible for helping me get my life together. And, to this day, I owe him that.

Lisa Sinha: He was a wonderful, awesome, hilarious guy. Sweet as can be-compassionate. But had this side...Rogers put it really good one time—"He has a devil on one shoulder and an angel on the other." It was true. The nicest guy—you never wanted to see anything bad happen to him. But just had issues, he really did.

Shelley Shaw: My greatest hope is that his daughter can get some sense of him, and not be screwed up. I think she has a great mom—I think she got married to a doctor, and they still live in Lafayette. Hopefully she'll manage the memory of the dad with care. I think she will—I really think she'll be objective and she's a really smart, balanced lady. That's my main thing—I hope that little kid can have some sense of him, because he would have been a great dad. She would have gotten a lot of pleasure with him being around. I think the music's taking care of itself out there. I'm really pleased.

Melissa Whitus: I think about Lisa, and the fact that she has two beautiful kids with Ray [Lisa's husband], and he's a great guy. Just how different things would have been too for her. She probably would have had at least four kids with Shannon by now. Nico—DNA-wise—it's amazing how a person can be so much like somebody that's not being raised by somebody.

Brad Smith: It just gets sadder, because Shannon isn't here to witness this kinda thing. He's not here to witness his daughter growing up—who's the spitting image of him. It's really sad. At the time, you get over that little hump where you're grieving, and you're like "Oh man, I really miss Shannon." You go through bouts of hating him for leaving you, like "What the fuck were you thinking, you asshole?" But it just gets sadder. In the back of your mind, all the time—"God, Shannon really fucked up." He didn't fuck up for the band, he fucked up for him.

Lisa Sinha: I have been real careful with [Nico]. I've tried my hardest just to make it as painless as possible. Because she's a very emotional child. You know what, I have to tame her—she is a 'Shannon Jr.' She'll flash me a look, say something, or even her humor is similar to his. Yes, she has listened to his stuff. Have I played it over and over for her? No, I haven't. And the reason is…I have all this stuff for her. I have videos after videos, and I've saved everything for her—when it's age appropriate and she is able to handle it. I had a really hard time with her at times, just being sad about Shannon—"I miss my Dad" and "Why did he do drugs?" She's a very passionate kid—like *him* in a lot of ways. She wants to be a drummer. And that was the other thing—I didn't want her to be pigeonholed into also feeling she had to be a singer. Some people feel like they have to fill their parents' shoes. I've been real careful. I've been kind of cautious with all that—I don't know what the right way to handle it is. She thinks it's the coolest thing ever—*it's her dad.* There's a lot of 'Soup' I wouldn't want her to listen to, because it's 'adult content.' I mean, she thinks it's *really cool* that there's an album named after her. She's such a tomboy and she's funny, she told me, "I'm kind of famous, because there's an album named after me!" She's quite a character.

Nel Hoon: After Shannon passed, I was looking through a lot of pictures, and I found a picture of the band—of all of the guys together. It was when they had gotten signed. And this was in Shannon's handwriting—Shannon said that they were all his brothers. He praised them so much. They probably don't even know about this—he wrote in the back of it. That was just sad, because it brought back the softhearted Shannon that he really was. It may have been about a year after he was gone—I just thought, "Oh, I'm just going to open up this frame." Something told me to. And when I read that—I wonder if the band knew how much he did care for them.

Epilogue

After the surviving members officially end Blind Melon in 1999, Chris-topher and Brad relocate to Los Angeles and form Unified Theory. The group eventually splits (after issuing a lone self-titled release in 2000), before the duo opens their own recording studio, Studio Wishbone (and produce such artists as Anna Nalick and Critter Jones, among others). Stevens moves to New York City and plays in a pair of bands, Extra Virgin and the Tender Trio (the latter featuring ex-Spacehog frontman Royston Langdon), while Graham moves to North Carolina, and plays in the Meek. Then, seemingly out of nowhere, singer/songwriter/Blind Melon fan Travis Warren comes into the picture in 2006…

Rogers Stevens: Brad wrote a fake press release and sent it to me—it was say-ing how we were back together and how Travis had brought us together. It was the first I'd heard of it. I called Brad and I was like, "What do you mean? You got the band back together without me?"

Travis Warren: I'm originally from Amarillo, Texas. Both of my parents are musicians. I grew up with it—there was always instruments laying around the house. I happened to pick up the guitar at a young age—six years old. About the time I was eight or nine, I was playing rhythm guitar for my dad's band. I got really into AC/DC, Metallica, Slayer, and Pantera—it went into really heavy things for a while. I was about twelve or thirteen, I remember walking into a record store, and the guy had Jane's Addiction 'Ritual' and Blind Melon's first record. I was going on a trip with my grandmother to visit family in south Texas, and I ended up taking the tape of Blind Melon's first record. That whole trip, I listened to that tape front and back. Blind Melon was always my favorite band out of that time.

I don't think I ever got teary eyed or cried when somebody died that I didn't know—I didn't have any direct contact with Shannon, but I remember when he passed away, I was heartbroken. Shannon always stuck out as one of my favorite influences. I ended up following my girlfriend out to California in '97—I had just turned 17 years old. I sold all my lesser guitar equipment, had an acoustic guitar, and that's when I really started to write music. I was living in San Luis Obispo, and the day after I turned 18, I got a tattoo of Shannon on my back—just a tribute to him. When I hit about 19 or 20, I started getting into some bands, and one of the bands, 00-Metro, I was writing all the music for, but we didn't have a singer. So I told the guys, "I'll just sing until we can find a singer." Slowly but surely, I started to find my own voice, and ended up being the singer in the band.

Rogers Stevens: His voice is in that higher register that Shannon's was in, but he doesn't sound like him. There are certain similarities, just because he's in that range.

Travis Warren: A few years passed, the band I was in at the time, Rain Fur Rent, ended up moving to Los Angeles. We got management and started showcasing for the majors. One of the labels we were working with was Atlantic Records. There was a guy there, Kevin Carvel—we were chatting one day, and he asked who my influences were. I mentioned Blind Melon, and he said, "Are you kidding me? I know Christopher and Brad really well—they're producing, they have a studio." He asked me if I'd like to meet them, and I said, "Absolutely." He took me by Wishbone Studios, and that's when I first met Christopher and Brad. It was a great experience, sitting there, kicking it with my idols. We had a gig at the Key Club that weekend, and Christopher and Brad both came and checked out the show. They liked what I was doing, and said something like, "Maybe in the future we can work together." I didn't really think twice about it, and went on with what I was doing.

Early 2006, Rain Fur Rent disbanded. My manager got a hold of Christopher and Brad, and set up a meeting. Meanwhile, my manager dropped off some demos that I recorded. They called my manager back and wanted to set up a meeting. We met up with Christopher and Brad, they were into what I was doing, and they wanted to work with me. When we originally started working together, they were going to produce my record and try to get me a record deal. But at the same time, they weren't just producing the record—they were going to play on the songs. Two or three months into that, Christopher had a barbeque over his house, and invited me over. Brought my guitar, not really thinking too much about it—just thought we were going to hang out and have a good time. Heather cooked dinner and we hung out. By the time I was about to leave, they both sat me down and said, "We want to talk to you about something." My initial thought was, "Oh shit—they don't want to work with me anymore." I was paranoid a little bit—they looked very intense when they said that. That's when they said, "How do you feel about singing for Blind Melon?" I took a double take, like *"What?!"* Of course, I said, "Yes!" On one hand, I was like, "Man, this is a great opportunity. I get to sing some of my favorite songs with one of my favorite bands." On the other hand, I knew it was going to be not an easy thing.

Rogers Stevens: We decided to get into a room and play—we thought it would be fun. I was really skeptical in the beginning about doing anything, and none of us are into doing any kind of 'nostalgia trip.' We started playing, and I knew within the first half of a song that [Travis] was nailing it. It was something about the way he did it that it immediately disarmed my skepticism.

Travis Warren: They'll tell you not to meet your idols because you'll be disappointed, but that definitely wasn't the case. These guys are so down to earth—it's like hanging out with my buddies back home in Amarillo. They're great guys. That's what makes it so much fun—there isn't egos floating around in this band. Everybody in this band wants the same thing. I think the fact that they're a little bit older, they've been through the shit, seen first hand what it could do to you, and they're just about making great music. It's a great vibe—there's not a lot of drama.

Danny Clinch: I was there when they got together. They had done two jam sessions with this guy. On the third day, I showed up. I went in the room, and they went into "Galaxie." I got completely overwhelmed. It was so fantastic to hear those four guys kick those riffs.

Travis Warren: "For My Friends" has got a special place in my heart—it was the first song that we worked on together. Rogers wrote the music to it. It was one of those nights when the stars were all lined up—he sent me the song at 9:00 or 10:00 New York time. I got the song, listened to it once, heard a melody for it, threw it on ProTools, and wrote the lyrics right there. Recorded it, and when Rogers woke up the next morning, I had sent the song back to him with vocals on it. That demo is exactly the same as far as the melody and lyrics go. Christopher would send me a song, and it just went by really fast—that's a good sign of chemistry. Obviously, *they* had chemistry. That was another easy part for me—I had grown up listening to them. I knew their styles—I know how Brad plays bass, Glen plays drums. It was not really a hard thing for me to come in and contribute. As far as the record [also titled 'For My Friends,' and issued on April 22, 2008] goes, I really believe in it, and I don't think that's wishful thinking or me being biased because I'm in the band. It's kind of like 'Soup'—the more you listen to it, the more it grows on you.

There's songs like "For My Friends," that has a heavy Blind Melon influence. And there's other songs, like "Sometimes," that we're venturing off. We don't ever want to be pigeonholed or just have one sound. We all respect bands like Radiohead and the Beatles—each record went completely left field, but was still a great record. We definitely want to experiment and do different things with music. Hopefully with [the next] record, it'll go completely left from where this record took off. But this record's a great rock n' roll record. You have the classic guitar riffs that you've heard in previous Blind Melon records. I think Glen plays—on songs like "Make A Difference"—heavier than he's every played. Glen is like Keith Moon on crack [laughs]! He just goes off.

If people give it a chance, as far as the old Blind Melon fans, I think they'll really come to like it. And we're hoping to get a whole new generation that missed out on the first record, 'Soup,' and 'Nico.' When I got turned onto AC/DC, Brian Johnson was singing. When I had gone back and bought their old records, then I was introduced to Bon Scott. I remember the first time I heard Bon Scott, I was like, "Oh my God, *this is amazing!*" That's what we're hoping—that we get a whole new generation of fans, and they're able to go back and experience Shannon. We've done everything on our own—we produced this record on our own, we have our own studio we recorded at. We're really trying to do it as 'grass roots' as we can.

Glen Graham: Travis has a remarkable ability to nail the old material without sounding like a Shannon clone or a singer in a cover band. He also has his own very distinct, engaging personality onstage and is accepted completely by our fans, old and new. Quite naturally, these strengths have served him well, as his ability to consistently find favor with female fans offstage is...considerably more than minor [laughs].

Rogers Stevens: On the stuff we're doing, his phrasing and whatnot is different than Shannon's. On the old songs, he can sing them really well. They are different, but he definitely was influenced by Shannon.

Travis Warren: The way I saw it, it was a very unfortunate thing that happened to Shannon. For Glen, Rogers, Brad, and Christopher not to perform again as a band...it's like torture. Those guys are *so* great. I feel like they didn't even really scratch the surface on the potential they had. I felt like if I can help them continue to write and create, it was a great thing. When we first thought about it, we were like, "Should we use the name Blind Melon? Should we not?" The way we saw it, it's going to be four out of the five members of Blind Melon, we're going to go out there, and in the papers it's going to say, "So and so, formerly of the band Blind Melon." And we're going to get up there and sing all Blind Melon songs. It ended up ripping off ourselves—we didn't really see the point. I don't think everybody's going to get it, and that's totally fine. I understand why, but I do think you should give it a chance.

Danny Clinch: [Travis] has got a lot of Shannon in him, because he was influenced by Shannon, but it's not contrived—it is who the guy is. It's part of who he is, and he's just doing his thing—living his life, and that's what his life is. He's got a lot of that same attitude as Shannon too, like, "Yeah, whatever—I'm just doing my thing. This is really cool and I'm psyched to be here."

Travis Warren: I think what is going to be great when we do the [next] record, we were all talking about renting a house—like 'Sleepyhouse.' Getting out of Los Angeles, maybe going to the east coast, renting a home, and getting to work on music together. Say, Brad has a riff, Christopher might have a great chorus to it. We'd actually get in a room and work together. The fact that we were able to work being spread across the country, working through email, I think it'll be even that much [better] when we're actually able to sit in a room and write the songs together.

Glen Graham: Andy Wallace once described working with us in the studio as "A thrill a minute." I'm pleased to say that with the addition of Travis, I think we have altered that ratio to somewhere around "A thrill a week."

Rogers Stevens: I feel like I'm back where I belong with these guys.

Travis Warren: That night in Chicago [on October 16, 2007, at the Double Door, when Nico Blue Hoon sang "Change" with the band] was really a magical night for me. That was one of the times where Nel and Nico really got to see each other. I got to go out to dinner with Nico. It was such a great experience—we're in the back of the bus and we were practicing "Change." She was getting a couple of verses mixed up, and Nico was like, "I want to sing this one part like my dad—let me show you." She gets on YouTube, and finds some bootleg version of "Change" that Shannon pulls off. That was a real highlight for me—sitting there on the computer, watching Shannon with Nico. Shannon was classic for never singing the same part the same—he would change it up every night—and Nico was wanting to sing it a different way. It was really cool. She's very intuitive—very smart for her age. Definitely has potential. As far as Nel goes, there's Blind Melon fans, and there's Shannon Hoon fans. The way I see it is Nel is kind of the 'queen bee.' If she doesn't support the idea of Melon getting back together—there's a lot of people that look at the way she sees things and goes by that. The fact that Nel did support it, and got up there and let the fans know that, I think there was a relief with a lot of the fans that maybe were not getting over the fact that Blind Melon was going on without Shannon. I've ended up becoming really good friends with Nel and Nico—it's just great. There was also a point when I was talking to Nico in Chicago, and I was seeing a piece of Shannon in her eyes...

Discography

Albums:

Blind Melon (Capitol)—September 14, 1992
"Soak the Sin," "Tones of Home," "I Wonder," "Paper Scratcher," "Dear Ol' Dad," "Change," "No Rain," "Deserted," "Sleepyhouse," "Holy Man," "Seed to a Tree," "Drive," "Time"

Soup (Capitol)—August 15, 1995
"Galaxie," "2x4," "Vernie," "Skinned," "Toes Across the Floor," "Walk," "Dumptruck," "Car Seat (God's Presents)," "Wilt," "The Duke," "St. Andrew's Fall," "New Life," "Mouthful of Cavities," "Lemonade"

Nico (Capitol)—November 12, 1996
"The Pusher," "Hell," "Soup," "No Rain" (Ripped Away Version), "Soul One," "John Sinclair," "All That I Need," "Glitch," "Life Ain't So Shitty," "Swallowed," "Pull," "St. Andrew's Hall," "Letters from a Porcupine"

Classic Masters (Capitol)—January 29, 2002
"Tones of Home," "Galaxie," "Change," "Paper Scratcher," "Mouthful of Cavities," "Walk," "No Rain," "Toes Across the Floor," "Soup," "2x4," "Pull," "Soul One"

Tones of Home: The Best of Blind Melon (Capitol)—September 27, 2005
"Tones of Home," "Change," "Paper Scratcher," "No Rain," "I Wonder," "Time," "Galaxie," "Mouthful of Cavities," "Walk," "Toes Across the Floor," "2x4," "St. Andrew's Fall," "Soup," "Pull," "Soul One," "No Rain" (Ripped Away Version), "Three is a Magic Number," "Soak the Sin" (live), "Deserted" (live)

Live at the Palace (Capitol)—April 4, 2006
"Galaxie," "Toes Across the Floor," "Tones of Home," "Soup," "Soak the Sin," "Change," "No Rain," "Wilt," "Vernie," "Walk," "Skinned," "Time"

For My Friends (Adrenaline)—April 22, 2008
"For My Friends," "With the Right Set of Eyes," "Wishing Well," "Sometimes," "Tumblin' Down," "Down On the Pharmacy," "Make a Difference," "Harmful Belly," "Last Laugh," "Hypnotize," "Father Time," "So High," "Cheetum Street"

DVDS:

Letters from a Porcupine (Capitol)—November 12, 1996
"Hello Goodbye," "2x4," "Galaxie," "Dear Ol' Dad," "Tones of Home," "No Bidness," "No Rain (Ripped Away Version)," "No Rain," "Wilt," "Change," "Lemonade," "Mouthful of Cavities," "St. Andrew's Fall," "Walk," "Skinned," "Dumptruck," "Time," "Soup," "After Hours" [also includes promo videos for "Dear Ol' Dad," "I Wonder," "No Rain," "Tones of Home," "Change," "Galaxie," "Toes Across the Floor," and "Soul One," as well as 'video press kits' for 'Blind Melon,' 'Soup,' and 'Nico']

Live at the Metro: September 27, 1995 (Capitol)—September 27, 2005
"2x4," "Toes Across the Floor," "Wilt," "Tones of Home," "Vernie," "Soak the Sin," "Lemonade," "Skinned," "Walk," "No Rain," "Galaxie," "Dumptruck," "The Duke," "I Wonder," "St. Andrew's Fall," "Soup," "Paper Scratcher," "Change," "After Hours/Time" [also includes three tracks recorded at MuchMusic from 1995—"Toes Across the Floor," "Change," and "Soup"]

WEBSITES:

www.myspace.com/blindmelon
www.blindmelon.com
www.beemelon.com
www.blindmelonforum.com
www.studiowishbone.com

Acknowledgements

I would like to thank the following colorful characters for their help in the creation of this book:

Brad, Christopher, Glen, Rogers, and Travis—thanks for responding to all the numerous phone calls and emails over the past few years. All of the people that were kind enough to grant me interviews and retell their Melon tales. All of the photographers who sent in great photos (Andy Martin Jr., Brooks Byrd Graham, Danny Clinch, Lyle Eaves, Marlon Stoltzman, and Nicholas Bechtel), as well as Danny Clinch's studio manager, Lisa Connelly. And thanks to Lloyd J. Jassin and Dan Weiss for publishing advice, and Linda Krieg for helping design the book.

Also, thanks to Bill Olivieri for being the first gentleman to play me Blind Melon back in '92, and to James Fleischmann and various other chaps for accompanying me to numerous Blind Melon shows.

And lastly, thanks to my wife Mary, my entire family, and all my friends, who have had to put up with me playing Blind Melon's music and pontificating about the band continuously over the years!

Source Notes

[All are quotes by Shannon Hoon, except otherwise noted as ***]

Shannon's Upbringing

"Why?" (MuchMusic Interview, September 1995)

"I'm from Lafayette...pull it out." ("Hoon Struck," Cree McCree, *Circus*, November 30, 1993)

"I was such...beat my opponent." ("Soup's On," Marc D. Allan, *The Indianapolis Star*, September 25, 1995)

"I have a...like my father." ("Rapping with Blind Melon," Robert Hunter, *Creem*, October 27, 1993)

"I was raised...important to me." ("Knee Deep in the Hoopla," Kim Neely, *Rolling Stone*, November 11, 1993)

"Nothing major...habitual-criminal charge." ("Knee Deep in the Hoopla," Kim Neely, *Rolling Stone*, November 11, 1993)

"My family was...other one's love." ("Heavy Mellow," Robyn Doreian, *Rip*, November 1993)

"I was a...about the place." ("Come On Feel the Melonheads," Martin Townsend, *VOX*, December 1993)

"I didn't realize...important to me." ("Are Blind Melon the Next Doobie Brothers?", Philip H. Farber, *High Times*, August 1993)

"Singing made me...alright to sing." ("Knee Deep in the Hoopla," Kim Neely, *Rolling Stone*, November 11, 1993)

"I remember we...pretty forgiving guy." ("Blind Melon: By Their Fruits Ye Shall Know Them," Sandy Stert Benjamin, *Goldmine*, April 1, 1994)

"I'd basically backed...anything by leaving." ("Knee Deep in the Hoopla," Kim Neely, *Rolling Stone*, November 11, 1993)

"Well, people in...understand it now." ("Blind Melon," Chuck Crisafulli, *Music Connection*, August 30-September 13, 1993)

Axl and Shannon

"We've been friends...live in Indiana." ("Home for the Blind: Blind Melon Know Why W. Axl Rose is Mad!", Jason Arnopp, *Kerrang!*, May 29, 1993)

"We're both from...going back home." ("Hoon Struck," Cree McCree, *Circus*, November 30, 1993)

"I still think...to talk about." ("Blind Melon," Chuck Crisafulli, *Music Connection*, August 30-September 13, 1993)

"I got to...that one track." ("Blind Faith," Nick Douglas, *Metal Hammer*, March 1993)

"It was just...fault, not mine." ("Come On Feel the Melonheads," Martin Townsend, *VOX*, December 1993)

"If I had...think everyone would!" ("Home for the Blind: Blind Melon Know Why W. Axl Rose is Mad!", Jason Arnopp, *Kerrang!*, May 29, 1993)

"They had one...at that thing." ("Big Melons," Chris Heath, *Details*, November 1993)

"I don't really...I'm doing now." ("Blind Faith," Nick Douglas, *Metal Hammer*, March 1993)

L.A./Blind Melon Forms

"I moved out...way they are." ("Blind Melon's Shannon Hoon: Meditative Musings," Karen Sidlow, *Rip*, January 29, 1996)

"It's hard to...meant to happen." ("Blind Melon: By Their Fruits Ye Shall Know Them," Sandy Stert Benjamin, *Goldmine*, April 1, 1994)

"L.A.—after being...was real refreshing." (Untitled, Georgia Tsao, *M.E.A.T.*, October 1993)

"Back then we...fit into it." (Untitled, Georgia Tsao, *M.E.A.T.*, October 1993)

Capitol Records/Chris Jones/'Sippin' Time Sessions'

"We knew we...signed our contract." ("Blind Melon: By Their Fruits Ye Shall Know Them," Sandy Stert Benjamin, *Goldmine*, April 1, 1994)

Durham/Sleepyhouse/Soundgarden Tour

"We established a...in the kitchen." ("Blind Melon: By Their Fruits Ye Shall Know Them," Sandy Stert Benjamin, *Goldmine*, April 1, 1994)

"My lungs are...the better brands." ("Are Blind Melon the Next Doobie Brothers?", Philip H. Farber, *High Times*, August 1993)

"Everybody slept all...must've been thinking." ("Blind Melon: By Their Fruits Ye Shall Know Them," Sandy Stert Benjamin, *Goldmine*, April 1, 1994)

"It was long...thought they were." (Untitled, Georgia Tsao, *M.E.A.T.*, October 1993)

Seattle/120 Minutes Tour/'Blind Melon'

"We weren't in...the band well." ("Organically Grown," Kim Neely, *Rolling Stone*, October 1, 1992)

"Anyone can go...and natural sound." ("Blind Melon: By Their Fruits Ye Shall Know Them," Sandy Stert Benjamin, *Goldmine*, April 1, 1994)

"I get asked...all of us." ("Blind Melon," Chuck Crisafulli, *Music Connection*, August 30-September 13, 1993)

"The song was...and lifestyles there." ("Blind Melon: By Their Fruits Ye Shall Know Them," Sandy Stert Benjamin, *Goldmine*, April 1, 1994)

328 A Devil on One Shoulder and an Angel on the Other

"I'm not about…us hasn't experienced." ("Blind Melon: By Their Fruits Ye Shall Know Them," Sandy Stert Benjamin, *Goldmine*, April 1, 1994)

"Songwriting has become…sick with it." ("Blind Melon," Chuck Crisafulli, *Music Connection*, August 30-September 13, 1993)

"I hope people…from repressed environments." ("Organically Grown," Kim Neely, *Rolling Stone*, October 1, 1992)

"Someone who tags…all that stuff." ("Hoon Struck," Cree McCree, *Circus*, November 30, 1993)

"When you hear…just the best." ("Rapping with Blind Melon," Robert Hunter, *Creem*, October 27, 1993)

Crammed in a Van Tour

"I annoy the…guys so bad!" ("Rapping with Blind Melon," Robert Hunter, *Creem*, October 27, 1993)

"Our strength is…we're 'above' anything." ("Blind Melon: By Their Fruits Ye Shall Know Them," Sandy Stert Benjamin, *Goldmine*, April 1, 1994)

"Going back through…it looks like." ("Big Melons," Chris Heath, *Details*, November 1993)

"I think the…that's sold out." ("Heavy Mellow," Robyn Doreian, *Rip*, November 1993)

"Since it was…was very shocked." ("Strange Fruit," Simon Witter, *Sky*, February 1994)

"The best shows…nervous breakdown together." ("Soul Searchers," Adrianne Stone, *Rip*, March 1994)

"Tiptoeing between sanity…to the next." ("Blind Melon: By Their Fruits Ye Shall Know Them," Sandy Stert Benjamin, *Goldmine*, April 1, 1994)

Success of "No Rain"

"This record's been…on the ground." ("Knee Deep in the Hoopla," Kim Neely, *Rolling Stone*, November 11, 1993)

"I don't like…buy our record." ("Soul Searchers," Adrianne Stone, *Rip*, March 1994)

"People chip away…that guy today." ("Ahhhhhhhhhhh! (Larvely) Blind Melon: Are They Taking the Piss or What?", John Aizelwood, *Q*, February 1994)

"Sure there's a…a time frame." ("Knee Deep in the Hoopla," Kim Neely, *Rolling Stone*, November 11, 1993)

Neil Young and Lenny Kravitz Tours/Rolling Stone Cover

"Sometimes I think…my knees buckle." ("Blind Melon," Chuck Crisafulli, *Music Connection*, August 30-September 13, 1993)

"It was worth…play every night." ("Rapping with Blind Melon," Robert Hunter, *Creem*, October 27, 1993)

"You're brought into…wrong with it." ("Strange Fruit," Simon Witter, *Sky*, February 1994)

"Customs is very…about my underwear." ("Soup Review," John Sakamoto, *Toronto Sun*, August 2, 1995)

Rehab/Euro Tour

"You know, I'd…a gold record." ("Hoon's Addiction," Steve Bloom, *High Times*, February 1996)

"I feel more…time was there." ("Big Melons," Chris Heath, *Details*, November 1993)

"I'm a terrible…your sleep, really?" ("Strange Fruit," Simon Witter, *Sky*, February 1994)

"I don't know…the Frolic Room." ("Blind Melon's Grass Roots Soup (Or, No More Bees Please)", Kristin Estlund, *Rip*, September 1995)

"You just don't…because of it." ("MuchMusic Spotlight: Blind Melon," 1996)

"I've never seen…catch them again." ("Slack to Basics," Howard Johnson, *Raw*, July 6, 1994) ***[Robert Plant quote]

Woodstock '94

"When it was…a complete high." ("Soup-er Unknown!", Steve Beebee, *Kerrang!*, August 1995)

"Yeah, it was…of that gig." ("Soup-er Unknown!", Steve Beebee, *Kerrang!*, August 1995)

'Soup' Recording

"That was a…home with me." ("The Modern Age," Eric Boehlert, *Billboard*, August 12, 1995)

"Andy was a…Real well." ("Dog, Man, Star," Mick Wall, *Raw*, May 10-23, 1995)

"There was so…are dangerously entertaining." ("From Bee Girl To Big Time," Michelle Cordle, *Music Monitor*, 1995)

"Recording in New…making this record." ("Soup-er Unknown!", Steve Beebee, *Kerrang!*, August 1995)

"When I think…album got made." ("Blind Melon's Grass Roots Soup (Or, No More Bees Please)", Kristin Estlund, *Rip*, September 1995)

"New Orleans is…your pores, man." ("Dog, Man, Star," Mick Wall, *Raw*, May 10-23, 1995)

"There's no way…a great song." ("Soup-er Unknown!", Steve Beebee, *Kerrang!*, August 1995)

"[Brad] wrote some…all the lyrics." ("Blind Melon's Grass Roots Soup (Or, No More Bees Please)", Kristin Estlund, *Rip*, September 1995)

"We're not all…for each other." ("From Bee Girl To Big Time," Michelle Cordle, *Music Monitor*, 1995)

"It's very hard...that was whole." ("Dog, Man, Star," Mick Wall, *Raw*, May 10-23, 1995)

"The end result...has been reinstated." ("From Bee Girl To Big Time," Michelle Cordle, *Music Monitor*, 1995)

'Soup'

"[The car] was...so far out." ("The Modern Age," Eric Boehlert, *Billboard*, August 12, 1995)

"'Skinned' though is...from their remains." ("Soup-er Unknown!", Steve Beebee, *Kerrang!*, August 1995)

"Well, obviously I...a kazoo solo." ("Soup-er Unknown!", Steve Beebee, *Kerrang!*, August 1995)

"There was a...great, great grandmother." ("Dog, Man, Star," Mick Wall, *Raw*, May 10-23, 1995)

"It was February...she wrote it." ("Dog, Man, Star," Mick Wall, *Raw*, May 10-23, 1995)

"I believe that...can't comprehend it." ("Soup Review," John Sakamoto, *Toronto Sun*, August 2, 1995)

"One night we...is all about." ("Dog, Man, Star," Mick Wall, *Raw*, May 10-23, 1995)

Shannon '94-'95

"I have a...turned out right." ("Blind Melon's Grass Roots Soup (Or, No More Bees Please)", Kristin Estlund, *Rip*, September 1995)

"No matter how...most exhausting, actually." ("Lust For Life," Jason Arnopp, *Kerrang!*, November 4, 1995)

"Lisa and I...go about it." ("Soup's On," Marc D. Allan, *The Indianapolis Star*, September 25, 1995)

"And I think...a happy life." (MuchMusic Spotlight: Blind Melon, 1996)

"Obviously now being...one of them." ("Lust For Life," Jason Arnopp, *Kerrang!*, November 4, 1995)

"I'm an old...farm into town." ("The Modern Age," Eric Boehlert, *Billboard*, August 12, 1995)

Release of 'Soup'

"I'm happy with...copies it sells." ("From Bee Girl To Big Time," Michelle Cordle, *Music Monitor*, 1995)

'Soup' Tour

"I would be...to be away." ("Soup's On," Marc D. Allan, *The Indianapolis Star*, September 25, 1995)

"It was just...the other day." ("Blind Melon's Grass Roots Soup (Or, No More Bees Please)", Kristin Estlund, *Rip*, September 1995)

"We can prepare…nothing to do." ("Lust For Life," Jason Arnopp, *Kerrang!*, November 4, 1995)

"I like outdoor…grass underneath you." ("Dog, Man, Star," Mick Wall, *Raw*, May 10-23, 1995)

"I was just…your alcohol problem." ("Lust For Life," Jason Arnopp, *Kerrang!*, November 4, 1995)

October 21, 1995

"It touches me…just a shame." ("Blind Melon's Shannon Hoon: Meditative Musings," Karen Sidlow, *Rip*, January 29, 1996)